T0222316

Creating Infographics with Adobe Illustrator: Volume 1

Learn the Basics and Design Your First Infographic

Jennifer Harder

Apress®

Creating Infographics with Adobe Illustrator: Volume 1: Learn the Basics and Design Your First Infographic

Jennifer Harder
Delta, BC, Canada

ISBN-13 (pbk): 979-8-8688-0004-7
https://doi.org/10.1007/979-8-8688-0005-4

ISBN-13 (electronic): 979-8-8688-0005-4

Managing Director, Apress Media LLC: Welmoed Spahr
Acquisitions Editor: Spandana Chatterjee
Development Editor: James Markham
Project Manager: Jessica Vakili

Cover designed by eStudioCalamar

Cover image designed by Freepik (www.freepik.com)

Distributed to the book trade worldwide by Springer Science+Business Media New York, 1 New York Plaza, Suite 4600, New York, NY 10004-1562, USA. Phone 1-800-SPRINGER, fax (201) 348-4505, e-mail orders-ny@ springer-sbm.com, or visit www.springeronline.com. Apress Media, LLC is a California LLC and the sole member (owner) is Springer Science + Business Media Finance Inc (SSBM Finance Inc). SSBM Finance Inc is a **Delaware** corporation.

For information on translations, please e-mail booktranslations@springernature.com; for reprint, paperback, or audio rights, please e-mail bookpermissions@springernature.com.

Apress titles may be purchased in bulk for academic, corporate, or promotional use. eBook versions and licenses are also available for most titles. For more information, reference our Print and eBook Bulk Sales web page at http://www.apress.com/bulk-sales.

Any source code or other supplementary material referenced by the author in this book is available to readers on GitHub. For more detailed information, please visit https://www.apress.com/gp/services/source-code.

Paper in this product is recyclable

Table of Contents

About the Author

Jennifer Harder has worked in the graphic design industry for over 15 years. She has a degree in graphic communications and is currently teaching Acrobat and Adobe Creative Cloud courses at Langara College. She is the author of several Apress books and related videos.

About the Technical Reviewer

 **Sourabh Mishra** is an entrepreneur, developer, speaker, author, corporate trainer, and animator. He is a Microsoft guy; he is very passionate about Microsoft technologies and a true .NET warrior. Sourabh started his career when he was just 15 years old. He has loved computers since childhood. His programming experience includes C/C++, ASP.NET, C#, VB.NET, WCF, SQL Server, Entity Framework, MVC, Web API, Azure, jQuery, Highcharts, and Angular. He is also an expert in computer graphics. Sourabh is the author of the book *Practical Highcharts with Angular* published by Apress. Sourabh has been awarded a Most Valuable Professional (MVP) status. He has the zeal to learn new technologies, sharing his knowledge on several online community forums.

He is a founder of "IECE Digital" and "Sourabh Mishra Notes," an online knowledge-sharing platform where one can learn new technologies very easily and comfortably.

Acknowledgments

For their patience and advice, I would like to thank the following people, for without them I could never have written this book:

- My parents, for encouraging me to read large computer textbooks that would one day inspire me to write my own books.

- My dad, for reviewing the first draft before I sent a proposal.

- My program coordinator, Raymond Chow, at Langara College, who gave me the chance to teach evening courses and allowed me to find new and creative ways to teach software.

- My various freelance clients whose projects, while working on them, helped me research and learn more about various topics.

- At Apress, I would like to thank Spandana Chatterjee and Mark Powers, for showing me how to lay out a professional textbook and pointing out that even when you think you've written it all, there's still more to write. Also, thanks to the technical reviewer for providing encouraging comments. And thanks to the rest of the Apress team for being involved in the printing of this book and making my dream a reality again. I am truly grateful and blessed.

Introduction

Welcome to the book *Creating Infographics with Adobe Illustrator: Volume 1*. This book is the first of a three-volume set.

What This Book Is About

In this book, we will be looking at how to create infographics, also known as "informational graphics," which are often used by various people in companies for the purpose of informing the general public in a quick at-a-glance way, without having to go into a lot of detail on a specific topic. Basically, they are complex ideas in a bite-sized format for those with short attention spans. However, you as a graphic designer, in order to accomplish this task of creating a successful infographic, must have a slightly longer attention span than the viewer and be willing to take time to craft an informative and engaging infographic that your audience will enjoy. This book is about how to go about doing just that and gain knowledge about the main Adobe applications that you will use to accomplish that task, which I will talk about shortly in this volume and the subsequent volumes.

This book is divided into nine chapters in which we will explore the history and beginning steps of infographic creation. Much of what you learn here in this book can also be applied to logo creation as well. However, as you will discover, infographic creation often requires more invested research and time due to many factors that I will try to break down in this book and later conclude in Volume 3. If you are a beginner to the idea of infographics, make sure to use this book to first focus on logo design or create a simple 2D infographic before moving on to more complex ideas like graphs, 3D, SVG, or general page layout with text, which we will explore in Volumes 2 and 3. As you work along in this book on projects, if you are a student, make sure to consult with your instructor about their thoughts on infographics as well as work with your fellow classmates to discover what makes an ideal infographic. They may have different thoughts on this topic than myself that will be insightful as well.

Here is a brief overview of the chapters in this volume:

- Chapter 1: What are infographics? In this chapter, you will look at an overview of the history of infographics as well as what is the difference between an infographic and a logo.

- Chapter 2: This chapter will focus on the preparation of creating a logo and infographic. Before working in a program like Adobe Illustrator, there is a bit of preplanning that needs to be done when you work with your client or team. We will also look at the Adobe Color online application.

- Chapter 3: When you begin creating an infographic, it is important to set up your application's workspace; however, before you start this task, I will give you some information on scanner basics for scanning a hand-drawn sketch that you will need to scan using Photoshop.

- Chapter 4: When you begin creating an infographic, it is important to set up your application's workspace and know how to save your files. This chapter is important if you have not done a lot of work in Adobe Illustrator or if you need to review the basics of setting up your area and an overview of old and new panels and tools.

- Chapter 5: This chapter focuses on how to work with your single or multiple artboards in Illustrator and how to save your files so that you can work on various projects in Illustrator but also between Photoshop.

- Chapter 6: If you are unfamiliar with which tools to use in Illustrator to begin to create your infographics, this chapter will give you a basic overview of working with Illustrator's basic shape tools as well as how to move and select those shapes and paths.

- Chapter 7: This chapter will give you a basic overview of how to use Illustrator's pen tools as well as how to combine various paths using panels and Object commands.

- Chapter 8: In this chapter, we will be doing a review of working with the Layers panel and look at how an illustration can be traced over while using various tools and panels to recolor paths and work with Type tools and related panels. Then we will look at brush tools as well as panels that are used for the creation of graphic styles and symbols. We will also be exploring a few new tools and some of the resources that these panels can offer if we need a starting point for infographic creation.

- Chapter 9: In this chapter, we will look at how you can start to create your first infographic on a topic that is of interest to you as well as some suggestions and examples of how this can be done using the skills you have acquired from the previous chapters.

Note: The data in this book that we will be using for the infographic design is purely fictitious and is subject to change. It is not meant to reflect any actual data, only act as a placeholder to display the graphic. For your own projects, you will want to have accurate and up-to-date data if you are going to present your infographic to the public.

In Volume 2, we will continue the discussion on two-dimensional and three-dimensional infographics using various graphing tools, effects, and the 3D and Materials panel but also look at other panels such as Image Trace and Perspective tools.

Volume 3 will focus on SVG interactivity and how it can enhance your infographic. This book also gives some additional ideas on infographics as well as additional thoughts on how to work with your client on your infographic project and what applications to explore next that are part of the Creative Cloud.

Adobe Illustrator

Adobe Illustrator is one of the many drawing applications that is part of the collection of the Adobe Creative Cloud when you have a subscription with the company. Refer to Figure 1.

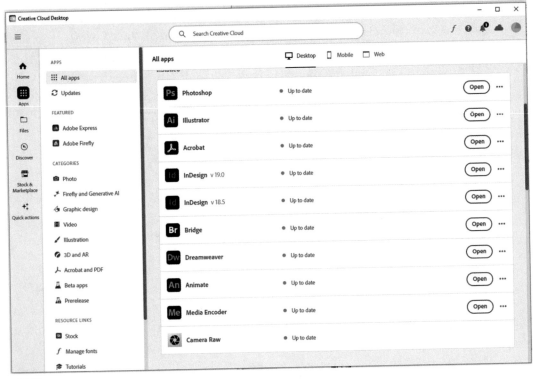

Figure 1. *Creative Cloud Desktop console and icon shortcut*

Note The topics in this book do not cover Adobe Illustrator for the iPad.

Here is a link so that you can learn more about Creative Cloud Desktop and its options. In my case, I use an individual license, but you may have acquired a subscription as a student/teacher or your company may have a team's or business license.

www.adobe.com/creativecloud.html

While some people like working with a single software like Photoshop, I prefer Creative Cloud because it offers you access to many applications including the web application Adobe Color, which you will see in Chapter 2. This is a useful application that takes the guesswork out of color theory and helps you create color themes for your infographics online. Refer to Figure 2.

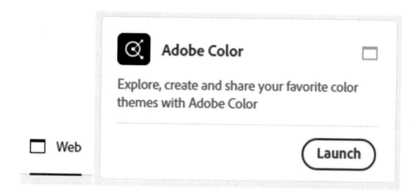

Figure 2. *Link to Adobe Color online application via the Creative Cloud*

If you have purchased and downloaded the Creative Cloud Desktop console from Adobe, you will want to Install Illustrator along with Photoshop and InDesign on your desktop computer. You can refer to the section "System Requirements" if you need to first check if your device can handle these applications. Refer to Figure 3.

Figure 3. *Desktop application icons for Photoshop, Illustrator, and InDesign that you can install*

System Requirements

If you are unsure if your computer meets the following requirements for running the latest version of Adobe Illustrator (version 28.0) on your Windows or macOS desktop computers, then please consult the following links:

```
https://helpx.adobe.com/download-install/kb/operating-system-
guidelines.html
https://helpx.adobe.com/creative-cloud/system-requirements.html
https://helpx.adobe.com/illustrator/system-requirements.html
```

With the Creative Cloud Desktop console visible, the installation steps are similar for all Adobe applications on your computer. I will, in the next section, "Install and Open Application Steps," give a brief overview of how to load and open your Illustrator application; however, not until Chapters 3 and 4 will we actually use the Photoshop and Illustrator applications. As mentioned, we will look briefly at Photoshop in Chapter 3 for the purpose of scanning and opening a scanned file. Photoshop will be mentioned briefly in Volume 2, and we'll look at Photoshop again in Volume 3, as well as InDesign.

In this book, by the time we get to Chapter 3, if you are planning on digitizing an infographic that you drew by hand, you may want to download Photoshop as well at the same time, and this will cause Camera Raw and possibly Bridge to download as well. That's OK. Though not required for this book, Camera Raw is a useful tool for color correction of photos, and Bridge is great for keeping your images and photos organized. I will mention Bridge again in Volume 3 as well, and then I will also discuss how InDesign is a great layout application that can be used for incorporating graphics to create your final publication. Refer to Figures 3 and 4.

Figure 4. *Adobe application icons Camera Raw and Bridge*

At this point, if you have not used any other applications before such as Animate, which comes with Media Encoder or Dreamweaver, you can wait on downloading them until Volume 3 as they are not required for this book, and I will merely be showing how these applications could be used at a later time to incorporate your original infographics for additional interactivity. Refer to Figure 5.

Figure 5. *Adobe application icons Animate, Media Encoder, and Dreamweaver*

Note   Though not required for this book, for myself and my personal workflow, I also install Acrobat Pro as this application can assist you in your graphics workflow for PDF file creation after completing your work in InDesign. In addition, if you are doing a lot of video work, then you may also want to later install Premiere Pro, After Effects, and Audition for video and audio work. Though none of these are required for the book, they will be mentioned again in Volume 3. Refer to Figure 6.

Figure 6. *Adobe application icons Acrobat Pro, Premiere Pro, After Effects, and Audition*

Install and Open Application Steps

If you have not already installed Photoshop or Illustrator on your computer, then do so now from the Creative Cloud console. Refer to Apps ➤ All Apps ➤ Desktop Tabs. Look for the area called "Available in your Plan." Click the Install button beside each application one at a time. Refer to Figure 7.

Figure 7. *Use the Adobe Creative Apps Desktop area to install Photoshop and Illustrator*

The installation may take several minutes. You will then receive a notification once the installation is complete, and then from time to time, the Creative Cloud will send automatic updates to you as well as bug fixes. Some installations may require a computer restart. In the installed area, Photoshop and Illustrator will appear "up to date." Then, to open, for example, Illustrator, just click the Open button on the same line. Refer to Figure 8.

Figure 8. *Open these installed applications using the button*

The Illustrator application will then open after a minute, and then you will be presented with a desktop interface. We will look at desktop interface areas more starting in Chapter 3. But for now, if you want to close the application, then choose, from the above menu, File > Exit or Ctrl/CMD+Q, and Illustrator will close. Refer to Figure 9.

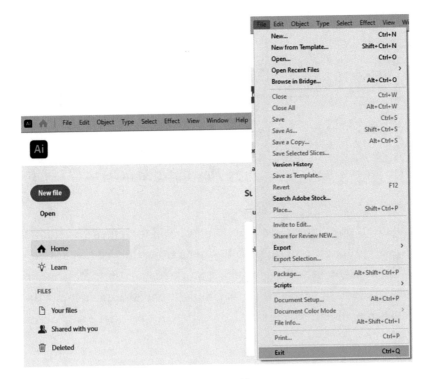

Figure 9. *Use Illustrator's File menu to exit Illustrator*

These are the same steps you can use with the Photoshop application, and then to close, use File ➤ Exit.

Additional Resources

While not required for this book, if you are interested in other related topics that I have written on Adobe applications, after you have read the three volumes on the topic of Infographics, you might also want to view one of the following:

- *Graphics and Multimedia for the Web with Adobe Creative Cloud: Navigating the Adobe Software Landscape*

- *Accurate Layer Selections Using Photoshop's Selection Tools: Use Photoshop and Illustrator to Refine Your Artwork*

- *Perspective Warps and Distorts with Adobe Tools: Volume 1: Putting a New Twist on Photoshop*

- *Perspective Warps and Distorts with Adobe Tools: Volume 2: Putting a New Twist on Illustrator*

- *Data Merge and Styles for Adobe InDesign CC 2018: Creating Custom Documents for Mailouts and Presentation Packages*: While this is an older book, you could certainly use it to incorporate some of your graphic designs in future layout projects that involve mass mail-outs.

Also, for the most up-to-date information, make sure to use Adobe online help links which can be found at

- https://helpx.adobe.com/photoshop/using/whats-new.html
- https://helpx.adobe.com/illustrator/using/whats-new.html
- https://helpx.adobe.com/photoshop/user-guide.html
- https://helpx.adobe.com/illustrator/user-guide.html
- https://helpx.adobe.com/photoshop/tutorials.html
- https://helpx.adobe.com/illustrator/tutorials.html

I will be referring to these help links throughout the book and subsequent volumes if you need additional information on a specific tool or panel. However, the focus of the book will be mostly on Illustrator, and it is assumed that you have some experience already with Photoshop.

You can also find the tutorials using the Creative Cloud Desktop console when you hover over them in the installed area and click the icon. Refer to Figure 10.

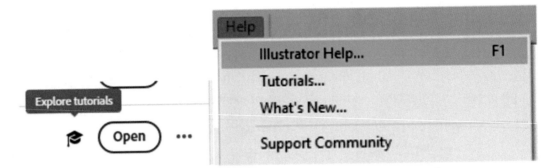

Figure 10. *Adobe Creative Cloud and Help menu links to additional resources*

Or you can access similar areas in the Illustrator Help drop-down menu or the Discover panel that can be accessed via a magnifying glass icon in the upper menu area when a file is open. The same settings are available in Photoshop as well, which are helpful for speeding up your workflow. Refer to Figure 11.

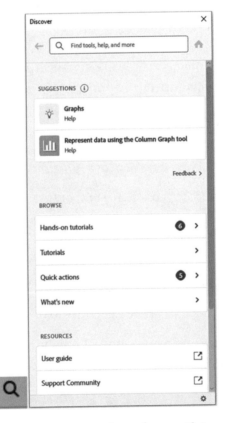

Figure 11. *Adobe Illustrator application icon (magnifying glass) and Discover panel*

Now that you are a bit more familiar with how to install and open Photoshop and Illustrator, let's begin our journey into infographic creation.

For this book, you can find the following project files for each chapter at this link:

`http://github.com/apress/illustrator-basics`

CHAPTER 1

What Are Infographics?

Before you begin deciding what kind of infographic to create, whether that be as a preliminary sketch or when you start working in Illustrator, it is important to have a firm idea about what exactly is an infographic. You may already know that an infographic needs to somehow convey information graphically. But how can that be done? Before you can understand that, we need to look at how long infographics and logos have been around. You might be surprised, they have quite a long history over thousands of years and basically began as soon as humans started to combine pictures and a form of writing together to create instructions for other humans. Though they have changed in structure over time, some kinds of infographics that were used hundreds of years ago have translated well into the digital computer age and continue to be used by us today. The history of infographics or graphic communication is a very broad topic and in no way could be fully discussed in this book. However, in this chapter, I think it is important to present some key events, cultures, and people in history who played a role in the creation and progression of infographics and logos into the present day. In turn, this will give you a better understanding of how to build your infographics later in Illustrator, as well as form a vision of how your design should appear.

Note This chapter does not contain any projects.

A Short History About Infographics

I will now present a few timelines to explain the progression of infographics throughout history. Refer to Figure 1-1.

© Jennifer Harder 2023
J. Harder, *Creating Infographics with Adobe Illustrator: Volume 1*,
https://doi.org/10.1007/979-8-8688-0005-4_1

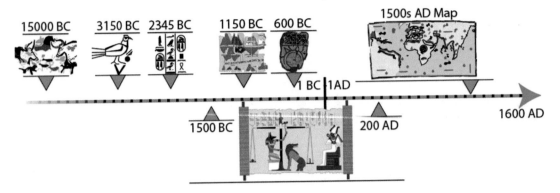

Figure 1-1. *Pictorial timeline of ancient history to 1600 AD*

Ancient History–Pre-1600 AD

One of the earliest forms of drawings that you are probably aware of is the cave paintings of Lascaux near Montignac, France. Some anthropologists believe them to be around 17,000 years old (15,000 BC). While this is considered an example of Paleolithic art, some anthropologists and art historians wonder, "Could this be a representation of a past hunting expedition or some type of mystical ritual?" For today's modern viewers, we cannot be sure as there is no text or familiar icons that come with the drawing, so we are left unsure as to the artists' true intentions. At the very least, it does give us a clue as to what animals existed in the ancient landscape. Refer to Figure 1-2.

Figure 1-2. *Recreation of animals in a cave painting in Lascaux, France*

Over the millennia, text has diverged out of the pictorial image. Yet pictures and text continued to be placed together to give clearer instructions. Instruction was something that became very important to ancient cultures such as the Egyptians. One example we can consider, besides the myriads of hieroglyphics painted or carved on pharaohs' tombs, would be the ancient Book of the Dead, possibly compiled around 1500 BC. Though the origins of the original writing of hieroglyphs are much older, about 3150 BC, the actual concepts of the ritual came about in 2345 BC, as its text and images appeared in the tombs of the kings. In 1500 BC, the Book of the Dead consisted of papyrus scrolls of priests' instructions appearing with pictures and hieroglyphics explaining various funerary spells that they felt could help the deceased person through the underworld into the afterlife successfully. This text continued to be used up until about 200 AD. Refer to Figure 1-3.

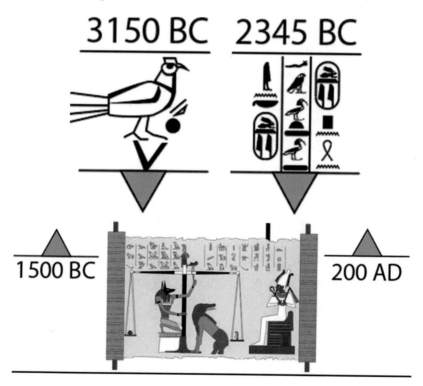

Figure 1-3. *Recreation of ancient Egyptian hieroglyphics and part of the scroll symbols in the Book of the Dead*

Other cultures and religions, such as Christian, Mayan, Tibetan, Buddhist, Hindu, and others throughout the world, if they had separate languages in written text and illustrations, often tried to compile sets of instructions on the topic of ritual, religion, or a way to live. These are the origins or roots of the first infographics.

However, over time graphic instructions changed into other ways to visually quantify knowledge; this included such topics as health, weather, agriculture, life cycle, and territory.

When we think of a group marking out a territory, we should consider maps. One of the earliest maps was created in Egypt in 1150 BC, known as the Turin Papyrus Map. One of the earliest world maps was created in 600 BC in Babylon on a clay tablet and is considered a flat earth diagram. Refer to Figure 1-4.

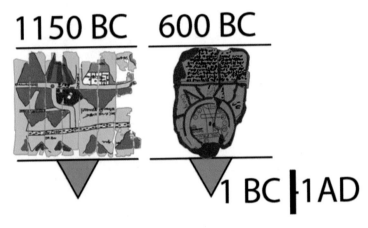

Figure 1-4. *Recreation of ancient Egyptian map and Babylonian clay tablet map*

Many other nations and cultures, in order to keep a record of their territories, continued to create maps that included typographical drawings and text explaining the regions depicted. Refer to Figure 1-5.

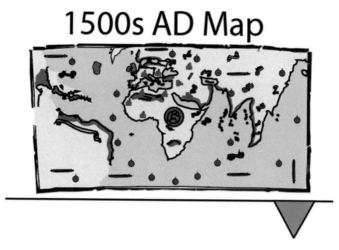

Figure 1-5. *Recreation of ancient map from the 1500s of the known world*

Ideas about how a map was to be depicted gradually changed over hundreds of years. Today we see these maps in the present day in books as well as folded road maps and the GPS we use in our vehicles.

1601 AD–1800 AD

During the 1600s–1800s, various artists continued to refine and define different ways to use the traditional map to display data on earth. Refer to Figure 1-6.

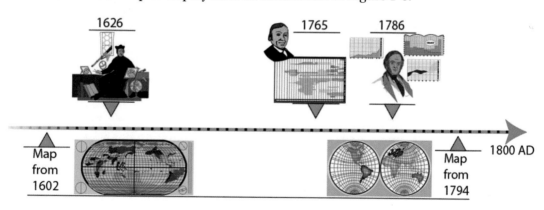

Figure 1-6. *Pictorial timeline of 1601–1800 AD*

Yet in the AD 1600s, the ideas of what an infographic was to appear like and what it was to represent began to change, and there were other topics on people's minds besides earthly maps. Refer to Figure 1-7.

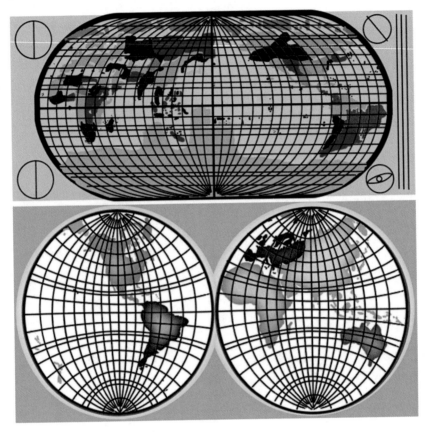

Figure 1-7. *Recreation maps from the early 1600s and late 1700s*

For example, in 1626, Christoph Scheiner (1573 or 1575–1650), who was a priest, physicist, and astronomer, created an infographic that involved the rotation of the sun and sunspots. This is considered one of the first modern infographics and was published in his book *Rosa Ursina sive Sol*. Refer to Figure 1-8.

Figure 1-8. *Pictorial sketch of Scheiner with his work on sunspots surrounding him*

In 1765, Joseph Priestley (1773–1804), a chemist and philosopher, had created the innovation of the first timeline charts. Refer to Figure 1-9.

Figure 1-9. *Pictorial sketch of Priestley and one of his timeline charts*

In 1786, William Playfair (1759–1823) was a Scottish engineer, political economist, secret agent, and founder of graphical methods of statistics. He was inspired by Priestley's timeline charts and, as a result, created the originals of many of the modern graphs and charts we see today. These include the line, area, and bar (column) chart of economic data. Playfair felt that a chart communicated an idea better than any data table could. Refer to Figure 1-10.

Figure 1-10. *Pictorial sketch of Playfair and examples of some of his charts line, bar, and area*

1801 AD–1900 AD

Playfair also began creating the circle pie chart to show the part/whole relationship in 1801, but this particular chart did not become popular until Florence Nightingale (1820–1910), the founder of modern nursing, began using it more frequently in 1857 in the form of a polar area diagram, or similar to a radial histogram. Nightingale's "Rose diagram" was used to explain patient mortality in the military field hospital she managed during a specific year. A copy of that chart was sent to Queen Victoria the following year. Refer to Figure 1-11 and Figure 1-12.

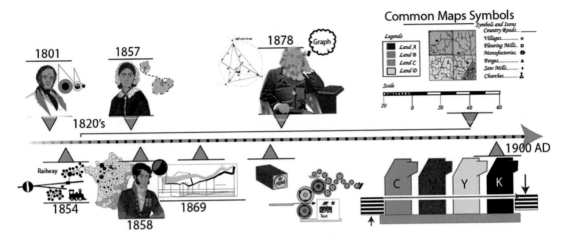

Figure 1-11. *Pictorial timeline of 1801–1900 AD*

Figure 1-12. *Pictorial sketch of Playfair with his pie chart and Nightingale with her "Rose diagram"*

In 1858, Charles Joseph Minard (1781–1870), a French engineer, used the more traditional pie chart in his map about cattle for consumption in Paris. He also, in 1869, created an infographic on the discussion of Napoleon's disastrous march on Moscow. Refer to Figure 1-13.

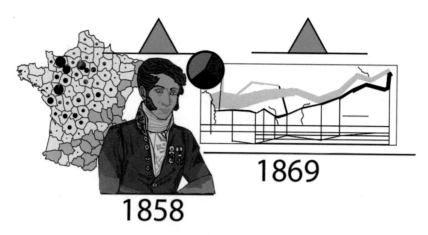

Figure 1-13. *Pictorial sketch of Minard with his map, pie charts, and infographic about Napoleon's march in Moscow*

You will look at how to create similar kinds of graphs using Illustrator in Volume 2 of this work.

However, the term graph, which was applied to diagrams, is attributed to James Joseph Sylvester, a mathematician in 1878, when he first used this term in the science magazine of Nature where he published some of the first mathematical graphs. Refer to Figure 1-14.

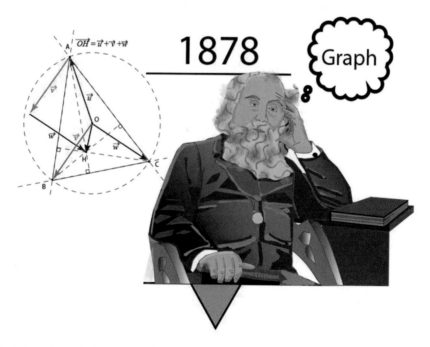

Figure 1-14. *Pictorial sketch of Sylvester and his coining of the word graph, the Sylvester's triangle problem on the left was later named after him*

The 1820s and onward also continued to see the development of the map and modern geography with, besides legends and scale, the addition of symbols and icons. Refer to Figure 1-15.

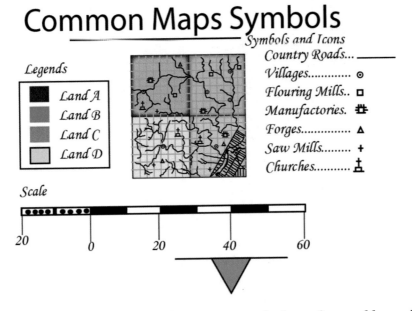

Figure 1-15. *Pictorial examples of some map symbols, scales, and legends that began to appear on maps after the 1820s*

We can see, at this point, the visualization of information or data was becoming very important to the general public, as these types of infographics were being more and more frequently published. Also, at this point, printing techniques were moving away from woodcuts and etched stone and were improved with hot metal type and later offset lithography on metal and rubber plates to facilitate easier and faster distribution of this data in books and magazines. Refer to Figure 1-16.

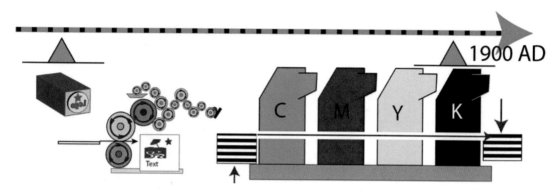

Figure 1-16. *Pictorial examples of print improvements in metal type and offset printing in the 1800s–1900s*

1901 AD–2000 AD

In 1900, charts and graphics continued to be popular and published. Refer to Figure 1-17.

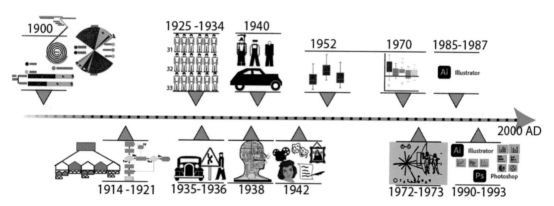

Figure 1-17. *Pictorial timeline of 1901–2000 AD*

Notable users include W. E. B. Du Bois where he and his team created 60 data visualization charts about the lives of Black Americans. Refer to Figure 1-18.

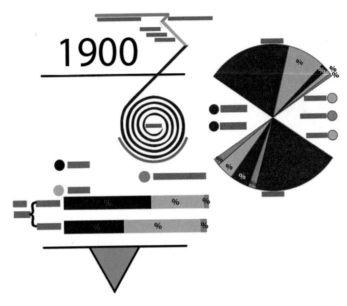

Figure 1-18. *Pictorial examples of three of Du Bois's data visualization charts*

While the first organizational chart was developed in 1854, it was not called this until 1914. However, it was not until the 1920s that they began to be used more frequently, along with the flow process chart in 1921. Though they are not as appealing with only rudimentary shapes, text, and colors, their main purpose is to show order and flow direction or an action or sequence of actions. Refer to Figure 1-19.

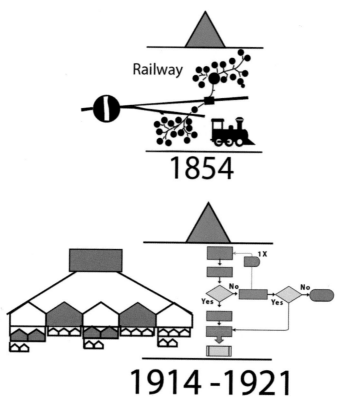

Figure 1-19. *Pictorial examples of org and flow process charts*

From around 1925 to 1934, Isotype or the International System of Typographic Picture Education developed out of the art movement, known as Cologne Progressives in Germany. Originally, it was called the Vienna Method of Pictorial Statistics, whose founding director of this museum was Otto Neurath (1882–1945). He was the initiator and chief theorist of the Vienna Method. Gerd Arntz (1900–1988) was the artist responsible for realizing the graphics. However, in 1935, the term for these types of graphics was changed to Isotypes after its key practitioners were forced to leave Vienna because of the rise of Austrian fascism and World War II. It was Neurath's partner Marie (later his wife) who chose the new name, and she worked together with him and Arntz. Refer to Figure 1-20.

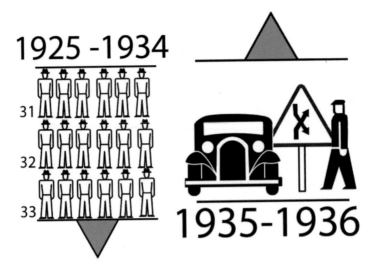

Figure 1-20. *Pictorial example of some of the Isotypes created by Arntz with Neurath and Neurath's wife*

During this time and into the 1940s, Rudolf Modley (1906–1976), a graphic designer, popularized, developed, and standardized these kinds of symbols in the United States where he was later to join an organization called Glyphs Inc. Refer to Figure 1-21.

Figure 1-21. *Pictorial example of some of the Isotypes created by Modley*

Isotypes are a method of showing standardized social, technological, biological, and historical connections in pictorial form. Some isotypes were later developed into the road signs and traffic symbol icons we see as we travel in the car today. We will look at developing some examples of Isotype creation or as they are now called icons and apply them to a layout in Chapters 6, 7, 8, and 9.

Fritz Kahn (1888–1968), a physician, was one of the main pioneers of the modern infographic from 1938 to the 1950s, comparing the parts of the body to machines, like cars or motors, in his commission illustrations. Refer to Figure 1-22.

Figure 1-22. Pictorial sketch of an infographic by Kahn and his team of artists

Though he did not create the drawings himself but worked with a team of artists as is often done today as part of design collaboration, this will be a discussion point in Chapter 2.

More on Kahn's work can be found on this page:

https://hekint.org/2022/03/31/dr-fritz-kahn-and-medical-infographics/

By 1942, besides politics, infographics were by this time covering other topics such as art, culture, poetry, and film. Refer to Figure 1-23.

Figure 1-23. *Pictorial example of the popular topics for infographics in the 1940s*

In 1952, data visualization specialist Mary Eleanor Spear (1897–1986) further expanded upon the bar chart with the range bar, which later became the box and whisker plot in 1970, created by John Tukey. Refer to Figure 1-24.

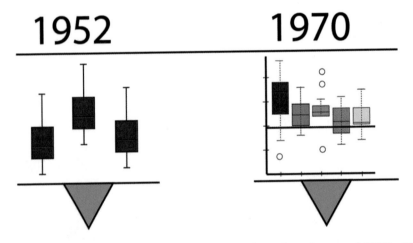

Figure 1-24. *Pictorial example of box and whisker plot charts of 1952–1970*

By 1972 and 1973, infographics on gold-anodized aluminum plaques became an important part of Pioneer 10 and Pioneer 11 spacecrafts, in the hope that their graphical meanings would be understandable to extraterrestrial beings, who would have no conception of our human language. Refer to Figure 1-25.

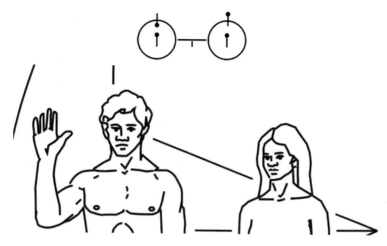

Figure 1-25. *Pictorial sketch of part of the infographic on the Pioneer spacecraft plaques*

However, as we will look at infographics later, that is one of the concerns, if not created correctly; they can be so visually appealing to the point of losing the point of the information contained within them. The second concern is that infographics, as data changes, can lose relevance. Since Pluto (Planet 9) was demoted to a dwarf planet in 2006 and some rings around the other gas giants were not known until later as well. Refer to Figure 1-26.

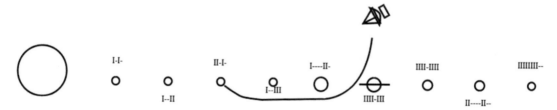

Figure 1-26. *Pictorial sketch of part of the infographic on the Pioneer spacecraft plaques in regard to the sun and our solar system*

Other notable people who joined the discussion and development of infographics in the twentieth century included visual artist Isidore Isou, philosopher Stephen Toulmin, lecturer/writer Edward Tufte, and Peter Sullivan, an infographic creator from 1970 to 1990 for the British newspaper, *The Sunday Times*.

In the years 1985–1987, as the computer was gradually becoming a popular drawing tool, Adobe Inc. created the scalable vector drawing program we know today as Adobe Illustrator. However, it was not until 1993 that graph creation was added to the program. Over the following years, many of the application tools that we use today to create our infographics were added. Refer to Figure 1-27.

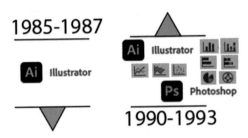

Figure 1-27. Introduction of Illustrator and its graphing tools along with Photoshop

Adobe Photoshop: It should be noted that was released in the 1990s and was not usually used for initial infographic creation and more for touching up photographs. It would over time become another key application in the acquisition of the sketch and then for the enhancement of the final infographic, where Illustrator, in earlier versions, could not add subtle shadows, gradients, and textures to its vector graphics. Photoshop was then needed to successfully create a raster or pixel-rendered version in a high resolution for final output for print.

2001 AD–Present and Modern Infographics

The 2000s and onward have seen many types of infographics being able to be produced more quickly using computer programs like Adobe Illustrator, which allows us to create scalable versions of a design, and Adobe Animate (formerly known as Flash until 2016), which allows us to animate those drawings. Other Adobe applications also added further 3D and video options for the graphic designer. Refer to Figure 1-28.

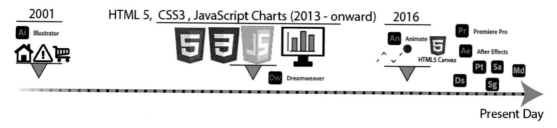

Figure 1-28. *Pictorial timeline of 2001 AD to the present*

For your website coding with HTML 5 and CSS3, along with JavaScript (jQuery) and Chart.js libraries and plug-ins that allow us to create charts and graphs quickly to display data in real time along with interactivity, I will discuss this more in Volume 3 in regard to Adobe Dreamweaver.

These are just some of the many innovations in recent years that have allowed graphic designers to display information visually on websites and various social media networks.

You can find more historical people and links to other historical information on the following page as well as searching on "infographic history" using your preferred search engine:

```
https://en.wikipedia.org/wiki/Infographic
```

How Did the Logo Come Along with the Infographic Historically?

The word logotype or logo originates from Ancient Greek words λόγος (lógos) meaning "word, speech" and τύπος (túpos) meaning "mark, imprint."

Infographics and logos for the most part were developed side by side.

For thousands of years, individuals and organizations have created a graphic mark, emblem, or symbol (whether it be abstract or figurative) to be used to aid and promote their public identification and brand recognition.

Ancient logos were often more pictorial and were imprinted into clay tablets, wax, or metal coins. The carved cylinder or stamp seal that contained the logo was often made of wood, stone, ceramic, or metal. Refer to Figure 1-29 and Figure 1-30.

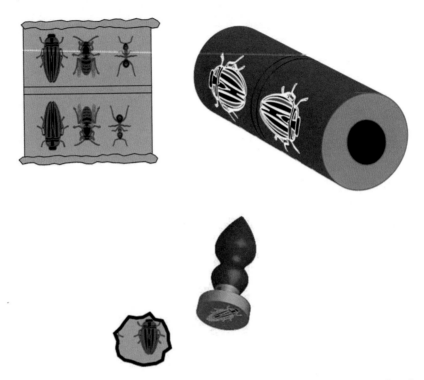

Figure 1-29. *Pictorial example of clay rolled with pattern from a cylinder or stamped seal*

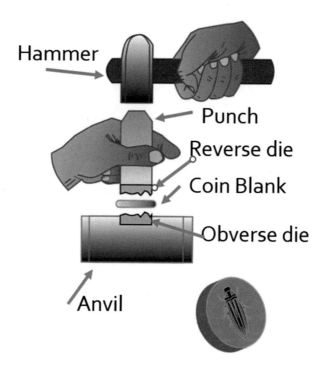

Figure 1-30. *Creating a metal coin*

However, what we consider modern and abstract logo design did not occur until the 1800s. Earlier in this chapter, we saw how this was true with the infographic as the distinct type of chart or graph we see begins to emerge. Logos and infographics became more standardized due to the improvement of printing techniques such as hot metal type settings and later offset lithography. Modern printing allowed logos to be mass produced as words and symbols could be cast or plated together as one unit or moved around to be added to another location in the page layout before printing begins. And so it was with infographics that could more easily appear in books, magazines, and other publications. Refer to Figure 1-31.

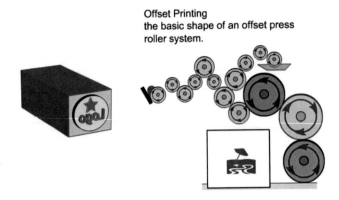

Figure 1-31. *Pictorial example of metal type logo and offset press roller system*

Later, in the electronic age of the 1950s, logos appeared more prominently on television, and some animated infographics in the form of cartoons appeared as well in advertisements.

By the 1980s, computer applications such as Adobe Illustrator were created that allowed the graphic designer to easily create and edit a logo as well as an infographic.

Logos appear today on many web and social media sites, often with bold and simplified designs, which are easily recognizable, no matter what digital viewing platform you are using. Refer to Figure 1-32.

Figure 1-32. *Pictorial examples of some common social media logos*

Here we can see a timeline of the logo in relationship to the infographic. Refer to Figure 1-33.

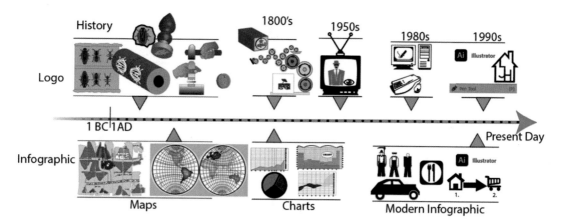

Figure 1-33. *Pictorial timeline of the logo and infographic developing together over thousands of years*

What Is the Difference Between an Infographic and a Logo?

Today's beginner graphic artist, who is training in graphic design, would likely develop a logo first before creating an infographic. Infographics must be more accurate factually, while a logo we can consider more like an ancient stamp. Yes, it represents a company, but in a more abstract and sometimes ambiguous way, it is just a design. What it actually represents may not be important as long as it satisfies the client. This is not to say that creating a logo does not take time and effort. But with an infographic, often the design is more elaborate requiring many components or steps, and you really need to do your research to get the information or data correctly displayed. We will discuss this more in Chapter 2. Refer to Figure 1-34.

Figure 1-34. *A basic pictorial logo and infographic with numerical steps*

An Infographic in Its Basic Form

An infographic does not need to be complicated, but it should in some visual way reveal data and answer most if not all the questions of who, what, when, where, why, and how.

Here I will explain briefly how a simple infographic could be constructed visually.

Let's begin with a drawing of three animals: a lion, a bear, and a parrot. These three animals appear to be placed among plant life that kind of resembles a jungle-type setting. Refer to Figure 1-35.

Figure 1-35. *A basic pictorial infographic with wildlife on a sign*

While it is a nice drawing, we really don't know what it means. To you, the viewer, it could mean or represent a number of things. Maybe you like animals or you like the colors or the general layout of the picture. Could it be something to hang on a wall as artwork? A parrot lives in the jungle, but what about the lion and bear, why are they represented here? If you saw this picture on a sign outdoors, what would you think it meant? The next thing we need to add, to give us some more clues, is an arrow. Refer to Figure 1-36.

Figure 1-36. *A basic pictorial infographic with wildlife on a sign and an arrow*

If the arrow points in some direction, it may tell us how to get there. This tells us that if we go that way, something involving possibly these animals will be there. But are these animals real, or are they only puppets or stuffed animal toys? The final thing we need to add is text, in this case, the text that could be added is "Zoo." Now it has become an official infographic and has given us many clues. Refer to Figure 1-37.

Figure 1-37. *A basic pictorial infographic with wildlife on a sign, an arrow, and the word zoo*

We know who we are going to see (lions, bears, and parrots), we know what is over there (the zoo with jungle plant life), and we know how to get there if we follow the arrow. Other questions like where and when can be answered though this requires extra text for streets, dates, and times. Refer to Figure 1-38.

Figure 1-38. *A basic pictorial infographic with wildlife on a sign, an arrow, the word zoo, and more text details*

Why, in this case, would likely be separate graphics such as when or why the zoo was established. Though, in this case, you should know why you want to go to the zoo to see the animals.

Yet, because we need to scan this sign quickly, we may not need to answer these questions precisely until we get closer to the destination. More detailed infographics could be presented within the zoo for each animal's habitat such as lions in savannah or bears in the forest though they can exist in jungle-type settings as well. This is just a general overview of what to expect at the zoo. Also consider if we had left off the graphic of the animals. Refer to Figure 1-39.

Figure 1-39. *A sign with the word zoo and an arrow*

Would the idea of the zoo be any more exciting if we saw a white sign with text and an arrow? Would you be compelled to see what or who was there? It might be a zoo of goats and sheep, but we would not know without the image. Again, if we just saw just the arrow, would we follow the path to the location? Refer to Figure 1-40.

Figure 1-40. *A sign an arrow*

As you can see, all of these items need to work together to create an infographic that the audience can scan quickly to get the relevant information they need on the topic.

Later in Volume 2, we will also see how similar questions can be answered with graphs.

Summary

In this chapter, you looked at an overview of the history of infographics, as well as how a logo is slightly different than an infographic. Later, you also looked at how a graphic requires certain other components like text and icons to guide the audience so that the information is quickly and clearly conveyed. In the next chapter, we will be looking at what kind of preparation goes into creating the overall mock-up of the infographic before you start designing it in Illustrator.

CHAPTER 2

Preparation for Creating a Logo and Infographics

When you begin to design your artwork, you need to consider that each logo and infographic that you create will be unique and different, and if you are creating them for a client whom you have not worked with before, it can be a challenge to know where to begin. You may also be used to creating logos in the past, and now you are creating an infographic for the first time. This chapter will look at some of the main considerations and steps that you can take, either independently or with your team, as you create an infographic for a client.

Note This chapter is a discussion on the process of logo and infographic creation but does not contain any actual projects other than a reference file in the Volume 1 Chapter 2 folder mentioned in this chapter. However, you can use the online application of Adobe Color in the chapter mentioned later if you want to follow along.

Design Considerations

With any type of data visualization, the goal of course should be to create an infographic that shows the data in an easy-to-understand way through a picture but at the same time causes the viewer to contemplate and compare what is being presented. In doing so, you, the designer, must avoid such things as causing a distortion of that data. Yet this can be difficult when you have a limited amount of space to incorporate a lot of information. The graphic may be very straightforward, but there also may be two or more levels of

© Jennifer Harder 2023
J. Harder, *Creating Infographics with Adobe Illustrator: Volume 1*,
https://doi.org/10.1007/979-8-8688-0005-4_2

detail in the data that you want the graphic and text to reveal. How can you incorporate a full story onto one page? The answer is to focus on the highlights or memorable moments as one might do in a trailer for a movie and remove any unneeded clutter, but to edit it down takes time, both in the data and various visual elements.

To review, designing a professional logo for a client is probably one of the main tasks that most graphic designers encounter when a client is starting a new business or refreshing their brand. If you have been lucky enough to have been chosen to do this task for the first time, as a new designer, it is definitely important that you practice your drawing skills in applications like Adobe Illustrator and Photoshop.

Note   An infographic will likely be required to be designed for a client after they have established their brand or logo. Their logo may be incorporated as part of the infographic on the page or not at all depending on what its topic will be. Nevertheless, similar requirements will apply as follows to working with your client, whether as a team or individually.

Once you have acquired some skills, such as the ones you will be reviewing in this book, before you get to work on any projects for your client, it's always important to spend some time meeting with your client. This first meeting should be done either in person or virtually, for at least an hour. Refer to Figure 2-1.

Figure 2-1. *Illustration of meeting with client in person or on the computer to discuss artwork*

During that time, it is good to ask them some questions as to

- What are their goals and expectations with the logo or infographic?

- What message they are trying to convey (such as values, mission statement, and accomplishments)?

- Who is their target audience? The graphic needs to reach a target audience, which could be defined by age, gender, and race as well as location, income, and core values. Logos are used as the company brand on a variety of media whether it be in print on paper and packaging or actual promotional items (T-shirts, water bottles, bags, etc.) or as seen on a website on the web page or in a video. However, infographics will mostly appear in a publication whether it be print or online. Still, you need to consider who will be viewing them and what message the graphic conveys.

- It's important to discuss with the client the various multimedia options, with regard to how the design will affect marketing channels and brand perception as well as what topics to avoid keeping good PR (public relations). We'll consider some of these factors later in the chapter.

Color Theory and Harmony Rules with Adobe Color Online

Using colors in your logo or infographic project can be a bit intimidating if you don't know what colors look best or coordinate well together. To understand colors, we need a brief overview of some of the science behind color.

The Science of Color

In our visually saturated world of images and graphics, for most sighted people, it's hard to imagine a world without color. Color plays such an important role in choices such as what to eat, wear, purchase, branding, and mood. Everywhere that we go, there is color. But what is color? When we turn off the lights, we can't see it. So, is color light? Yes, this is part of the story, but not all of it. To see colors, you do need light. Light is made up of electromagnetic radiation. The main light source is the sun, but a light source could also be a candle or even a light bulb. The wavelengths or frequency that it emits and its intensity give us light. However, the human eye is only able to see certain wavelengths. This is known as the visible "spectrum" or visible light. Refer to Figure 2-2.

Figure 2-2. *The sun shines through a prism, and a person sees a blue circle on a paper*

Pure "white" light, for example, from a light source, is then broken down into the various rainbow colors within the spectrum (red, orange, yellow, green, blue, indigo, and violet) when it goes through a prism or lands on a substrate like paper or an object. In most cases, an object contains a pigment.

A pigment is a material that changes the color of reflected or transmitted light as a result of wavelength-selective absorption. For example, a blue object will absorb all other light in the white spectrum. But it will reflect back the blue of the object. So, as you can see, just having light is not enough to see color, we also need a pigment and a surface to separate the colors of light; otherwise, everything would be white.

Once the pigment is reflecting a color, we see the color; the information goes into the eye, and the receptor in our eye and our brain processes what color of "blue" based on the visible spectrum.

This is how it should be for all normal-sighted people "in theory," but as we'll see later, there are a few other factors going on, so we don't all come to the same conclusion. What we need to know at this moment is that to see color, we need light, a surface with pigment, and a person to view the effect that is produced.

Now let's look at how color is classified.

Light or objects that emit light, like our computer screen, use what is known as additive color. Refer to Figure 2-3.

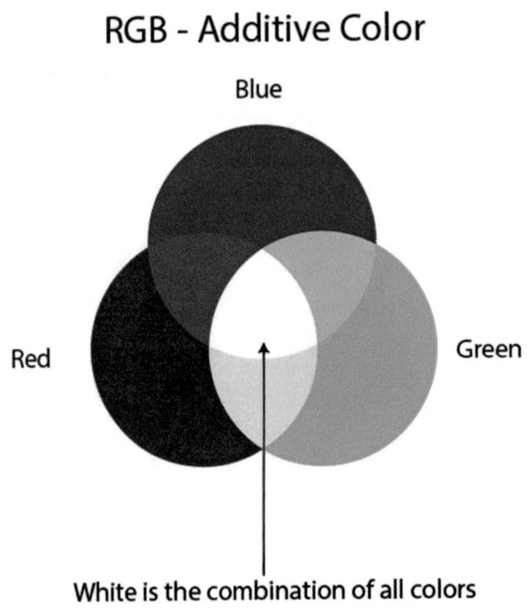

RGB - Additive Color

Figure 2-3. *RGB additive color diagram, white is a combination of all colors*

In the case of the computer screen, the light primary colors are red, green, and blue, and a full combination of all three when added together produces white light. In combinations of two, we get secondary colors, such as combining red and blue, we get magenta; or blue and green, we get cyan; and red and green surprisingly, we get yellow. Depending on the technology used, LED, LCD, or plasma pixel lights, in their respective wavelengths on the screen, are so small that our mind is fooled into believing that we are seeing only one solid color, but we are not. RGB color mode is one of the most common modes and is used not only for the computer color screen but for all devices that emit light or need to capture color using light, like digital cameras, scanners, smartphones, and TV sets. Websites are built using the RGB color mode.

Subtractive color deals with colors that are produced using pigments. This includes most printed material that we see every day. Subtractive color systems start with light, presumably white light. Colored inks, paints, or filters between the viewer and the light source or reflective surface subtract wavelengths from the light, producing the color you see. Refer to Figure 2-4.

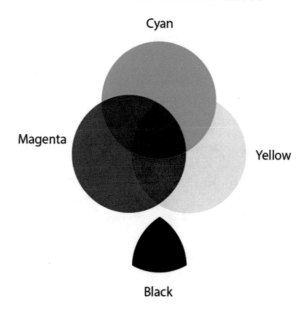

Figure 2-4. *CMYK subtractive color diagram*

On a piece of pure white paper, we lay down the pigments of cyan, magenta, and yellow, commonly referred to as "CMY," using an inkjet, laser, or offset press. This should in theory produce a black. The problem is it does not. It looks more like a muddy dark gray because, unlike light, pigments have impurities. So a fourth pigment is required, black, also known as K, to compensate for any totally black or shaded areas in the advertisement you are reproducing. The black on its own is known as grayscale and moves from white (no pigment) to 100% black or full pigment. Refer to Figure 2-5.

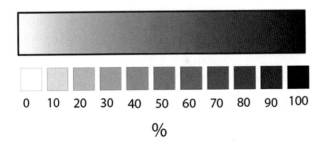

Figure 2-5. *Grayscale chart showing 0%–100%*

In the CMYK color mode, cyan, magenta, and yellow are the primaries with black to compensate. To create secondary colors, you need magenta and cyan to create blue, magenta and yellow to create a red, and cyan and yellow to create a green.

Unfortunately, RGB (additive) mode for digital and CMYK (subtractive) for print cannot capture all colors in the visible spectrum. This is what is known as falling out of gamut, which we will look at in more detail later in the chapter. But you can refer to this comparison or compression chart. Refer to Figure 2-6.

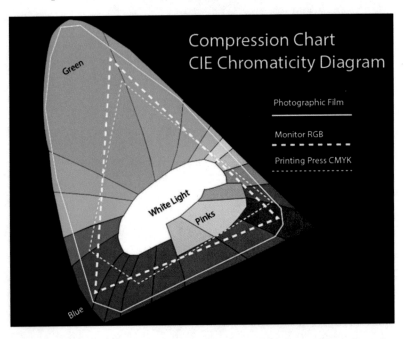

Figure 2-6. *Color compression CIE chromaticity diagram chart for photographic film, monitor RGB, and printing press CMYK*

RGB can capture more colors than the CMYK model, but the area doesn't equally overlap in all cases, and that is why your monitor (additive) cannot accurately tell you how a printed (subtractive) item will look. These ranges can vary from media to media depending on what is trying to reproduce the color range.

Over time, some designers have tried to find ways to compensate. For example, to capture yellow better on a TV screen, they have attempted to add a yellow light to the RGB known as Quattron (QuadPixel technology) to get a higher range of colors in the yellow. However, this technology only apparently lets through more red and green light resulting in less than accurate color. In CMYK printing, booster or spot colors like reds or orange and greens are added as additional inks to the inkjet printer and offset presses to achieve a higher range of the visible spectrum. However, in the case of the press, unless you know how these colors will interact with one another, you can get some undesirable results. Due to this and economic reasons, it is why most offset press projects stay within the four colors of CMYK.

To work with color theory on our computer, we need to look at a blend of the two color wheels. To do that, we will be looking at the traditional color wheel that blends both the ideas of RGB and CMYK and what is seen by the human eye into one wheel. Shortly we will look at Adobe Color, and then later you can use the Photoshop and Illustrator applications to deal with the exact interpretation of the pigments if you plan to print or use them online. Refer to Figure 2-7.

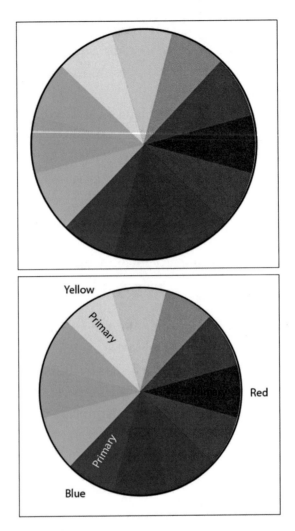

Figure 2-7. *Color wheel and primary colors on the wheel*

If we remember from school, we were taught red, yellow, and blue are primary. Here on the wheel, they are spaced evenly.

You can mix red and yellow to make orange, yellow and blue to make green, and blue and red to make a purple violet. These are known as the secondary colors of the wheel. Refer to Figure 2-8.

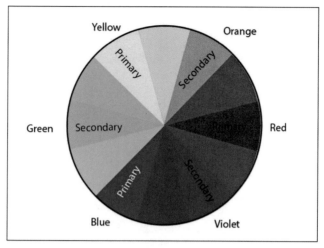

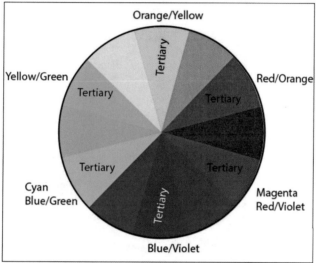

Figure 2-8. *Color wheel with primary, secondary, and tertiary colors*

You can then mix the colors between a primary and a secondary to create a third set of colors known as tertiary. Refer to Figure 2-8.

So that these colors on the wheel blend with traditional and modern views, I have classified the names as such: orange/yellow, red/orange, red/violet (also known as magenta), blue/violet, blue/green (also known as cyan), and yellow/green. Refer to Figure 2-9.

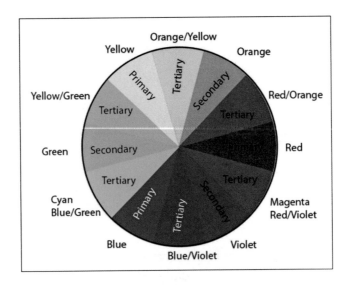

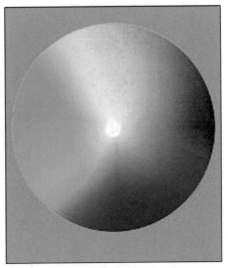

Figure 2-9. *All colors listed on the wheel and as they appear as a gradation*

However, it is important to remember that color does not fall into neat zones and this is a rough approximation of how color falls. In reality, outside of the computer, color is more graduated. Who really knows precisely where one color begins or another ends?

Some clients may already have picked out some colors for you which you can use in your project. However, if it's up to you to choose the colors, where should you begin? How can you easily learn some rules about color theory and harmonies? Adobe has an online app called Adobe Color that you can use to adapt five colors to several harmony rules.

Working with the Adobe Color App

To locate this application, you need to use your Creative Cloud Desktop console. Choose the Apps tab. Refer to Figure 2-10.

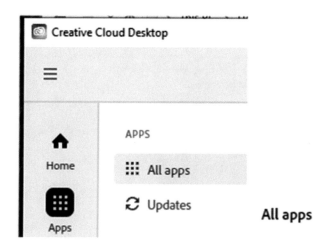

Figure 2-10. *Creative Cloud Desktop with All Apps tab selected*

Then on the left, select All Apps, and from the middle section, choose the Web icon tab. Refer to Figure 2-11.

All apps   Desktop   Mobile   Web

Figure 2-11. *Creative Cloud Desktop with All Apps tab selected and Web icon tab selected*

Scroll down the list of applications and locate Adobe Color and click the Launch button. Refer to Figure 2-12.

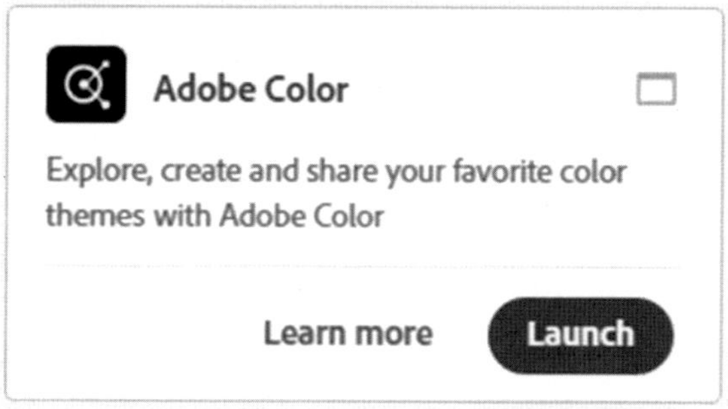

Adobe Color

Explore, create and share your favorite color themes with Adobe Color

Learn more   Launch

Figure 2-12. *Link to Adobe Color online app*

45

This will bring up the Adobe Color Application in your browser and you can begin to start working with the Color Wheel and apply Color Harmony Rules. Refer to Figure 2-13.

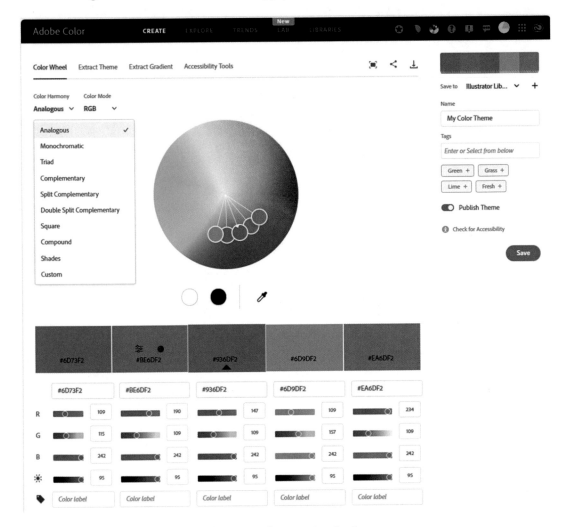

Figure 2-13. *Adobe Color online app layout in the browser*

Note   Due to the application being online, the layout is subject to changes and new features being added frequently.

In this example, we are in the Create section on the Color Wheel tab.

Other sections like Explore, Trends, Lab, and Libraries will allow you to look at images in relationship to color or past color themes in Libraries that you have created. Refer to Figure 2-14.

Figure 2-14. *Create section is currently selected for Adobe Color*

Lab, which is a new feature, will allow you to recolor vector artwork from an SVG file. While not relevant to this book, you may want to explore this option when you work with SVG files in Volume 3. For now, remain in the Create section.

Also, in the upper right of the dark bar are additional settings to link with other features, adjust how you preview the colors on a white or dark interface theme, color game, help, forum, feedback, login settings, web and apps services, and other Creative Cloud settings. You can ignore these for this book. Refer to Figure 2-15.

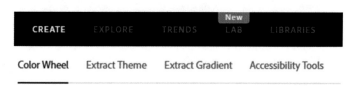

Figure 2-15. *Adobe Color additional resource links*

For now, remain in the Create section on the Color Wheel tab. Refer to Figure 2-16.

Figure 2-16. *Create section in Adobe Color with Color Wheel tab selected*

This area has a section called color harmony where you can choose various rules from the drop-down menu. Adobe says you can use the color rules to ensure a harmonic balance of colors based on the color you have set as the base color. Currently in this example, analogous has been selected, and the base color is the middle one in the bar of five with a black or white upward-pointing arrow depending on the color it overlays. Refer to Figure 2-17.

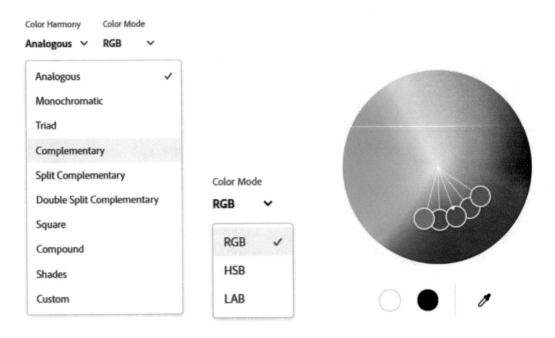

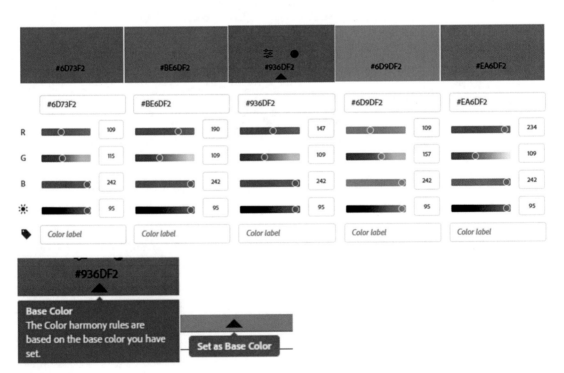

Figure 2-17. *Adobe Color Wheel selection with current layout setup and default harmony rule*

I'll mention more about base color and other settings including color mode in a moment as seen in Figure 2-17. However, let's take a moment to review how each of these harmonies is based on the color wheel. Refer to Figure 2-18.

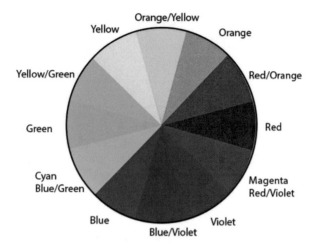

Figure 2-18. *Review of the color wheel and its segment names*

To understand color, it's important to know that the 12 colors or hues in our wheel fall into two main categories, warm or cool. This is collectively known as temperature.

Warm colors fall in the red to yellow range, and we associate these hues with activeness, warm seasons (summer), or aggressiveness. Refer to Figure 2-19.

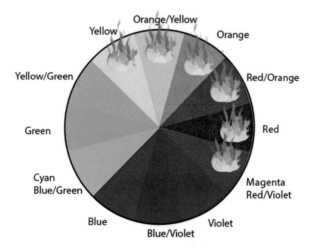

Figure 2-19. *Colors that fall into the warm zone on the color wheel*

Cool colors fall in the green to violet range, and we associate these hues with passiveness, the cool season (winter), or something that recedes. Refer to Figure 2-20.

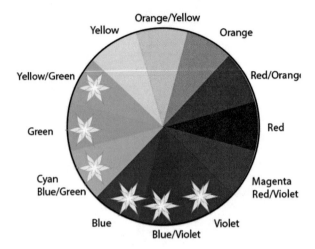

Figure 2-20. *Colors that fall into the cool zone on the color wheel*

However, when we design with color theory and harmonies, we don't just stay within these rules. There are other rules and combinations that mix warm and cool colors in a harmonious or discordant blend.

Color Harmony Definitions

- Analogous (analog): A color combination where two, three, four, or even five hues can be touching or adjacent.

  First, a base or active color is chosen, and then the other colors move based on the placement of that color. You can then move to other colors together on the wheel as you cycle around; this is true for all color themes and harmonies. A variation on analogous is known as split analogous, which you could create if you drag on one of the outer colors on the wheel using the custom option. This makes the hues one step apart. A good tip to remember about analogous is this combination is good for blending or gradation of one color into another. Refer to Figure 2-21.

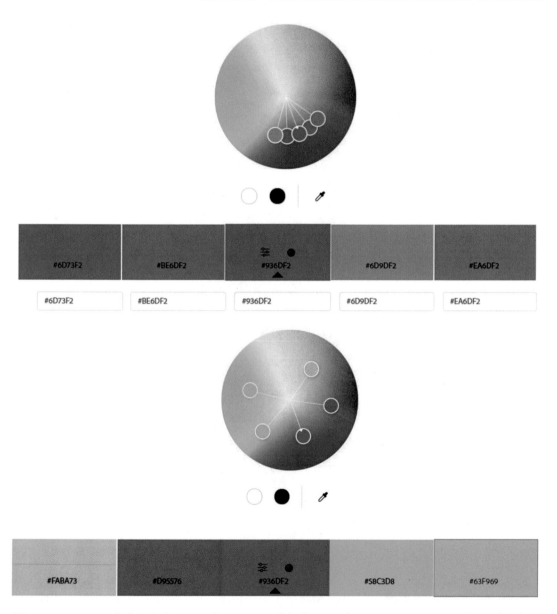

Figure 2-21. *Adobe Color Analogous and Split Analogous options on the wheel and resulting swatches based on base color selection*

- Monochromatic: Is when color stays in one hue like red or green or in this example purple. The color does not go beyond those boundaries and stays within a very strict zone. At least five swatches can be dragged out. If you are working with just black and white, this would be known as achromatic which uses the grayscale. Though the grayscale technically lacks color, it can create some very striking effects in art. In Adobe Color, it is also related to another harmony theme called shades, which we will look at later. Refer to Figure 2-22.

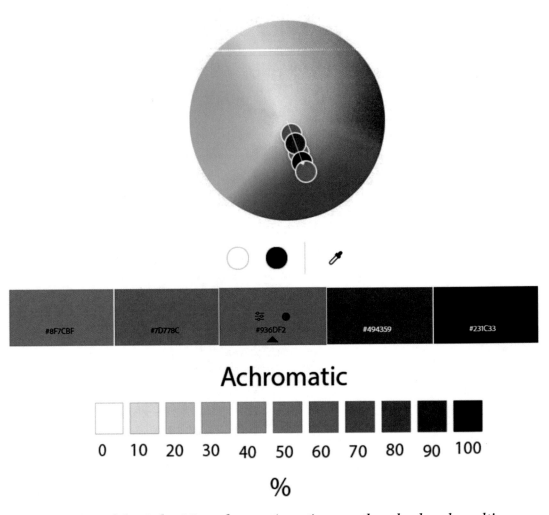

Figure 2-22. *Adobe Color Monochromatic options on the wheel and resulting swatches based on base color selection and achromatic diagram*

- Triad (Triadic): Uses three evenly spaced hues set at about 120 degrees on the circle. It has some similarities to the split complementary, which you will look at later, but in this case, the arms of the hues are farther apart on the left and right and create a greater variety. Notice how red, yellow, and cyan/blue could form a triad, but at least one or two muted colors are a part of the harmony as well. Refer to Figure 2-23.

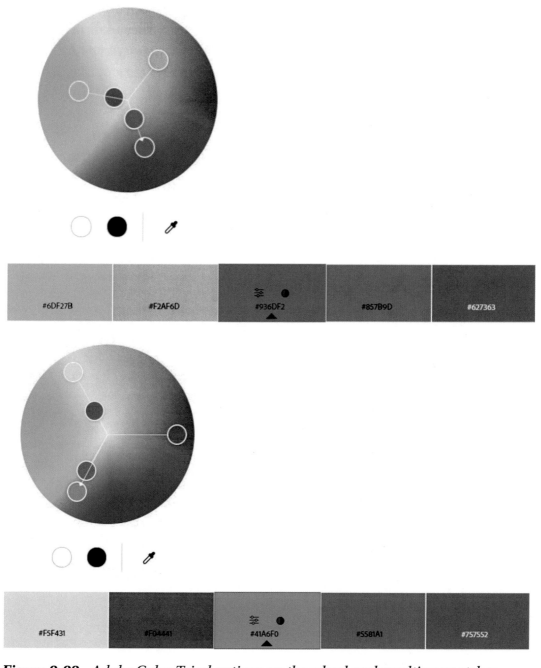

Figure 2-23. *Adobe Color Triad options on the wheel and resulting swatches based on base color selection*

- Complementary: For the most part, it uses two hues at opposite ends of the color wheel. For direct complementary colors, when using the purest hues, they can sometimes clash, or what feels like a vibration with the eyes and causes an afterimage when stared at too long. The eye is fighting for what color should be seen; it wants to blend colors, and this causes discordancy. To deal with this, try using at least three transitionary graying of hues and add them to the mix so that the colors blend and transition with the eye. However, in some cases, this may still not be enough to achieve harmony. Refer to Figure 2-24.

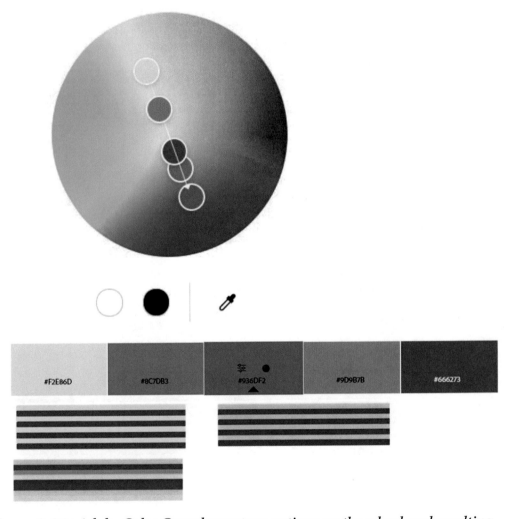

Figure 2-24. *Adobe Color Complementary options on the wheel and resulting swatches based on base color selection and examples of vibrating color and making transition muted colors*

- Split Complementary: To deal with this intenseness, you can create a split complementary that uses three hues, where one hue in the original complement is split to hues over to the left or the right, and these arm swatches can be moved closer or farther from the base color inward or outward. Refer to Figure 2-25.

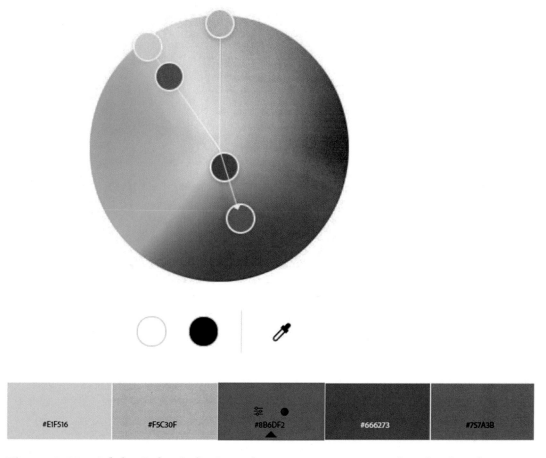

Figure 2-25. *Adobe Color Split Complementary options on the wheel and resulting swatches based on base color selection*

You can then choose to use only the hues on the left or the right or on both sides of the complement. One thing to remember, when dealing with complementary, is you need a good contrast of dark and light for legibility when adding text onto contrasting backgrounds. Otherwise, the text will be difficult to read and cause eyestrain, especially with larger amounts of text. We'll talk about this later in the chapter. Refer to Figure 2-26.

Figure 2-26. *Good contrast on the left but may not work well with smaller fonts due to complementary colors and may need further adjustments; on the right, contrast is bad, and colors cause eye strain at any font size*

- Double Split Complementary: Splits the complement in two, moving over a step to the left or right. Currently, you can recreate this using this option from the list. Refer to Figure 2-27.

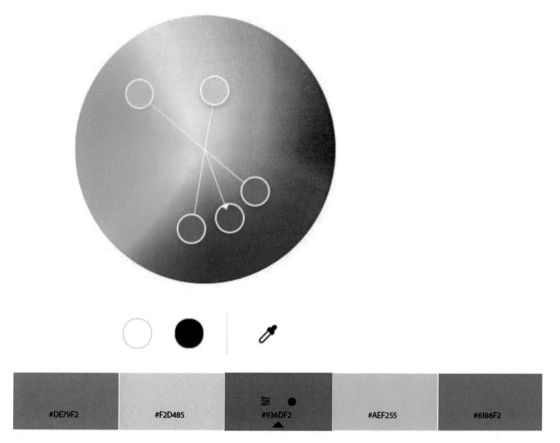

Figure 2-27. *Adobe Color Double Split Complementary options on the wheel and resulting swatches based on base color selection*

However, if you want the split to be more analogous, create a double analogous complementary instead by using the custom settings, which you can alter by choosing the custom option in the color harmony list and move the swatches independently. Refer to Figure 2-28.

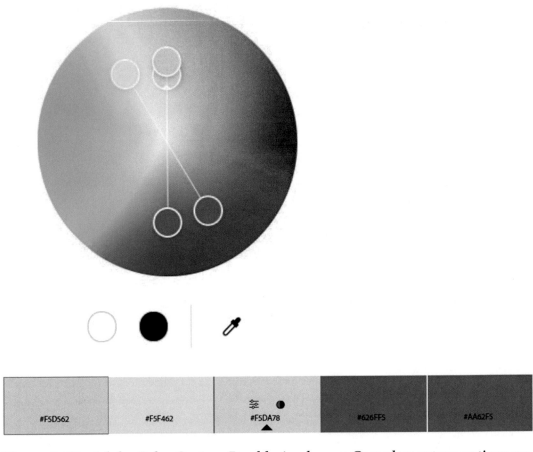

Figure 2-28. *Adobe Color Custom Double Analogous Complementary options on the wheel and resulting swatches based on base color selection*

Another custom variation on this is known as the alternate complement. This uses a triad with alternate colors in the middle. Use the triad option to set this one up and then move to the custom option and adjust at least one of your swatches. Refer to Figure 2-29.

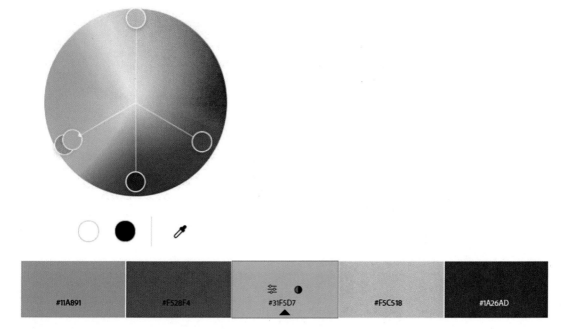

Figure 2-29. *Adobe Color Custom Alternate Complement options on the wheel and resulting swatches based on base color selection*

- Square: When dealing with four or more colors, there are a few harmony variety themes that can be created. The most common is the tetradic or double complement (square). Each color is set at 90 degrees to the other and then complements the opposite color. Note that another variation on this tetradic theme is the double split complementary, which is more rectangle-like than you looked at earlier, but this time, using the custom from the color harmony list with one of the swatches together with the other, you could create the custom setting. Swatches for the square can be moved inward and outward and spun around while keeping the harmony. Refer to Figure 2-30.

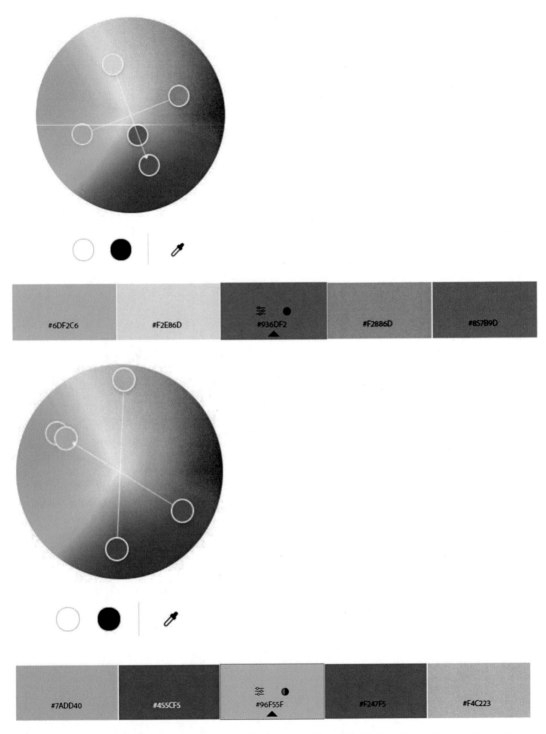

Figure 2-30. *Adobe Color Square and Custom Double Split Complement options on the wheel and resulting swatches based on base color selection*

- Compound: A separate or more complex color harmony with four or
  more colors. It uses a combination of analogous and complementary
  and can fall either to the left or right as you spin the swatches using
  the base color. The swatches can be moved inward or outward on
  the wheel. You can alter this later using the custom option. Refer to
  Figure 2-31.

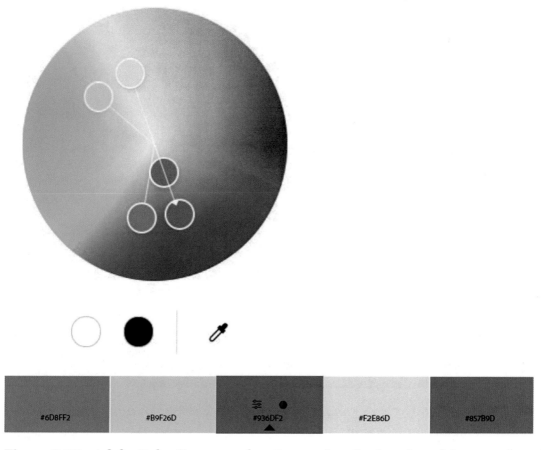

Figure 2-31. *Adobe Color Compound option on the wheel and resulting swatches
based on base color selection*

- Shades: Similar to monochrome but deals more with a narrow range of colors, usually one or two swatches on the wheel depending on the base or another color is selected, unlike monochrome which uses five. However, five swatch bars will be created. Refer to Figure 2-32.

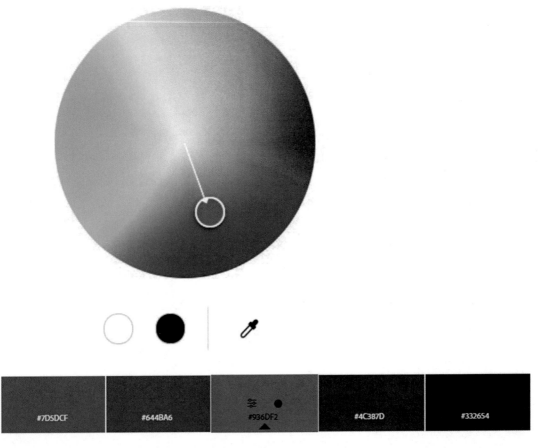

Figure 2-32. *Adobe Color Shades option on the wheel and resulting swatches based on base color selection*

- Custom: Another unique color harmony that is not as well-known as the pentagram, and this uses five colors at various spaced points on the color wheel. You can create this and your other custom harmonies with the custom setting as each color swatch moves freely. Refer to Figure 2-33.

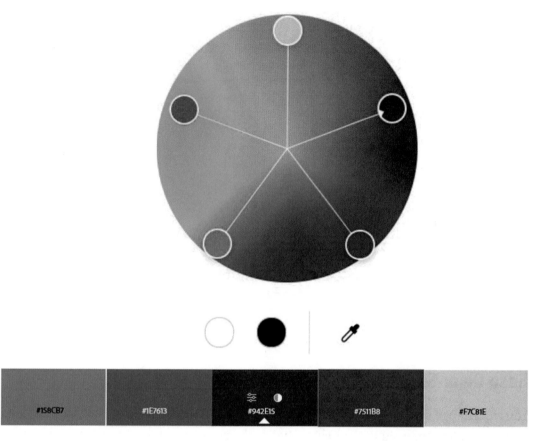

Figure 2-33. *Adobe Color Custom Pentagram option on the wheel and resulting swatches based on base color selection*

When using all color hues, you can refer to this as **polychromatic.** Using text or artwork in all colors is often more for kids than adults as children like things that are multicolored and are not so concerned with things that appear busy or vibrating. Refer to Figure 2-34.

Polychromatic

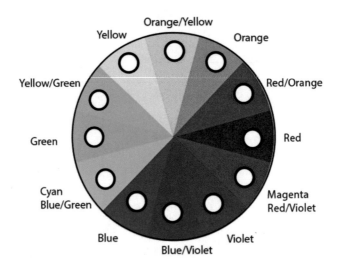

Figure 2-34. *Example of a polychromatic layout on a color wheel*

Base Color Settings and Eyedropper

You can change the base color that you base all your other colors on by clicking one of the other five colors in the bar colors below the color wheel to add a white or black triangle. Refer back to Figure 2-17. This will attach a white triangle to that swatch in the color wheel, and then you can move the color slider around on the wheel to make the other colors complement it. Below the color wheel, you will see the white and black dots on the left; these will allow you to select and set all colors one at a time when selected, which you will see the change reflected in the lower sliders, back to a base of white or black, which also reflects in the wheel or bars. Refer to Figure 2-33 and Figure 2-35. We will look at the lower slider in a moment. However, I will just point out that the eyedropper on the right can be used when selected to magnify and select colors on the screen for a more accurate pixel color selection for your base color or current selected swatch. Refer to Figure 2-35.

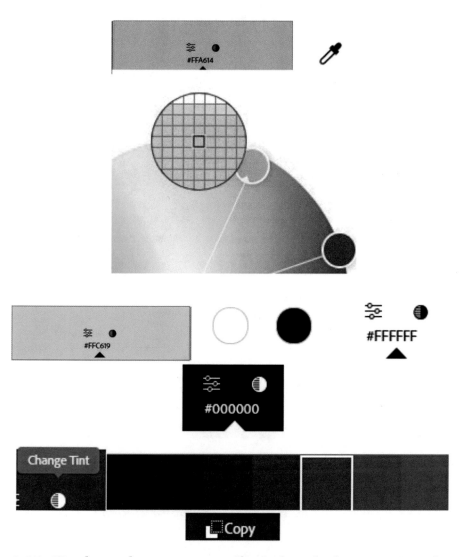

Figure 2-35. *Use the eyedropper to magnify pixels and select a precise color*

On the lower five swatch bars that display the HEX color as you hover over them, you will now notice a few new settings that were added. You can now drag and move the order of the bars, use the change color icon to hide and show the lower sliders, use the change tint icon to see bars of variations of tint option that you can easily switch, and also copy the HEX color code number to the clipboard if you need to add it to a document for web design. Refer to Figure 2-35.

Color Modes RGB, HSB, and LAB, HEX Color Codes, and What About CMYK?

Below the five swatches in the bar are the lower sliders which also react to changes in the wheel and base color section. Refer to Figure 2-36.

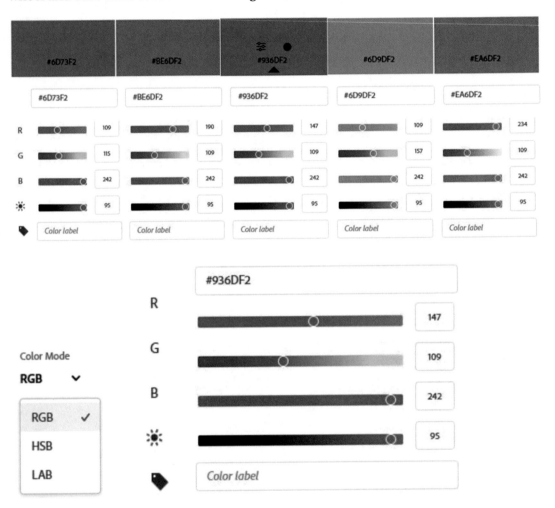

Figure 2-36. *Adobe Color swatches and sliders currently in HEX number and RGB color mode for base swatch*

Each of the five colors is set with a color mode menu on the upper left; in this example, we can see first the web HEX color which is very useful for working on websites. Then we can see the color mode that is currently RGB (red, green, and blue) (0–255) or additive color, and the lower sunlight slider is controlling the lightness and darkness or brightness (0–100) of that swatch and controls the other RGB sliders. Understanding this can be hard to visualize unless seen in 3D which I will mention shortly. You can also add a custom color label for each of the five colors as well.

Other color modes that can be set are HSB or hue (0–360), saturation (0–100), and brightness (0–100), which I will explain in more depth later, and LAB longitude (0–100), latitude (-128,0,127), and altitude (-128,0,127), which is preferred by some photographers for color correction. Refer to Figure 2-37.

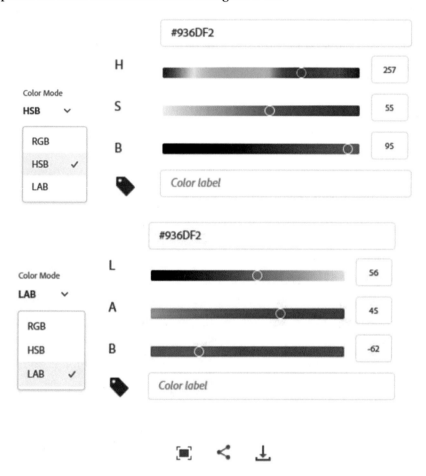

Figure 2-37. *Sliders for swatches can be set to HSB or LAB color modes and new icons for viewing, sharing, and saving colors*

You cannot use Adobe Color to currently find a color mode for CMYK (cyan, magenta, yellow, black) (subtractive) equivalents. However, once you know the RGB or HSB, you can use your Color Picker dialog box in either Photoshop or Illustrator to calculate this number. Note that while in the Color Wheel tab, a few new icons have been added to the right of the window; these include full screen view for viewing the bars on the screen at a larger size which you can exit when clicking the close button, share for sharing with others, and download as JPEG if you need a graphic of your current swatches with color text information. Refer to Figure 2-37 for reference to these new icons.

Color Science 2D and 3D visualization

From what you have seen so far about the color wheel, it may seem like color is pretty two dimensional, but this is not so. Just like in nature which has three dimensions, so is the range of color. Some colors, while we can see them in the visual world, just can't be reproduced on the screen or in print. They go out of gamut or out of range. To imagine three-dimensional color, we need to know what the three dimensions are. Earlier in the chapter, we looked briefly at a compression chart CIE chromaticity diagram for comparison. Refer back to Figure 2-6.

This figure showed a spread-out color wheel in a more triangular image because the color is in actuality, not evenly displaced. From this diagram, we can see that the full-color range would represent visual light. Next might be photographic film that light passes or filters through. Next would be the RGB or the computer screen and finally the CMYK printing press. Colors that are not within the respective boundaries are considered out of gamut by that device, and additional colors would have to be added to increase the range. This can vary from one printing device to another. Like an inkjet printer that may have a greater range than an offset press, this printer as well as your monitor must be calibrated to achieve optimum results.

However, the three dimensions of color can be better understood in the shape of a sphere or cylinder.

The first is hue or pure color, and we looked at this in the last segment as we went around the color wheel choosing color harmonies in Adobe Color.

Here I have turned the hue on its side so that it can be better visualized with the next two dimensions. Refer to Figure 2-38.

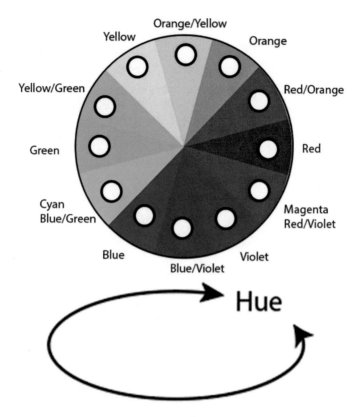

Figure 2-38. *Color wheel and diagram explaining hue*

The next dimension is known as saturation. This controls how intensely vivid, muted, or pure the colors will be in relation to graying. Another name for this is chroma, or some artists refer to it as tone. Saturation moves out from the center point in percentages or steps to its purest point on the very outside of the color wheel. Refer to Figure 2-39.

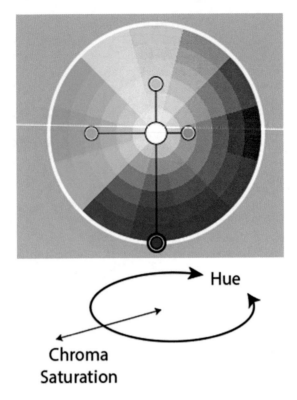

Figure 2-39. *Color wheel and diagram explaining chroma/saturation*

This is very useful to know when dealing with complementary color harmonies, as we saw earlier, so that the color options are not too intense. We can add a few saturations of gray of the same color in between to make the combination more visually manageable.

The final dimension that we need to be aware of is brightness or lightness. It is also known as value or the purest forms of black and white on the grayscale also known as shades and tints when added with a specific hue. Brightness affects luminance and the amount of light reflected. Here we are moving up and down. Refer to Figure 2-40.

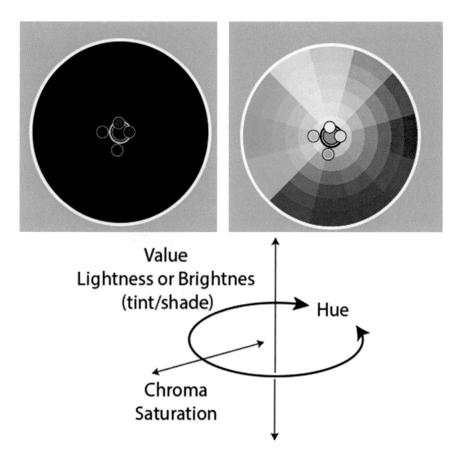

Figure 2-40. *Color wheel and diagram explaining brightness/lightness*

Neither Adobe Color nor Illustrator's Color Guide shows a three-dimensional model, rather they use a slider, which we will look at in the next segment, to control the brightness level.

This three-dimensional model uses what is called hue/saturation/brightness, also known as HSB in the computer. Here is how it looks in three dimensions and in RGB color mode as well. Refer to Figure 2-41.

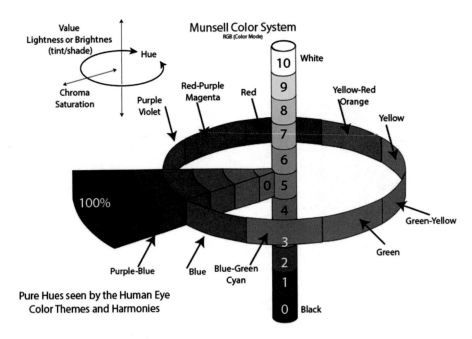

Figure 2-41. *Munsell color diagram imagining color to be displayed as a perfect cylinder*

Note   Ten in this case represents 100% or purest brightness moving down in increments of 1. One is 10%. Refer to Figure 2-42.

Figure 2-42. *Munsell color diagram imagining color to be displayed as a perfect cylinder with many layers*

Before the age of computers, this system was developed by Professor Albert H. Munsell. Starting in 1905, he continued to work on this until his death in 1918 and was used later in the 1930s by the United States Department of Agriculture (USDA) as the official color system for soil research. However, soil or dirt is one of the basic forms of pigments used in ink, and so because Munsell's model best separate hue, saturation (chroma), and value/brightness, it was eventually adapted for use in other color industries like printing and later in the digital computer age. The system was further developed and refined by CIELAB.

Now based on the way this model appears, you would think that color moves in a nice cylindrical fashion up and down all the way around the color wheel.

And in a world where you'd be able to view the whole spectrum of color in nature or any device that would be the case, but as you can see in the lower area of the brightness, you can't even see all colors—it's all black. In the upper area of white, those are out of gamut even though I have represented them on the screen.

Let's look at a two-dimensional slice so we can see this better. Refer to Figure 2-43.

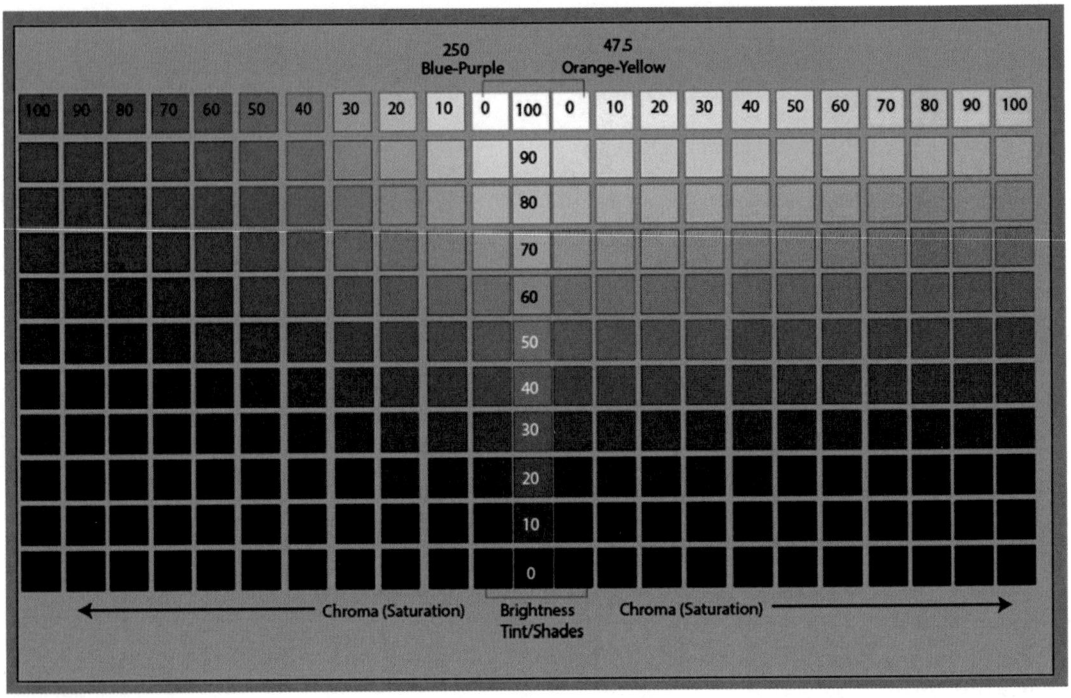

Figure 2-43. *Part of Munsell color diagram, a section of it laid flat in a complementary layout of swatches*

This is a cross section of the hue blue-purple at approximately 250 degrees, and it is running through its complement orange-yellow at an approximate of angle 47.5 degrees according to Adobe Math. This is an approximate complement. As you can see, pure white has a setting of 100, and purest black has a setting of 0. This is how brightness is determined by numbers of percentages. The same is so for chroma or saturation as it spreads out to the left or right of the core. What we can see here is that there are a lot of blacks that repeat and are out of gamut as well, most of the color at 100 of saturation, and values are also out of gamut. It's just not possible to replicate them in RGB monitor light, so once this is taken into consideration, the Munsell model looks something like this, which I have visually simplified in this illustration so that you can see both sides. Refer to Figure 2-44.

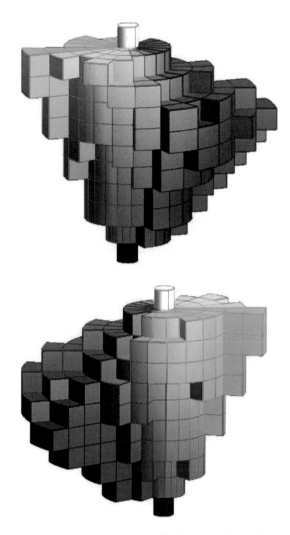

Figure 2-44. *3D diagram representation of color on the wheel and its range in areas it is not out of gamut to us*

You can see how yellows appear in a higher area in the upper saturation and tints but decrease as you enter the shades. The opposite is true for blue-purples, more in the shades but less in the upper tints. Yet they never quite reach the upper or lower value brightness and are at that point out of gamut.

With this knowledge of the color wheel, let's take time to practice with the Adobe Color Themes online app. You should later be able to create some swatches in Illustrator as well as work with its Color Guide panel later in Chapter 8.

Adding Your Color Theme

Returning back to the Adobe Color app, on the right side is the ability to add your color theme to a select library, create a new library, and name the theme. You can also add tag and publicly publish your color theme to Adobe Color as well as check for accessibility which we will look at in a moment. When done, you can save the theme, and it is added to your library, and you can access it in applications such as Photoshop, Illustrator, and InDesign as well as other Adobe applications that have access to the Libraries panel which we will look at in Volume 3. Refer to Figure 2-45.

Figure 2-45. *Adobe Color adding and saving a color to your libraries*

Other Options: Extract Theme and Extract Gradient

While not required for this book, Adobe Color also has options for extracting color or gradient from an image based on the tab you select. This could be useful later when trying to match a specific color. Select a file or drag and drop an image. Refer to Figure 2-46.

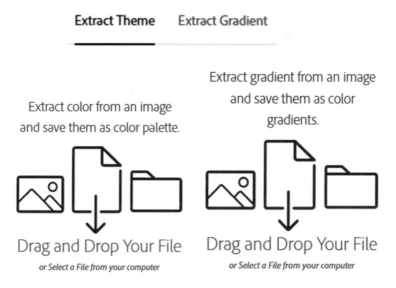

Figure 2-46. *Adobe Color allows you to extract a theme and a gradient from the image that you upload by first selecting one of the tabs*

Accessibility Tools for Contrast and Color Blindness When Dealing with Text and Graphics

One final thing to keep in mind when working with the color wheel is contrast. Are you using colors that have enough contrast? Are the colors distinct enough that they don't blend into one another and disappear?

You will know the difference because high contrast colors give a good range, while low contrast colors start to become difficult to tell the difference between. Here I am using six different colors in this fish, but if all the colors become too dark, each color becomes difficult to see. Refer to Figure 2-47.

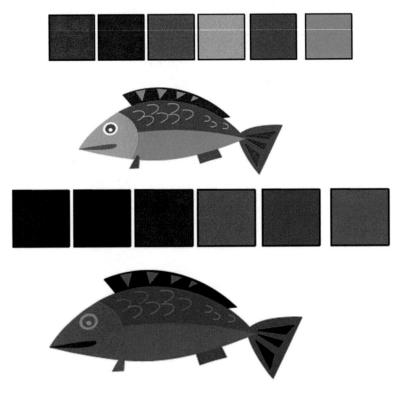

Figure 2-47. *Fish images with high and low contrast swatches*

A good range of high contrast text is more legible. However, with low contrast, colors become moody, somber, and muted as with the fish. With text, it becomes difficult to read. Refer to Figure 2-48.

Figure 2-48. *Text with high and low contrast; the text on the right is hard to see*

You can use this knowledge to create variations on the analogous, complementary, triad, or tetradic themes later with Photoshop and Illustrator. And as you learn more about the rules, you will see where you can alter these themes and make your own variation choices.

Remember, hue interacts with saturation and brightness to create colors that can be of high and low contrast. Also keep in mind how we saw complementary colors earlier affecting readability and contrast.

We can see this more clearly when we work with the Adobe Color Accessibility Tools tab. Samples of text can be reviewed against the contrast or color blind safe checker. In the first example, look at the Contrast Checker tool. Refer to Figure 2-49.

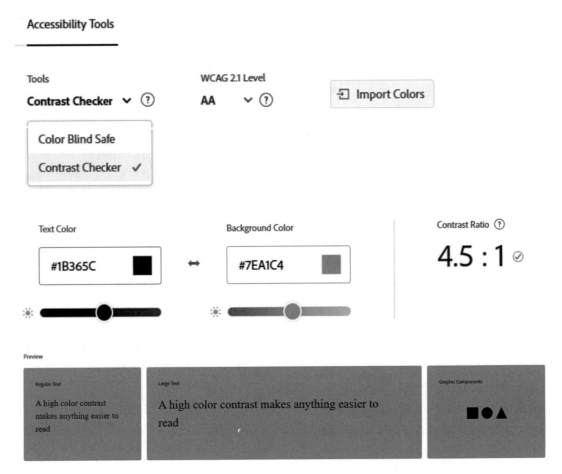

Figure 2-49. *Adobe Color Accessibility Tools tab and some of its options to determine pass or fail*

Once that option is selected, you can set the WCAG 2.1 Level. This refers to the Web Content Accessibility Guidelines, and it can either be Level AA or AAA. This area has an info button for more details that explain the criteria for how large regular text, which is 18pt and above, or 14pt and above for bold font weight, as a different ratio to qualify to when set to the AA or AAA settings. This also applies to regular text that is 17pt and below or 13pt and below for bold font weight. One color setting may pass for large text and graphic components (icons and actionable graphics) but fail for smaller text. Refer to Figure 2-50.

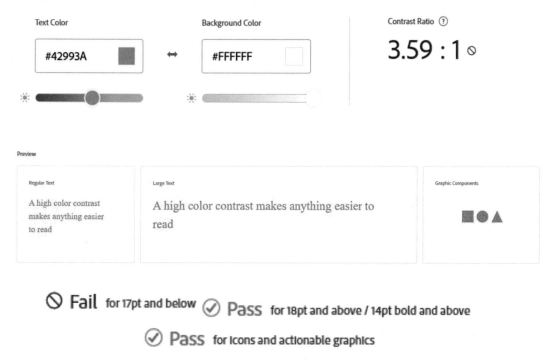

Figure 2-50. *Adobe Color Accessibility Tools tab and some of its options to determine pass or fail—some text will not pass at a small size*

More details can be found on the following page:

https://helpx.adobe.com/creative-cloud/adobe-color-accessibility-tools.html

The Import Colors button allows you to upload an image to check the color contrast between text and background colors and then import the colors. Refer to Figure 2-51.

Figure 2-51. *Adobe Color contrast checker allows you to import color or a file so that you can check the contrast in it*

You can then adjust the colors in the #HEX color or RGB color mode with the sliders to adjust the contrast ratio. You can then reverse the colors using the two-way arrows and continue to adjust the brightness/contrast setting slider, which will then show a pass or fail, and this can be applied to basic graphic components as well. Refer to Figure 2-52 and Figure 2-53.

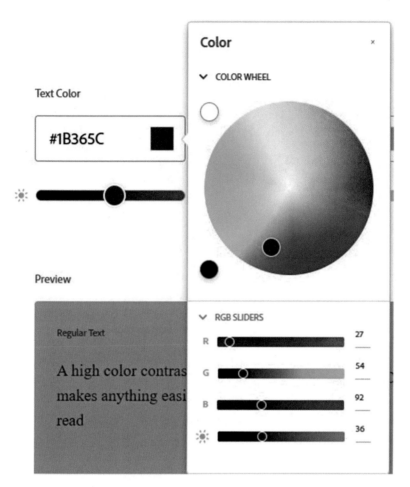

Figure 2-52. *Adobe Color adjusts the color in the contrast checker using the color wheel*

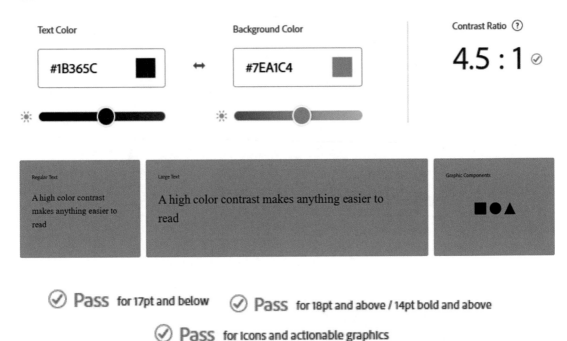

Figure 2-53. *Adobe Color adjusts the color in the contrast checker and then sees if the contrast passes or fails*

As well as on the right side, it can check against a background color and how it can be altered by a ratio with recommendations and saved to libraries. Refer to Figure 2-54.

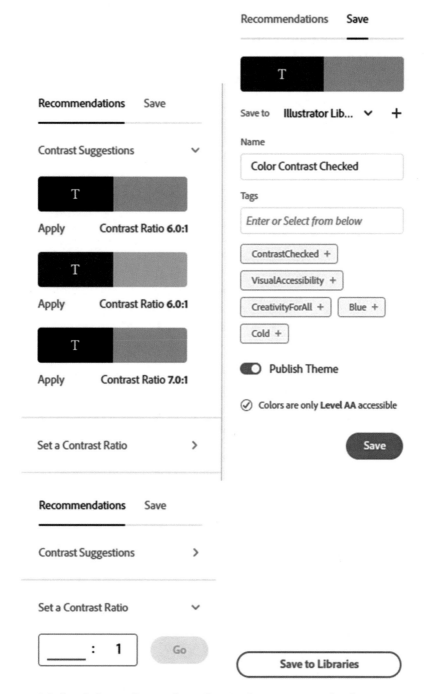

Figure 2-54. *Adobe Color adjusts the color in the contrast checker, reviews suggestions, and saves to your libraries*

The second Accessibility tool or color blind safe allows you to see when some colors are in potential conflict for those with sight issues in columns (A, B, C, D, E). When a theme is not color blind safe, you will be alerted in the RGB, HSB, and LAB color modes. Dragging around the color points will allow you to correct the color settings with any conflict lines as well as show sliders for the color mode to make further adjustments if that is your preference. Refer to Figure 2-55, Figure 2-56, and Figure 2-57.

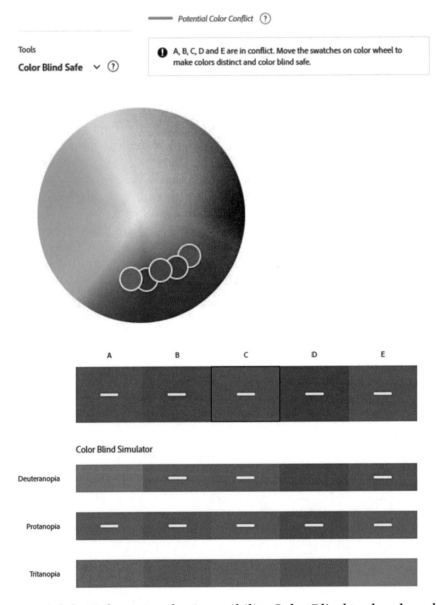

Figure 2-55. *Adobe Color using the Accessibility Color Blind tools color wheel and swatches to find the correct settings*

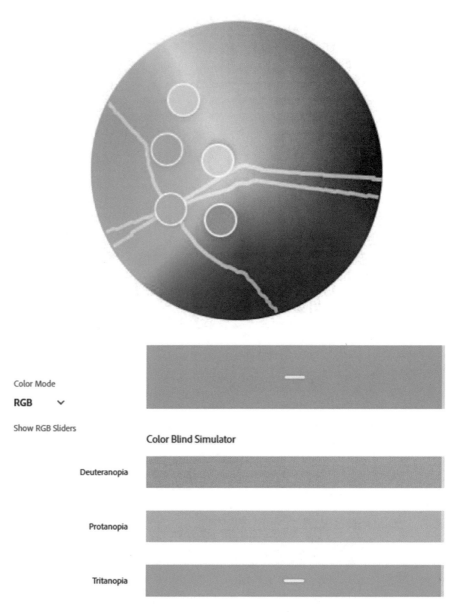

Figure 2-56. *Adobe Color using the Accessibility Color Blind tools color wheel and swatches to find correct settings and moving swatches to make correction and remove conflict*

Figure 2-57. *Checking and saving your color blind safe theme with a warning if it is safe or still not safe*

Before you save the library on the right side, you will be alerted if the theme is or is not color blind safe.

You will see the three main types of color blindness, using the color blind simulator: deuteranopia, protanopia, and tritanopia. Though color blindness only affects roughly 8% of the population, more men than women, it's good to make sure your design is easily readable and accessible to all. So continue to move the sliders around to adjust if you want your colors to be color blind safe if this is critical to your work.

Note   Vision is a key factor in how color is perceived by our brain. For normal-sighted people, as we age, the lens in the eye begins to yellow, and this may be due to cataracts or macular degeneration. In some cases, the lens can be removed and replaced, and then the individual can once again see true whites. Refer to Figure 2-58.

Figure 2-58. *Illustration about how as eyes age we do not see color the same*

However, this is not the case with a person who is color blind. It does not mean that they are actually blind, only that they have trouble distinguishing between certain colors that a normal-sighted person can easily see. In some cases, the person is born this way due to genetics or some trauma, with faulty or inactive photoreceptor cells, known as cones, found in the area of the retina. The ones that control our night vision are known as rods. Cones come in three types known as red (long-wavelength), green (medium-wavelength), and blue (short-wavelength). As light passes through the pupil, it hits the retina and activates the receptors and then the rods and cones. Refer to Figure 2-59.

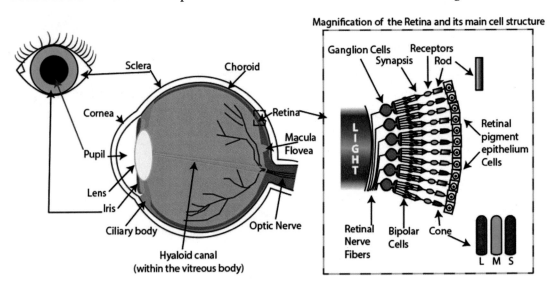

Figure 2-59. *An illustrated eye diagram showing where color receptors rods and cones are located*

If all the red receptors fail to work, this is called protanopia. Refer to Figure 2-60.

Figure 2-60. *Illustration of how protanopia would affect someone seeing red and green*

When green receptors fail, this is known as deuteranopia. Refer to Figure 2-61.

Figure 2-61. *Illustration of how deuteranopia would affect someone seeing red and green*

If blue receptors fail, it is called tritanopia. This person may be OK with red, but green or yellow may not come to the eye accurately. Refer to Figure 2-62.

Figure 2-62. *Illustration of how tritanopia would affect someone seeing red, green, and yellow*

When all cones fail, and the rods are all the eye relies on, which is rare, this is called rod monochromacy (achromatopsia). High and low contrast colors would definitely be important to check for this individual. Refer to Figure 2-63.

Figure 2-63. *Illustration of how rod monochromacy would affect someone seeing red and green*

In some cases, a person may have only partial color blindness, and some of their cone receptors continue to function. Nevertheless, it will affect how they see color. If color correctness is crucial to your job and people tell you you're having difficulty distinguishing colors, it might be a good idea to consult your doctor if you need your eyes tested for color blindness.

Note   In these current examples, we are looking at the printed colors of red, green, and yellow based on a CMYK to emulate RGB on paper. However, keep in mind that the interpretation of actual pure red, green, and blue on a monitor may appear different than pigment inks, and color accuracy will vary even for the color-blind person.

Tip   Photoshop and Illustrator also have viewing and proofing options for testing at least two types of color blindness if you are working in the application.

For Photoshop and Illustrator, refer to the menu:

View ➤ Proof Setup ➤ Color Blindness

Additional Tips on Color and Fonts

Here are some additional things you should keep in mind about fonts before working with a client.

Make sure to keep the text letter characters legible. A font should not be too small so you can read it or too large so that it overwhelms the infographic or logo. Also, the more styles, a font comes in the better, but you should at least have access to the main four: regular, bold, italic, and bold italic. However, keep in mind that handwritten script fonts or special fonts may have readability issues on the screen or in print. Refer to Figure 2-64.

Regular Text
Bold Text
Italic Text
Bold Italic Text

Script Text

Fancy Text

Figure 2-64. *Graphics of different font families with styles of text*

As you saw earlier, think about how color and readability work together. Most times, for an infographic or logo, you will stick with a font that is just going to be black or a dark color. Refer to Figure 2-65.

Figure 2-65. *Logo appearing with some basic text*

However, with logos, some text might be in a different color or style if it is to be on a business card or used in another multimedia project, so it is important to have options and see what works and what will not.

Yellow, light, or neon colors do not show up well on white and are better on a dark background. Refer to Figure 2-66.

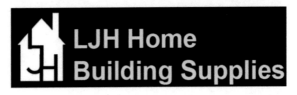

Figure 2-66. *Logo appearing with yellow text on a white and black background and bold text with enlarged logo*

A bold italic style could give the feeling of movement, yet if too bold, it could overwhelm the graphic unless it is enlarged as well. Refer to Figure 2-46.

Dark colors are better on light-colored backgrounds. Magenta may be OK for both light and dark backgrounds, but consider whether that color is present in a current design or does it clash with the design or message you are trying to convey. This suggestion could apply to any newly added color. Refer to Figure 2-67.

Figure 2-67. *Logo appearing with dark blue and magenta text on a white and black background and bold text with enlarged logo*

Also ensure that the background is not patterned or at the very least a faded pattern so that the text and graphics are clearly visible. Refer to Figure 2-68.

Figure 2-68. *Logo appearing with black text on a patterned and faded patterned background*

In most situations with a lot of data, a solid background is best.

Note: There are other lesser-known external and internal factors that influence color perception and how your graphic will be viewed. These include

External:

- Exterior or interior lighting which has varying cast from red, yellow, to blue

- Reflective color cast of another object, paper, pigment

- The camera you use to take your pictures

- The color mode you save your file in

Internal perceptions can be influenced by the following:

- Age (child and adult)

- Gender

- Personal preference

- Mood

- Cultural classification of color

- The era in which we currently live

If you are finished with the Adobe Color application, you can close it in the browser. Later, in Chapter 8, we will see color harmonies again in Illustrator.

How Research Plays an Important Role in Your Infographic Creation

As mentioned in Chapter 1, both the logo and infographic require you to research your topic thoroughly to know what the client wants for the final design. In the case of the logo, it may be a better understanding of the history of the company or client or what processes are involved or what is manufactured in the company or what the company is associated with to give you an idea of what the final logo will be. However, with an infographic, more research is required as you may be showing a process at the company or maybe something beyond what the company does. If you do not understand the process or nobody explains it to you, how will you design a successful infographic? Often, getting literature from the company library or online resources even if they are from competitors can be helpful in the research of your infographic.

What Topics Are Good for an Infographic?

Many topics are good candidates for an infographic, often in the topics of science or instruction, yet it takes a skilled artist either working independently with the client or with a team to be able to interpret how the graph can be displayed. Science and instruction fall into many categories, but here are some that you may want to consider an infographic for, some of which I will be exploring in this book in the later volumes as well.

Science

- Medicine

- Nutrition and food

- Human body

- Nature (plants and animals)

- Climate change

- Oceanography

- Political and historical

- Human culture, population, and agriculture

- Geography

- Geology

- Astronomy

- Languages

- Income, investment, finance, and housing

- Popular trends (pop culture, social, and fashion)

- Comparison of things (height, size, age, and how often something occurs)

Instructional

- Recipes

- Product assembly

- Complex technologies made easier to understand (cars, electronics, and robotics)

This is not necessarily an exhaustive list; it merely just shows there is a wide range of topics that you can draw from if you want to start creating an infographic.

However, there may be some topics that are easier than others to explain as infographics. Nevertheless, being creative in your display and researching the topic is important as we will look at in the next section, later chapters, and Volumes 2 and 3. Other topics may not be that interesting for the general public to pay attention to and so may not result in a highly successful infographic. It's all in how you arrange the topic. For example, what would be more interesting to the public, knowing visually about the history of the fax machine or the general history of technology which might include one reference to the fax machine? Again, topics to avoid would be those that have a discriminatory bent that draws attention to things like intellect of a specific race or demographic such as making the data appear like some people are more superior than others in a specific field. These would likely bring up negative connotations and emotions.

Collecting Your Data

As you collect your data for your infographic from various sources such as libraries, books, and your client's data, as well as other sources, you need to consider the sources of the data and how it will be applied to the infographic and the information you are trying to convey. Refer to Figure 2-69.

Figure 2-69. *Illustration designers in a team researching their data for infographics*

Here are some things to consider:

Will the data match the infographic I am creating? This might be something you may not know until you start designing, but if the client has given you some preliminary ideas of what they would like, do they match the data? Refer to Figure 2-70.

Figure 2-70. *Illustration of missing data in a pie and bar (column) graph*

Is the data misleading? If you find that as you create the infographic with data that is not clear, appears to have missing gaps, areas of no value, or adds up incorrectly, then you need to express this to your client. Consider with your team or client ways to get the missing information or ways to make it more relevant to the audience. If the topic is not particularly interesting, how can you creatively make it exciting without losing the truth and ensure the facts are clear? Refer to Figure 2-71.

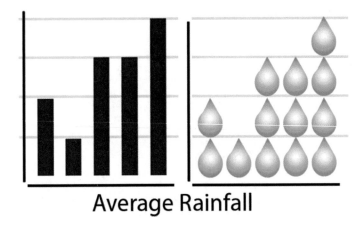

Average Rainfall

Figure 2-71. Illustration of a column graphic regular and more creative with the same data

You may have to do your own research on this topic as long as you let the client know that this is part of the budget and timeline.

Also, as mentioned earlier, as you review the data, try to eliminate data that may bring up negative connotations or emotions with the general public, but always discuss your reasons with the client.

Working with Your Team and Your Client in Design to Create a Mock-Up Sketch and Mood Board and Keep the Theme

As a designer, you certainly want to keep your designs as original as possible and not copy others' work or at the very least reference them. Nevertheless, it is a good idea to review what others have done on similar topics so that you know how and where you can improve your own artwork.

In your case, you want to make sure that you or your team can come up with a successful infographic. One member of the team may have done the research and you may be the designer, you would then need to consult with your client to ensure that you understand the process they want you to convey visually whether it be a chart or a graphic with many components.

A few more important things for the graphic designer to consider are as follows:

As mentioned earlier, knowing the eventual graphics colors and fonts is crucial for creating a rough sketch of a logo or infographic.

However, before you create a concept or mood board that will meet the client's standards/styles and expectations, you need to discuss the budget and a timeline to create the artwork for the graphic. Refer to Figure 2-72.

Figure 2-72. *Reviewing with the client a project time and when to sign off for approval*

During this discovery phase, you need to determine who needs to sign off for final approval of the design and at what stages. To lessen any confusion, these are just some of the topics you need to discuss before you start a project with your client. This will assist you in keeping the project within the approved timeline.

For reference, I have supplied a basic checklist in the project folder. For your own project, use this as a starting point to review and/or modify as you work with your client. From the list you create, you can glean information on how to begin the process of creating a rough draft sketch of your graphic, also known as a wireframe. For your own project, you may also want to create a mood board with the client as well. Refer to the file Client Preparation Logo_infographic_Check List.docx. This text can be applied to logo creation and adapted for infographics as well.

Just to clarify on these design terms

- Mock-Up Sketch or Wireframe: In this example is what you would
draw, usually with a pen or pencil on paper, for the client as you listen
to what their concerns and ideas are about the graphic. However, you
may want to use your digital tablet or stylus as well, and this could be
an easier and faster way to get your design digitized so that you are
ready to start designing without the extra step of scanning. However,
if you are more comfortable with paper and pencil, then in Chapter 3,
I will present how to scan your mock-up using Photoshop and your
scanner. Refer to Figure 2-73.

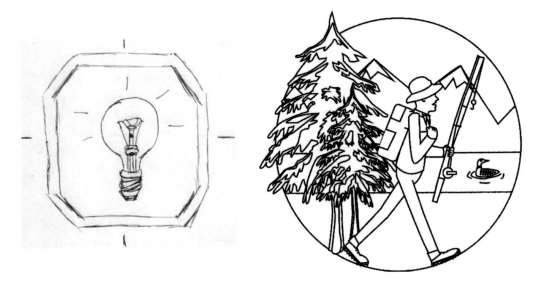

Figure 2-73. *Examples of a mock-up sketch*

- Mood Board: Whether it be on an actual paper board or in digital
format is usually a collection of your and the clients' ideas of visual
elements that you would like to see as part of the design. In this case,
it may be swatches of color, font typography choices, and various
images that are related to the topic or data as well as words or
phrases. In the case of images, it may be ideas that your clients like or
you would like to share. Regardless, they are all points of discussion
in your meeting and will give you a chance to eliminate or add to the
board. Refer to Figure 2-74.

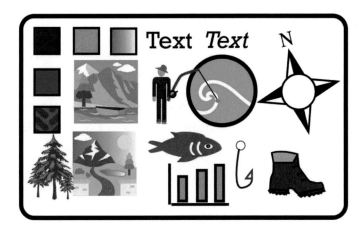

Figure 2-74. *Illustration of an example of a mood board*

- Style and Theme: Your client will want the graphic to have a theme, and your mood board will express it. But what is a theme? As a designer, you may have a certain style of drawing, just like you have a signature. When you write or draw, that is how you express your artistic skills. Some artists express one or two styles of art, while others can be very versatile and develop more styles over time. Are you very structured or are you more abstract? Can you be both? You must be able to understand your style and express that in your portfolio which your client should review before they begin a project with you. They will then be able to visualize how your style fits with their theme. In the case of you working in a team and there is more than one graphic designer, perhaps one of you is more suited to that client's particular theme/narrative elements for that project. Questions to ask here are

  - Will the style be artistic/abstract, realistic/technical, futuristic, minimalistic, or something else?

  - How does one style fit better with the topic (e.g., climate change, medicine, building a motor, travel) with the data you have collected and then apply it to your audience and demographic?

Other Design Considerations

As you work with your team or client on the design of the mock-up sketch and mood board, you need to consider the following as the design progresses:

- Lack of Design: The term "less is more" might be fine for your logo as you take a minimalistic approach. However, with the infographic, you need to consider whether the data matches the design. Is there a balance between the images and the story you are trying to convey? Refer to Figure 2-75.

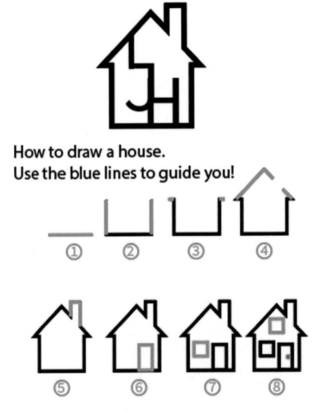

Figure 2-75. *A simple logo and an infographic with instructions*

- Too Much Text (Information): Often even with graphic considerations, there may be too much text or arrows surrounding the infographic. In other layout design work, you can encounter this issue, for example, when you try to cram too much text around a logo on a one-sided business card. Refer to Figure 2-76.

Figure 2-76. *Infographic and business card with logo that has become too cluttered*

The logo and infographic need space or room to breathe, so maybe you need to consider a second infographic, the other side of the page, or less data.

- Besides too much text in the wrong area, you may have clashing fonts and colors. These can certainly throw off any design as you work with your client. If new elements are being added, you need to consider how the fonts and colors are affecting reliability. Show a few proofs in different fonts and styles that match the message that your client is trying to portray with the graphic. Each font can invoke a slightly different feeling, some of which you might want to avoid. You may have to go back and forth a few times with your client to agree on the correct font size and wording. Refer to Figure 2-77.

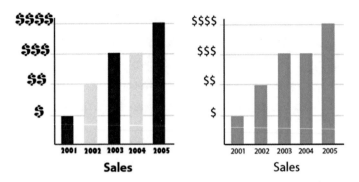

Figure 2-77. *Illustration of a graph idea of how certain fonts and color combinations on the left may not be best for a graph and then on the right with less fonts and one color*

Once approved, create a visual guide of the styles in relation to the logo or infographic. Refer to Figure 2-78 and Figure 2-79.

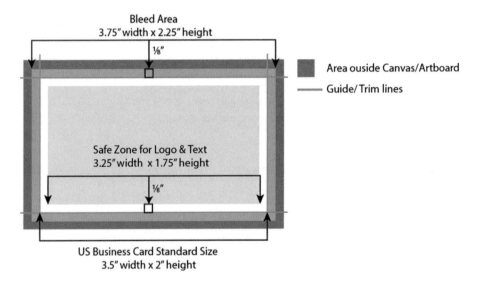

Figure 2-78. *Creating a general layout for a business card*

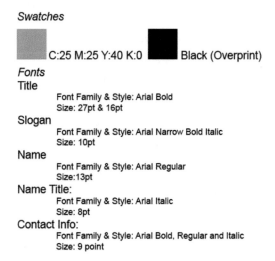

Figure 2-79. *Arranging graphics text and colors on the business card in a balanced layout with a style guide for reference*

- Wrong Type of Chart for Data: As you develop the infographic with the data, you may start to discover that the type of chart or graph you are using does not support the data visually. For example, you may start with a pie chart and then discover that a bar or column chart was a much better idea because you need to look more closely at individual parts by year and the numbers will not add up collectively to 100%. Along with this, you need to make sure that you check that your chart design has accurate scales and that your placement of the x and y axis is correct. We will look at charts (graphs) in more detail in Volume 2. Refer to Figure 2-80.

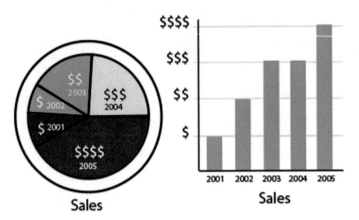

Figure 2-80. *Discovering that a pie chart (graph) may not be the best solution and later using a bar or column graph instead*

- Symbol and Shape Meanings: As you add symbols to your logo and infographic, you need to consider their meaning or representation in combination with colors. In the case of logo ambiguity, it might be OK for the audience if it means something to the client. However, this is not the case with an infographic; that is for the audience that is reading the publication. Consider if there are any parts of the symbol or isotype-like graphic icon that hinder the viewer from understanding it. There are many isotypes or icon symbols that are built into our daily lives that over time we recognize to mean something. Some of these we can see on street signs, emojis, or other illustrations. Refer to Figure 2-81.

Figure 2-81. *Icons that have meaning in our lives as we read and travel*

An arrow means a direction, and a light bulb means an idea; when we go on a trip, we see the following road sign icons and know what they mean such things as lodging, food, camping areas, or a picnic area. But some icons that people have designed or maybe you will invent don't really have a universal meaning to your audience. If you create one outside of the traditional shapes, will they understand what it means? Does the meaning cause your client to guess, or do they know instantly? Does it have the right association with the rest of the infographic? Should supplemental text be added? In these examples, what extra text would need to be added to explain what this is if it were part of an infographic? Refer to Figure 2-82.

Figure 2-82. *Icons that we may not know the meaning of without some supplemental text*

We'll look at these types of isotypes and icons as part of a creation and design layout in Chapters 6, 7, 8, and 9.

- 3D and Extra Enhancements: You can make an infographic appear 3D-like or add a drop shadow, feather, or glow to an icon, and that can certainly enhance the look of the design, but these should always be a final consideration. Looking at the infographic with and without these extra additions is certainly a good idea, as well as how they appear in print or on screen.

With graphics that contain text, you must keep a level of moderation for readability. If the effect is the spice, then use it sparingly. Adding effects will be looked at in more detail in Volume 2. Refer to Figure 2-83.

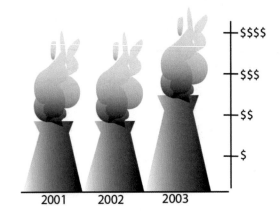

Figure 2-83. *2D and 3D examples of a graph as well as how text can appear in 3D in two different font families*

- Placement of the Graphics Parts: Layout of the final design as
  separate parts and then combining them as a whole is another
  consideration. As you move parts of the infographic around, you do
  not want them to appear scattered, such as a graph far away from its
  legend or the legend and graph having too many complex numbers
  and colors. You want to be cohesive, but at the same time, you do not
  want them to be too crowded as well. Refer to Figure 2-84.

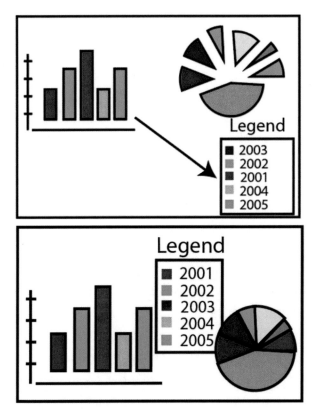

Figure 2-84. *Items that are part of an infographic should not be too separated nor should they be too close if the data is not related*

- Understand It at First or Second Glance: As the design progresses,
  whether in sketch or digital infographic, you need to keep refining
  and working with your team to discover whether the audience can
  take in the basic topic they are seeing at a glance. This again comes
  back to the point of symbols and meaning, but now you are looking
  at the layout as one unit and how it causes the eye to flow through

its parts. Can you scan through it quickly, or are you stalled at a certain point and then lose interest or become confused? You should not have to force the viewer to understand the process. Refer to Figure 2-85.

Figure 2-85. *Adding extra items to an infographic that are not necessary will only confuse the viewer*

Note   The topic of project management and working with clients is broad and requires its own separate training course. However, based on the clients you encounter, each situation can be a unique experience that you will learn from as you navigate your client's needs. In this book, and due to brevity, let's assume that the client has at this point already approved a basic wireframe sketch and any mood board ideas. Nevertheless, in Chapter 3, I will briefly give you a basic tutorial on how you might go about making your sketch into a digital format that you can later use in Illustrator for tracing over.

Time Frame Considerations: How Long Will Your Infographic Be Relevant to Your Audience?

Having looked at a variety of infographics over time and then returning to an older publication or magazine years later, you may notice that the infographic that was once relevant then is not as relevant today. I often see a parallel when I go back and look at old historical or political cartoons. If you have read these in the newspaper or online, you will understand what I mean. At the time, when we see the one-panel comic, we are living in the historical context, and we understand the meaning behind what the artist is saying; it may be funny or bring up any variety of emotions. Yet a year or years later when we look at that same comic, and unless we lived then or can remember the feeling we had when we first read it, the context gradually loses its value. The world has changed, and the topic then is not as important or relevant now, and the words and images are unfamiliar if we have not studied that particular history.

The same is true of many infographics depending on their topic. For example, years ago, from 1930 to 2015, people imagined what the dwarf planet Pluto might look like, and pictures were drawn to describe what it looked like there. However, in 2015, once the New Horizons interplanetary space probe arrived and took pictures closer than ever before, only then did we see most of what Pluto actually looked like. Now those old images that the artist created are not that relevant today. The data is old, and now we have new data. We saw earlier how this happened with the Pioneer plaque in Chapter 1. This is quite common in the study of science, technology, and astronomy as people learn more information on various topics via experimentation and updated images. This is also true of many topics that infographics are based upon, where more data can make them more accurate, but in the process, the old infographic will need to be discarded and replaced.

However, some infographic data may remain relevant for many years. Such images and text may describe instructions for a recipe or how to construct a historical piece of furniture or a part of a machine. However, at the same time, we must consider in these situations whether it is the design and not the data that needs to be updated for the general audience to make them want to continue to review it.

So how long will your infographic be relevant? It all depends on time, relevant data, and your audience's interest. For example, unless you were talking about the history of the telephone, which icon would you use in a modern infographic? Refer to Figure 2-86.

Figure 2-86. *The change in design of the telephone over the years*

How Simple or Complex Should You Make Your Infographic?

This is often a question that varies from project to project depending on the topic or audience and where the infographic will be viewed. It may be something that people will want to spend time to examine and study for a long period of time at home, perhaps as a poster for their wall, in a classroom setting, or in a book. Then the infogrpahic, with text incorporated, could be more complex and detailed especially if it is for academic learning and may be used by many people in the field. For example, the diagram earlier in this chapter of the eye, if we look at it again, could certainly be even more complex in the magnification area of the retina, with more types of cells because the eye is a very complex organ. Such a detailed infographic would be helpful in a medical journal. Refer to Figure 2-87.

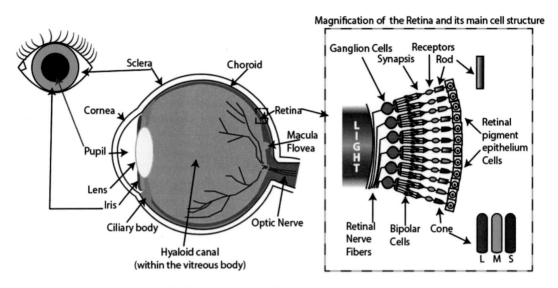

Figure 2-87. *Semidetailed diagram of the eye*

But again, we must consider the attention span of the general reader as an infographic generally appears only as part of a spread, on one side of a page or on a section of a page. If it is in a magazine or online publication where the reader just does a quick scan of the topic and surrounding text, you would likely want to keep the topic as simple as possible. In some cases, maybe just the eye in the upper left would be enough. In other situations, a simple bar chart or a few icon-like isotypes with minimal text may be all that is required. Again, even in simplicity, keeping text readable and graphics not crowding, not overly patterned, or with distracting colors are all factors to consider to not overwhelm the reader. Yet you do not, as we talked about in Chapter 2, make the graphic so simple that the reader is unable to decipher what the topic is and questions if they are just seeing an illustrated picture.

A search online on "bad infographic topics" will display examples of what others judge as unhelpful data or design. This can certainly help you visualize what kinds of design faux pas to avoid.

What Kinds of Media Will You Use to Display the Infographic?

As you will see later on in Volume 3 Chapter 3, there are other Adobe applications that you can use to assist you when you decide to display your infographic creation in print or online. In this case, we have been mainly focusing on print, but your infographic may be displayed on a website and in television or video format as well as for additional advertising purposes.

In the case of movie or video format, you may want to later consider if this static infographic may need to be animated with visual effects and sounds. An infographic may also need to be animated for a website. While video animation is not the topic of this book, we will look at some basic interactivity in Volume 3 Chapter 1 for a web page. Refer to Figure 2-88.

Figure 2-88. *Logo and graphics can appear online or in videos*

I would recommend that you work with your client and spend time finding out what other types of multimedia your client plans to use for their advertising as additional items could affect the budget and timeline. Then sit down with your team and consider if you have the skill to accomplish that type of additional work. Refer to Figure 2-89.

Figure 2-89. *When extra multimedia or items are required by your client beyond the budget and project, you need to consult with them again*

Summary

In this chapter, we reviewed the following. We looked at design considerations, whether creating a logo or infographics, and we saw how color theory plays a role in design and how we can use an online Adobe Color application that is part of the Creative Cloud to experiment and learn more about color. You also saw the importance of research and why you need to collect and check your data and review it with your client or team leaders to make sure that it is accurate and up to date but also keeps with the intended theme and does not become too simple or overly complex when viewed by the general public. You also considered the shelf life of an infographic—is it perpetually relevant? Lastly, you looked at what kinds of media are used to display an infographic.

In the next chapter, we will be exploring the basics of scanning your document in Photoshop for later work in Illustrator.

CHAPTER 3

Scanner Basics

In this chapter, as part of setting up your workspace, it is important to know how to use Photoshop to make a digital scan of your artwork should you have started your logo or infographic from a mock-up sketch. If not, feel free to move on to the section "Creating a New Document in Illustrator" in Chapter 4 where you will start working in Illustrator. Later, in Chapters 5 and 8, I will describe how to link your digital mock-up to the artboard so that it will display for tracing over should you need to and then conclude with how to save your Illustrator file and other design considerations.

Note This chapter does contain project files that can be found in the Volume 1 Chapter 3 folder, or you can just follow along and create a new scanned file on your own. This chapter was adapted from my book *Accurate Layer Selections Using Photoshop's Selection Tools*.

Making Your Sketch into a Digital Format

The simplest ways to digitize your sketch, depending on what hardware you have available, are listed here:

1. Use a digital camera, set up with a tripod, take the pictures, and then insert the camera's memory card into your computer and download the images.

2. Or use your smartphone and a scanner bin to take the pictures, and then email them to yourself and download them onto your computer. If you are interested in this idea, I'll mention this option a bit later in the section.

© Jennifer Harder 2023
J. Harder, *Creating Infographics with Adobe Illustrator: Volume 1*,
https://doi.org/10.1007/979-8-8688-0005-4_3

3.   In the following section, "Scanner Basics," I present a third option with some steps for making a digital scan of your image using a flatbed scanner or your all-in-one copier using Photoshop.

Scanner Basics

Most flatbed scanners can be acquired at an office supply store or online. For basic photos, artwork, and scans, they are quite affordable, and many brands are compatible with Photoshop. Refer to Figure 3-1.

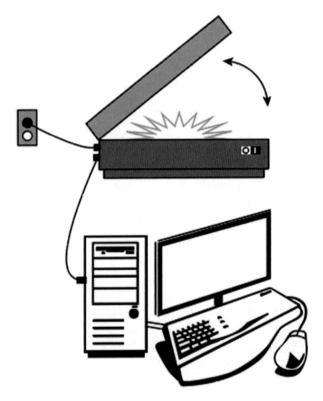

Figure 3-1. *An illustration of a flatbed scanner connected to the tower of a computer and wall power supply*

As with any electronic purchase, make sure you do some online research of the product first and check out the reviews of the product before you buy. A flatbed scanner allows you to acquire the scan of a flat sheet of paper without the presence of outside light which could cause color distortions to your artwork. Some flatbed scanners will allow you to adjust the top lid so that it sits better on an artbook that has a higher raised surface. Other scanners have just a hinged lid, so the bed might be exposed to outside light. Ultimately, if you're dealing with a sketchbook that is either raised or has binding that does not bend well, I would recommend placing a dark cloth sheet over your scanner to prevent any outside light from coming into the scanner as well. Refer to Figure 3-2.

Figure 3-2. *An illustration of a flatbed scanner covered with a black cloth to prevent shadows and gutter shadow on a sketchbook near the spine*

With a sketchbook, you may get a gutter shadow between pages during the scan if it is not a coil bind that can lay flat (refer to Figure 3-2). You may have to use the lid of the scanner, and with your hand, gently press down to press the book a bit flatter. Some scanners have software that can correct this gradient discoloration. However, you can use Photoshop and its adjustment layers afterward to clean this up and other issues, using a combination of selections and masks, though that is not required for this book. See my book *Accurate Layer Selections Using Photoshop's Selection Tools* on this topic, mentioned in the introduction, if that is a topic of interest to you.

Scanners come in various sizes. The most affordable is usually a bit larger than a Letter size, 8.5 × 11.7 inches. If you are planning to scan artwork larger than 11 × 17 inches, then you would need to check if the company you work for, your college, or your local print house might have a larger scanner you could use to scan the artwork.

Alternatively, as mentioned earlier, taking a picture with your smartphone or digital camera can get around this issue as long as it is on a stable tripod. Alternately, you can scan your artwork in sections or separate images, but this will require you to "stitch" the image together again in Photoshop. If you plan to do that, just make sure you have enough of an area to move your artwork around the scanner to accommodate the paper size so that nothing collides or bends the paper. Refer to Figure 3-3.

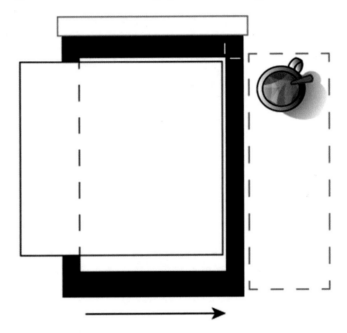

Figure 3-3. *An illustration of a paper that is too large for the scanner: it needs to be moved to scan twice, but there is a coffee cup in the way that should not be there as they may collide*

If you have a scanner already, be aware that over time, the light in the scanner ages. A scanner over ten years old, while it still may be operational, very likely is not the best for color photo scans where color is crucial for print or the Web. However, artwork or sketches that are just black and white, where color reproduction is not critical, may be alright for acquiring the image on an older scanner. However, I do recommend as you upgrade your computer or monitor every five to ten years, if it's in the budget, it's good to do the same with your scanner as even the software and drivers may be out of date and the scanner may cease to connect with your computer.

Scanner cleanliness is important. Make sure whatever scanner you are using that the scanner bed is free from dust and smudges. Refer to Figure 3-4.

Figure 3-4. *An illustration of a person cleaning the flatbed scanner class and removing smudges and dust before use*

You can use a glasses lens cloth to clean the surface of the glass and, if required, a mild glass cleaner if recommended by the manufacturer. Be careful not to scratch the glass as this can happen if you press down the scanner lid and your booklet's coil has any rough metal edges. Also, you should not have your scanner in an area of high humidity as the glass surface inside the scanner can fog up, leaving streaks which are difficult to clean.

Take a moment to review your scanner's manual or online specs as everyone is built slightly differently, depending on the manufacturer. Your scanner should be able to scan at least 300–600 dpi (dots per inch) or higher up to 2400 dpi for good quality. Some scanners also have the option of being able to scan film slides or film negatives, but this is not a topic of this book. For this book, a scanner without that option is fine.

In Photoshop, to connect to your scanner, you would make sure your scanner is plugged in and that it is turned on and connected to a USB port and that your computer is recognizing the device and the drivers are up to date. Most scanners have their own quick menu as well that you can access if you're not able to connect to Photoshop at first.

Adobe gives some helpful information on this topic of connecting to Photoshop. Depending on whether you are using a Mac or Windows computer, go to

https://helpx.adobe.com/photoshop/using/acquiring-images-cameras-scanners.html

However, let me demonstrate how the typical procedure of image acquisition might go though there may be slight differences depending on your computer or scanner version. I demonstrate the steps I use for my scanner in Photoshop CC 2024 on the Windows 10 computer. Refer to Figure 3-5.

Figure 3-5. Photoshop icon

Scanning a Sketch

1. Once open in Photoshop, go to
   File ➤ Import ➤ WIA Support
   Refer to Figure 3-6.

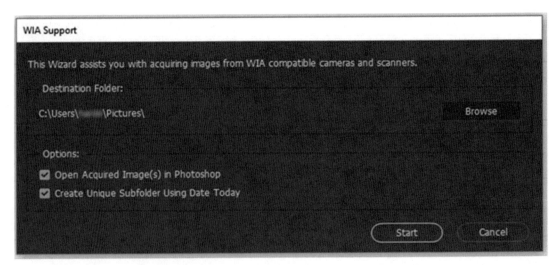

Figure 3-6. WIA Support dialog box

You will be presented with a dialog box where you will use the Wizard assists or Windows Image Acquisition (WIA) to help you decide where you will place your scans. You can also use this area for compatible digital cameras should you be using a USB cable to connect. You would then browse for a Destination folder where the images will be stored and then choose to enable or disable options such as

a. Should the acquired images appear and open in Photoshop and when acquired by the scanner.

b. Should each image be stored in a unique, created subfolder using today's date so that you can review them later. Refer to Figure 3-7.

2023-06-24   2023-06-24_0001   2023-06-24_0002

Figure 3-7. *Subfolders containing individual scans*

2. When you have made your selections, click the Start button to move to the next dialog box, or click the Cancel button to exit and not save your changes.

3. When you click the Start button, you will then be presented with the Select Device dialog box; in this case, it lists the scanner that is selected and its properties which will vary depending on the manufacturer and driver setup as per setup instructions. Even if it is an older scanner, always make sure your drivers and software are up to date so the scanner will be recognized and appear here. Refer to Figure 3-8.

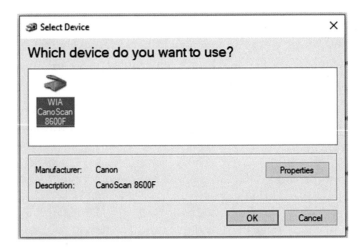

Figure 3-8. *Select Device dialog box where you can choose a digital camera or scanner that you want to acquire images from*

4.   While it is selected, click OK. This should then take you to the scanner dialog box, and you will be presented with various options on how to scan. Refer to Figure 3-9.

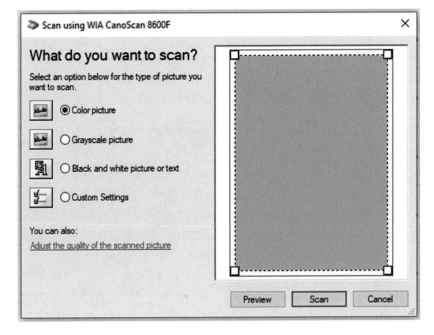

Figure 3-9. *Scan using WIA (Scanner name) dialog box with its various options*

In my case for this scanner, I can scan a

- Color picture

- Grayscale picture

- Black and white picture or text

In most cases, the default quick selections of color picture or grayscale are adequate, but I will choose those via the Custom Settings radio button and then click the lower link that says Adjust the quality of the scanned picture.

5. This brings up the Advanced Properties dialog box which gives me more options so that I can adjust the resolution to 300 dpi (dots per inch) up to 600 dpi. As well, I can adjust the brightness and contrast of the image. This can be reset as well. I generally leave those settings at 0 and do that type of appearance correction in Photoshop, but depending on your scanner after some experimentation, you may want to move these sliders or whatever other settings are available for you. Refer to Figure 3-10.

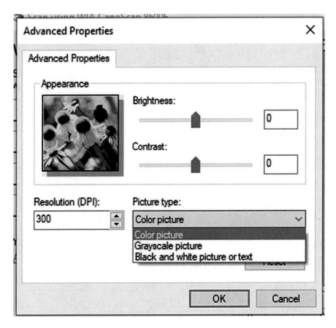

Figure 3-10. *Advanced Properties dialog box and various options with more options*

6. I will then choose the Picture type from the drop-down menu, which is the same as the earlier choices, and click OK to confirm.

7. I would then place the image I want to scan on the scanner bed face down, close the lid, and in the Scanner WIA dialog box, press the Preview button. Refer to Figure 3-11.

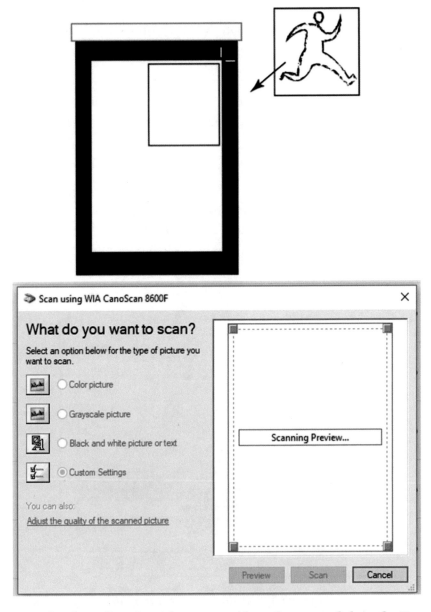

Figure 3-11. Sketch is placed on the scanner face down, and then the Preview button in the dialog box is pressed to get a preview of the sketch

In this case, Preview does not create a copy of the image yet, it is just stored in memory until you are ready to press Scan. If you notice that your image is a bit slanted or rotated, you can always open the lid, move the sketch a bit to the center or to the left or right so it's up against an edge, close the lid, and press the Preview button again. Some scanners will recognize the area of how large your artwork is and then will use their bounding box handles to crop or marquee to fit around that area, so you don't have to scan the whole bed. You should have the option of being able to drag the handles to the area you want to scan, and some scanners will allow you to scan more than one area on the page into separate files, if required, by allowing you to draw more than one bounding box. Refer to Figure 3-12.

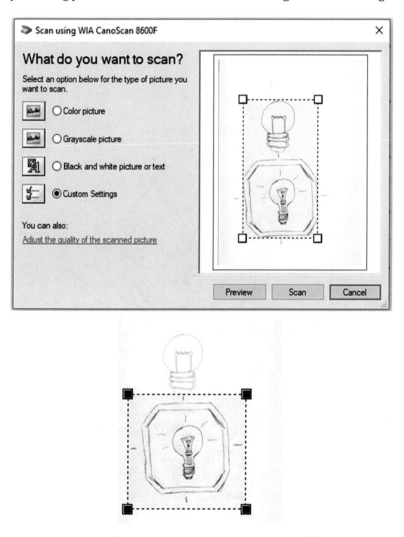

Figure 3-12. *Preview of the sketch appears, and I can use the bounding box to crop how much of the sketch I want to scan*

Scanner Color Modes

Now, depending on the setting you choose, different file color modes will be generated via the basic or advanced properties. For my scanner:

A color picture will produce a .bmp 8-bit bitmap file in RGB color mode. The file is generally larger than a camera .jpg file, but it is as good as a .tif file, and it will not lose quality as a .jpg would and can be stored for archival purposes. Refer to Figure 3-13.

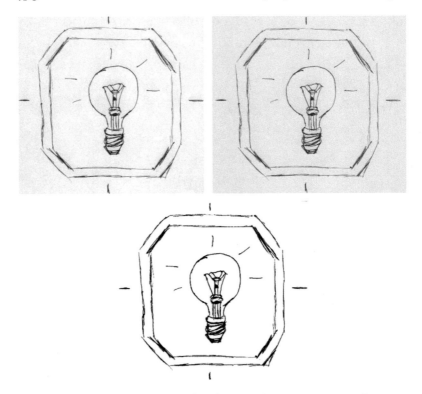

Figure 3-13. *Scanner results left to right, for a color picture on white paper, grayscale, and black and white picture or text*

A grayscale picture produces a .bmp file; however, in this case, the color mode is Index and 8 bit. You can always convert it afterward in Photoshop, choosing from the menu Image ➤ Mode ➤ RGB color. Refer to Figure 3-13.

The black and white picture or text produces a .bmp file but this time the color mode is Bitmap. I find this option to be the worst setting for my sketches as the image is very grainy and broken. In most cases, even if the image is in black and white, I will generally choose the advanced properties of color picture as this produces artwork with the same or better detail than a digital camera. Refer to Figure 3-13.

1. Once you have made your setting choices, Click the Scan button
    (Figure 3-12), and the file will be transferred and appear in
    Photoshop and be saved in the destination subfolder that you
    set up earlier. You can check that it is 300 dpi under the Image ➤
    Image Size dialog box, and it will show the resolution to be 300
    (pixels/inch), which is the same as the dpi setting. Click Cancel to
    exit that dialog box as you are not making any size adjustments.
    Refer to Figure 3-14.

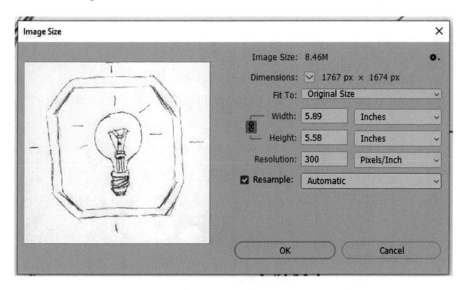

Figure 3-14. *Checking the resolution of the document using Image Size*

Adjusting Scanned Image

If your scan is sideways, you can always choose in Photoshop Image ➤ Image Rotation
and rotate the image in Photoshop 90° clockwise or 90° counter clockwise. Refer to
Figure 3-15.

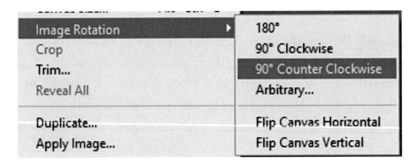

Figure 3-15. *Location in Image drop-down menu of Image rotation options*

Or you can double-click the Background layer in your Layers panel to make it Layer 0, and from the main menu, use your Edit ➤Transform. Then use your Move tool "Show Transform Controls" check box in the Options panel bar and then use the bounding box, surrounding the image, to manually rotate it from a corner. Refer to Figure 3-16 and Figure 3-17.

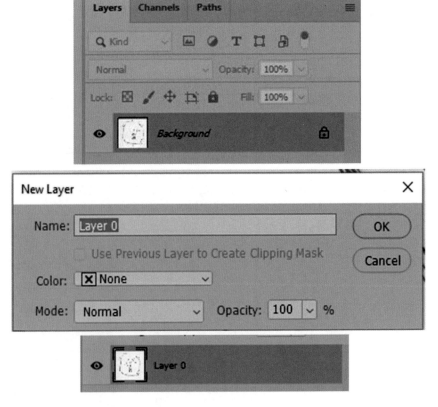

Figure 3-16. *Use the Photoshop Layers panel to change your Background layer into Layer 0 in the New Layer dialog box and the result in the Layers panel*

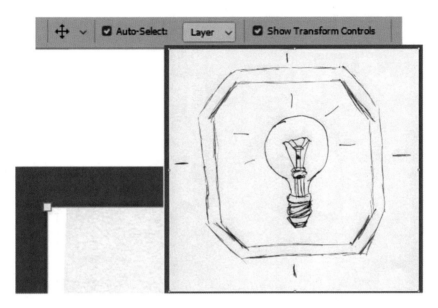

Figure 3-17. *Photoshop Options panel bar with settings and bounding box around the picture using the Move tool*

Once done, you would then check the commit check in the Options panel area. Then use the Layers panel menu or Layer> Flatten Image to flatten your image back to a Background layer. Refer to Figure 3-18.

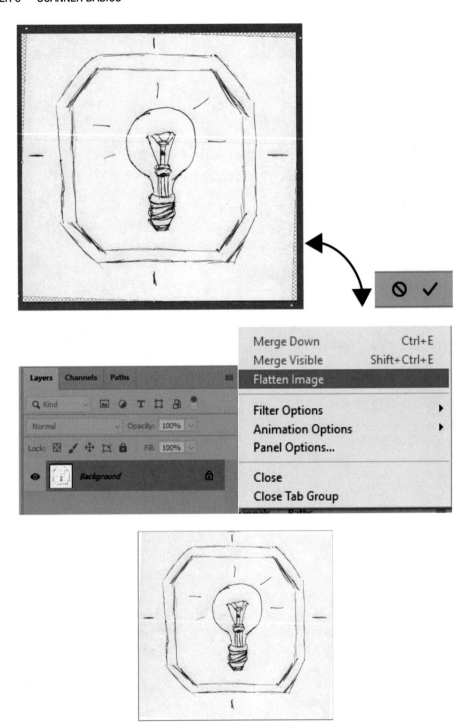

Figure 3-18. *Photoshop rotated image: click the Check in the Options panel to confirm*

So, as we can see, acquiring an image of your sketch via a flatbed scanner is very easy. You would then repeat these steps if you had any additional sketches to scan.

Saving Scanned Files

At this point, you may want to File ➤ Save (Ctrl/CMD+S) the files that you scanned to your desktop, a USB flash drive stick, or an external drive as a backup.

Also, it should be noted here that like any other image, you do not have to keep it in the .bmp file format if you plan to work with the file in Photoshop. You can always save an Image ➤ Duplicate, click OK to confirm, and then File ➤ Save as a .tif file or, as I plan to, a .psd (photoshop document) in case I plan to work with multiple layers. Refer to Figure 3-19.

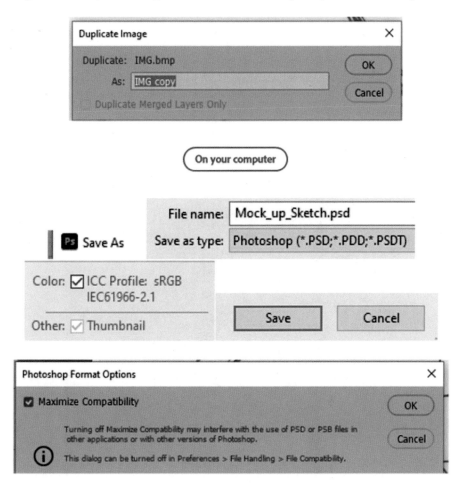

Figure 3-19. *Duplicate Image dialog box and saving your file as a (.psd) somewhere on your computer*

Make sure to confirm or click OK on any Photoshop settings of Maximize Compatibility as you save the file somewhere on your computer. Refer to Figure 3-19.

Later you could then use Photoshop adjustment layers to do any color correction and clean up the file with your eraser or selection tools or cropping tools. For use in Illustrator, again create an Image ➤ Duplicate, click OK, then flatten that image using your Layers panel menu as in Figure 3-18, and File ➤ Save and browse for a location to save your file of the graphic as a .jpg. Then click save and set your JPEG Options at Maximum image quality 12 and a Format Options of Baseline ("Standard"), then click OK. This will be later used as a linked file in Illustrator for tracing purposes. Refer to Figure 3-20.

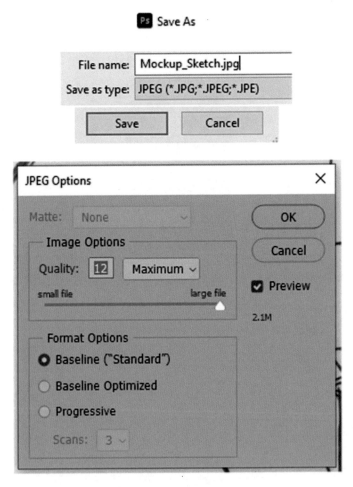

Figure 3-20. *Save As settings and JPEG dialog box*

Note   When you click File ➤ Save, you may be presented with some options as to whether to save to your computer or the Creative Cloud. I usually save to my computer and click "On your computer" button. Later, you can save to the Cloud or a drive for backup. Refer to Figure 3-21.

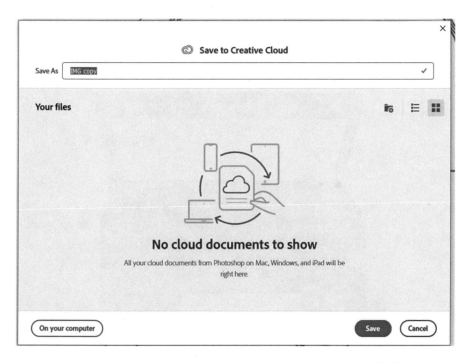

Figure 3-21. *Save on your computer or on the Creative Cloud dialog box*

Now, if you don't have room for a flatbed scanner in your office, here are some other options to consider.

Photocopier or All-in-One Office Printer

With limited office space, you might consider instead a photocopier or an office all-in-one printer that can copy, scan, and fax. This can turn your images into a PDF file format that could contain multiple pages stored together. However, I would not recommend using the auto document feeder to load your sketches into the machine as based on the type of paper, it could cause a jam, smear, and ruin your artwork. Refer to Figure 3-22.

Figure 3-22. *An illustration of an all-in-one, Scan Fax Print and lid top to scan your drawings*

If the all-in-one printer has a lid that you can lift to place the scan on the glass as you do with a flatbed, that is best, and then scan the artwork using the basic guidelines I have described earlier and the manual that comes with the devices to scan the sketches one at a time. You may then be able to place the image on a USB stick, or they may be sent wirelessly to a computer drive on your network, and then you can store them in a folder on your computer.

A Digital Camera

As mentioned before, for larger artwork such as murals or art that cannot fit in your scanner that you may want to incorporate into an infographic, you can use a digital camera. You may have to experiment with a few shots until you get the best quality. Refer to Figure 3-23.

Figure 3-23. *Capture your artwork with a digital camera*

For example, if the camera needs to be close or the surface is shiny, do not use a flash as it will cause a reflection and the image will disappear. Use a tripod to avoid shaky images even if your camera has an auto stabilizer. Set up the image in a vertical or horizontal position. Also check if your tripod has an option where the camera can point straight down on the table without tipping over when taking the picture. Refer to Figure 3-24.

Figure 3-24. *Photo examples of how you could use a tripod and a digital camera like a scanner for larger sketches*

Your camera should be at least 12 megapixels or higher. You can also experiment on a macro setting as this may produce a better quality resolution. The image will likely be. jpg (JPEG) in RGB color mode and 8 bit. To acquire the image, you can then use the method that Adobe describes using a USB port drive connected to the camera.

https://helpx.adobe.com/photoshop/using/acquiring-images-cameras-scanners.html

Or just take out the camera's memory card, insert it into your computer's drive, and copy the images that you want into a folder on your computer.

Your Smartphone Camera, an Additional Adobe App, and a Scanner Bin

One final scanning suggestion that I will mention is to use your smartphone in combination with the Adobe Scan app for mobile scanning and a scanner bin or scan box that you can purchase or build cheaply.

Smartphones, as we know these days, have a built-in camera app that can store photos and import the images and add them to the Cloud. Adobe and a number of other companies offer mobile scanning apps that you can use to scan documents. Adobe Scan comes with your Creative Cloud subscription, and Adobe gives instructions on how you can set up a link on your phone so you can download the app and use it for scanning. Refer to Figure 3-25.

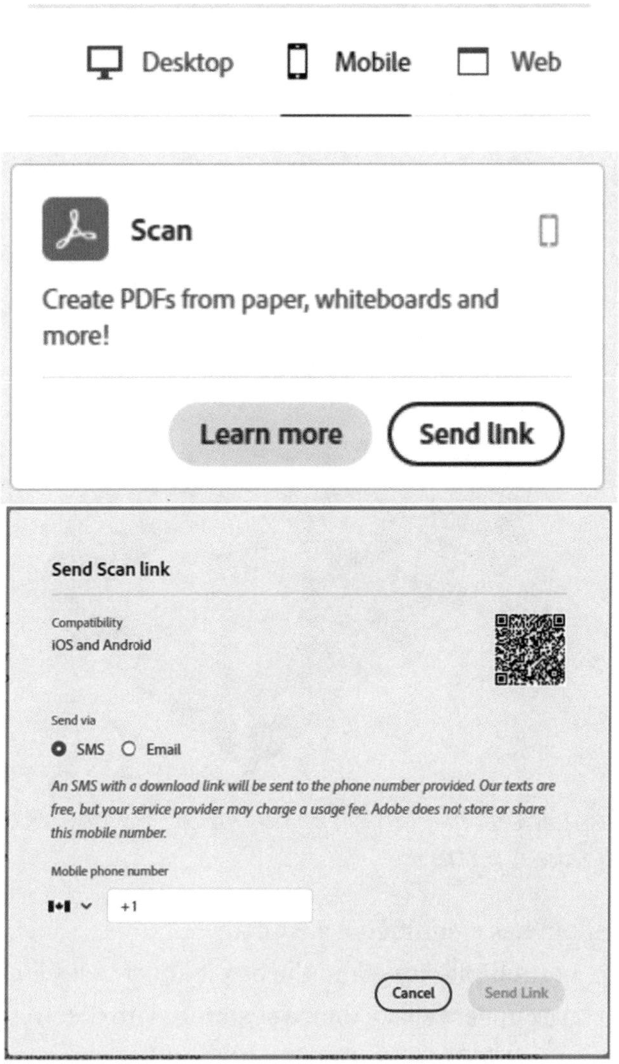

Figure 3-25. *Adobe Scan app that is part of your Creative Cloud subscription and can be added to your mobile phone or tablet*

You can find those instructions here:

https://helpx.adobe.com/mobile-apps/help/adobe-scan-faq.html
www.adobe.com/devnet-docs/adobescan/android/en/
www.adobe.com/devnet-docs/adobescan/ios/en/

Now, in combination with the app, I would suggest that you either make or purchase a scan box or scanner bin as this will allow you to keep your smartphone steady and at the correct distance from the artwork so it does not become smudged as it might with some sketches. You take the picture through a small hole in the top of the box. Refer to Figure 3-26.

Figure 3-26. *A scanner box used to keep your smartphone steady and at the right distance when you take a picture*

Also, the scanner bin has a number of advantages; like a scanner, it can block excess light from coming in on multiple sides, and the box in most cases is collapsible, so it can be easily stored and takes up less space than a scanner. With the Adobe Scan app, the file is saved as a PDF and uploaded to your Document Cloud account, and you can retrieve it from there later. However, keep in mind that with the Mobile Scan app, while you can resize images, there does not appear to be an option for setting in the instructions for the scan resolution, so it is likely dependent on whatever your smartphone's resolution allows.

Note   A similar form of Adobe Scan is also available via Adobe Acrobat Pro on your computer. Through the tools called Create PDF or Scan & OCR, you can also access your scanner this way should you not have access to a Photoshop application and wish to create just PDF files. Refer to Figure 3-27.

Figure 3-27. *When you open Acrobat Pro on your computer, you have access to the following tools and can connect to your scanner*

Unlike the Mobile Scan app, because you are connecting to your scanner, you can reset the default settings using the gear icon to a higher resolution.

Though many of the settings, as in Photoshop are similar, we will not be delving any deeper into Acrobat Pro in this book. However, I have supplied a link should you want to explore this option in more detail on your own:

```
https://helpx.adobe.com/acrobat/using/scan-documents-pdf.html
```

Either way, I have presented you with a variety of options for acquiring a digital image of your sketches, and the choice is up to you.

If you need to refer to my final scanned images in Photoshop, File ➤ Open Mock_up_Sketch.psd and Mockup_Sketch.jpg.

You can at this point close any files you have open in Photoshop and then File➤Exit the application as well.

Summary

This chapter is a starting point for learning about designing infographics by scanning and digitizing your images so that you can later use them for tracing in Illustrator.

In the next chapter, in Illustrator, you will look at how to create a new document and set up your workspace and you will discover how to work with some of the basic panels and tools that you will encounter in the following chapters, as well as Volumes 2 and 3.

CHAPTER 4

Setting Up Your Workspace

In this chapter, you will begin to review and set up your workspace in Illustrator beginning in the section "Creating a New Document in Illustrator" where you will start working in Illustrator. The next section is an overview of a workspace that I commonly use when I start creating a new document in Illustrator for a project, but you can later adapt it into your workflow if you need to add more panels later on. Later in Chapter 5, I will also describe how to link your digital mock-up to the artboard so that it will display for tracing over should you need to and then conclude with how to save your Illustrator file and other design considerations.

Note   This chapter does contain project files that can be found in the Volume 1 Chapter 4 folder see reference files NewDocument_Practice.ai and practice_document.psd, or you can just follow along and create a new file.

Creating a New Document in Illustrator

Return now to Illustrator to begin your project.

Make sure that your Adobe Illustrator program is open.

To get started and set up your workspace, from the main menu, Choose File ➤ New or the New file button. Refer to Figure 4-1.

© Jennifer Harder 2023
J. Harder, *Creating Infographics with Adobe Illustrator: Volume 1*,
https://doi.org/10.1007/979-8-8688-0005-4_4

Figure 4-1. *New file button in Illustrator*

You will for now, just practice, click the Print tab, and use the preset blank document of Letter. Refer to Figure 4-2.

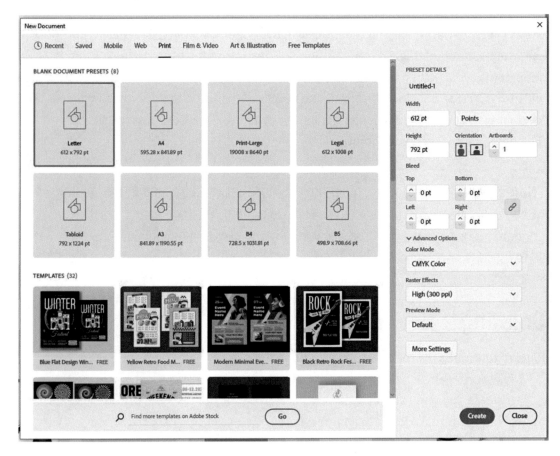

Figure 4-2. *Illustrator New Document dialog box and blank document presets*

You will notice on the right in the Preset Details that the name will be currently Untitled-1.

Change the increments menu from Points to Inches, but with the drop-down menu, I can choose other measurement settings. Refer to Figure 4-3.

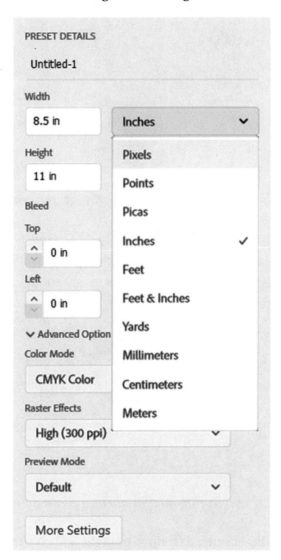

Figure 4-3. *New Document dialog box with various increment settings*

Now the width is 8.5, the height is 11, and this is now in inches.

The orientation is portrait, but it can be switched to landscape by clicking the button icon next to it. I can add additional artboards, but I will leave that option a 1 for now. Refer to Figure 4-4.

Figure 4-4. *New Document setting for Orientation and number of Artboards*

We will discuss artboards in more detail later in this chapter.

Leave the Bleed setting for top, bottom, left, and right at the default of 0 inches and link enabled. In this case, we do not need to add any additional spaces around the artboard. Refer to Figure 4-5.

Figure 4-5. *New Document dialog box for current Bleed settings*

At this point, open the Advanced Options triangle, and you have the option of setting the color mode from CMYK Color to RGB Color. I will leave it at CMYK for now for print work, but if you are planning on using the file in an RGB Photoshop file for the Web or additional filter and texture adjustments, then set it to RGB Color. Likewise, you can change the color mode of a copy of your file later on if you realize that you want to use it in this color mode later. I will show you how to do that in Chapter 5. Refer to Figure 4-6.

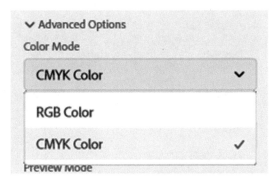

Figure 4-6. *New Document dialog box for Advanced Options and Color Mode*

The Raster Effects resolution is high (300 ppi) (pixels per inch), which is a good resolution for working with graphics that will have filters or 3D effects applied to them. I prefer to keep my Illustrator files in the highest settings. Refer to Figure 4-7.

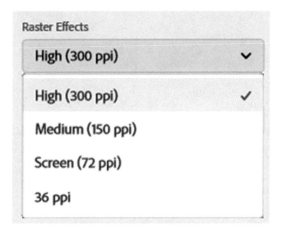

Figure 4-7. *New Document dialog box for Raster Effects*

I'll leave the Preview Mode set to default. Similar settings can later be accessed in Illustrator's View menu. Refer to Figure 4-8.

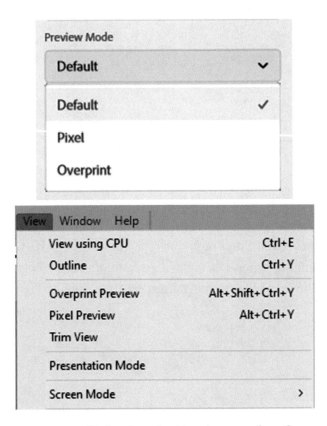

Figure 4-8. *New Document dialog box for Preview modes also seen in the View menu*

The More Settings button brings up the same settings with more detailed artboard options but also allows you to access Templates, but you can skip that button for now. Click Cancel if you opened this dialog box. Refer to Figure 4-9.

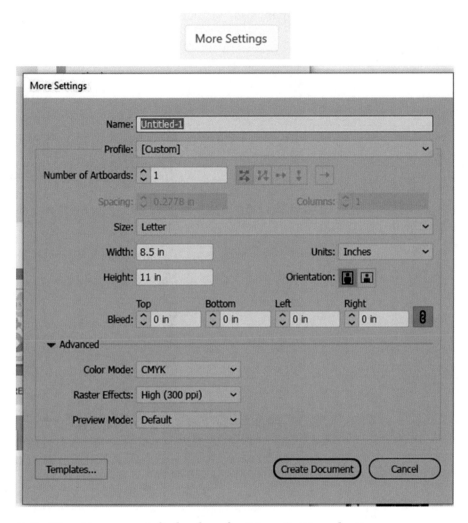

Figure 4-9. *New Document dialog box for More Settings button*

And click the Create button to commit the Preset. Refer to Figure 4-10.

Figure 4-10. *New Document dialog box for Create and Close button*

The new blank document will open, and you will see the current Illustrator workspace. Refer to Figure 4-11.

Figure 4-11. *Adobe Illustrator app current workspace*

Next you will want to begin setting up the workspace and review some of the main panels and tools within Illustrator.

Workspace Options

You can then begin to set up your workspace, either using the main menu Window ➤ Workspace or from the Workspace button found on the far right of the main menu area. Refer to Figure 4-12.

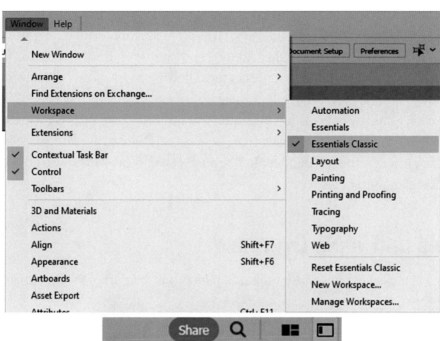

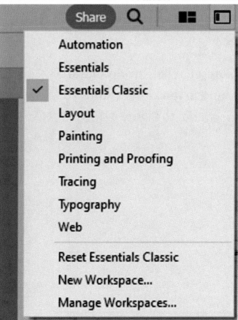

Figure 4-12. *Set your workspace using one of the menus to Essentials Classic*

For my work, I generally like to choose Essentials Classic as this gives me all the tools that I need in the Toolbars panel as well as other essential panels. Many of these following panels I discuss in my other Adobe Photoshop and Illustrator books, but I will present an overview of those panels in the following pages as well as a few recently added items. Refer to Figure 4-12.

If you have already been using Illustrator, you can reset Essentials Classic using the menu so that you can follow along with the notes in this book. This workspace will not affect your current artboard, but later in Chapter 5, I will show you how to adjust and modify it within the workspace.

Panels and Tools Overview

Now we will look at the Illustrator tools and panels that are part of the Essentials Classic workspace.

Illustrator Panels

Panels can be opened, collapsed (click the double arrows on the top of the panel), and undocked by dragging around in the application so that they are closer to your artwork as you work on your project. Refer to Figure 4-13.

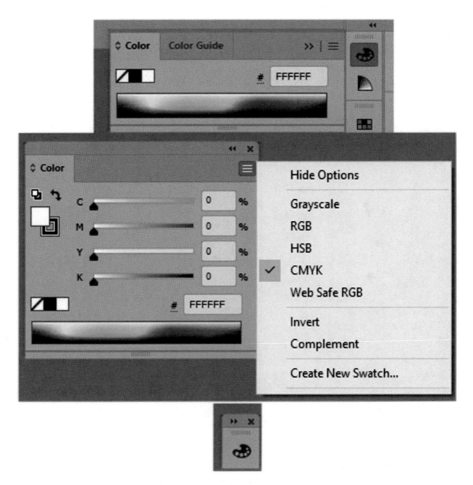

Figure 4-13. *Color panel collapsed and opened with its menu and then undocked from the Color Guide panel*

Most panels often have their own menu which gives you other options while working with the panel. You can find these panels again, as well as additional panels, in the Window drop-down menu. Refer to Figure 4-12 and Figure 4-13.

However, I will just do a basic overview of the key panels that are useful, from this workspace. Remember, you can reset your Essentials Classic workspace by choosing Reset Essentials Classic from the Workspace menu at any time. Refer to Figure 4-12.

Toolbars

The Toolbars panel contains all the tools that you need to work on your Illustrator projects. As you can see in Figure 4-14, there are many.

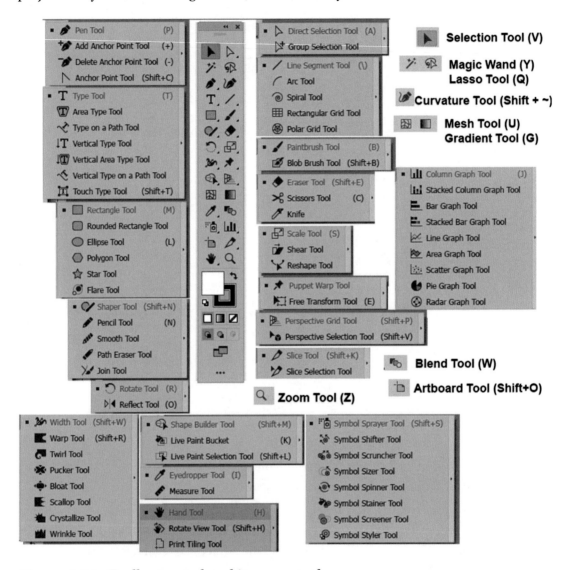

Figure 4-14. *Toolbars panel and its many tools*

Some of these tools, if you have worked in Photoshop, will already be familiar to you, and some are very unusual. However, for the moment, the main tools that you need to know about in this chapter are the Selection tool, Direct Selection tool, Zoom tool, and Hand tool. We will explore some of the others later in regard to infographic creation in the following chapters.

Selection Tool (V): The black arrow allows you to select click and move objects around on Layers with your mouse as you can drag the contents around. Refer to Figure 4-15 for a comparison to the similar tools in Photoshop.

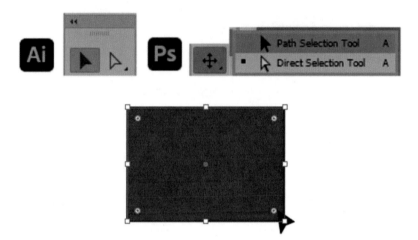

Figure 4-15. *The Selection tool next to the Direct Selection in Illustrator and Photoshop's Move, Path Selection, and Direct Selection tools, a rectangle selected with the Selection tool in Illustrator*

It is similar to the Photoshop Move tool, as well as the Photoshop Path Selection tool, which is used for moving your vector shapes layer around and for scaling. Refer to Figure 4-15.

Direct Selection Tool (A): The white arrow is basically identical to the Photoshop Direct Selection tool and is used to move and edit individual points on a vector path. Refer to Figure 4-16.

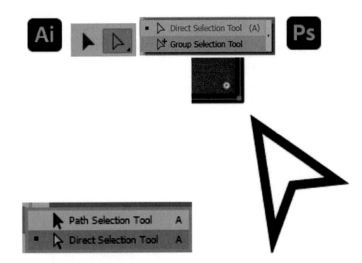

Figure 4-16. *A point on a rectangle in Illustrator has been altered with the Direct Selection tool which is similar to Photoshop's Direct Selection tool*

We'll review these Illustrator tools including the Group Selection tool further in Chapters 6, 7, 8, and 9. However, these two mentioned tools work best with Illustrator's Layers panel which we will look at shortly in this chapter and later chapters.

Zoom Tool (Z): Allows you to zoom in and out of an image. To zoom in, click once with the tool, and to zoom out, Alt/Option+Click with the tool, or you can use your key commands of Ctrl/CMD + +, Ctrl/CMD+ –, or Ctrl/CMD +0 to zoom in or out. Refer to Figure 4-17.

Figure 4-17. *Zoom tool*

Hand Tool (H): This is great to use when you are zoomed in. You can drag your Hand tool and navigate about the Canvas without moving or disrupting the layers or points on a shape while drawing it. If you hold down the spacebar key while using the Selection tool or another tool, you can access this Hand tool. Refer to Figure 4-18.

Figure 4-18. *Hand tool*

Note   If you find that a tool is missing in the Toolbars, it might be in the Edit
Toolbar button in the pop-out panel. You may need to drag and add it back to the
main Toolbars panel. In this workspace, however, all tools should be in the Toolbar.
Make sure, using the panel's menu or the Window menu, to set the Toolbars setting
of Advanced. Refer to Figure 4-19.

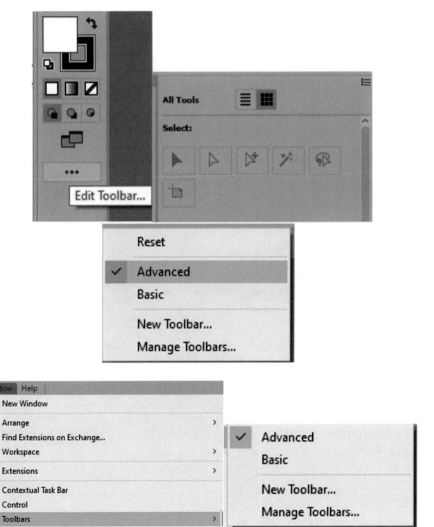

Figure 4-19. *Use the Edit Toolbar button in the Toolbars panel to locate missing
tools and use the Window menu to make sure that the Toolbars is set to Advanced*

Remember, because we are using the Essentials Classic workspace currently, no tools should be missing.

Note   Recently a Window ➤ History panel has been added to Illustrator which is very similar to the one found in Photoshop, and you can learn more about it later in this chapter; for now, make sure to use your Edit ➤ Undo (Ctrl/CMD+Z) if you make a mistake.

Control

The Control panel does have some similarities to the Options panel in Photoshop and does work with some of the tools in the Toolbars panel. However, this is usually when the object has been selected first with, for example, the Selection tool; many of its options are found in the Properties panel as well which we will look at later. Refer to Figure 4-20.

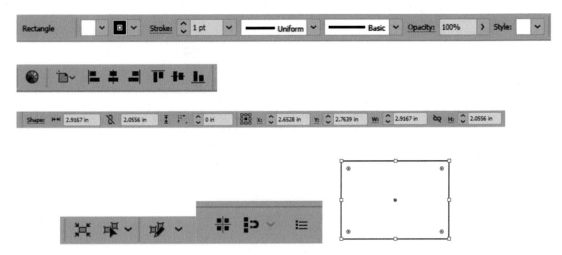

Figure 4-20. *How the Control panel appears when a rectangle is selected with the Selection tool*

Color

The Color panel allows you to select and set colors for select paths using its pallet without having to double-click on a stroke or fill in the color picker in the Toolbars. However, this new color is added to the stroke or fill, whichever is in the front color in the Toolbars panel. Refer to Figure 4-21.

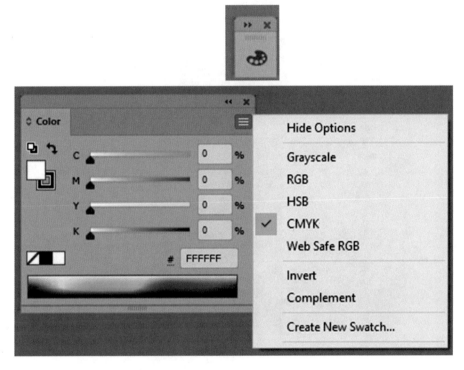

Figure 4-21. *Color panel collapsed and open with its menu*

Note   If you need to reset the colors in the Toolbars panel, press the D key which is a white fill and black stroke. To switch what is in the foreground or current selected color of the fill or stroke, press the X key on your keyboard. And Shift + X to swap fill and stroke color. Refer to Figure 4-22.

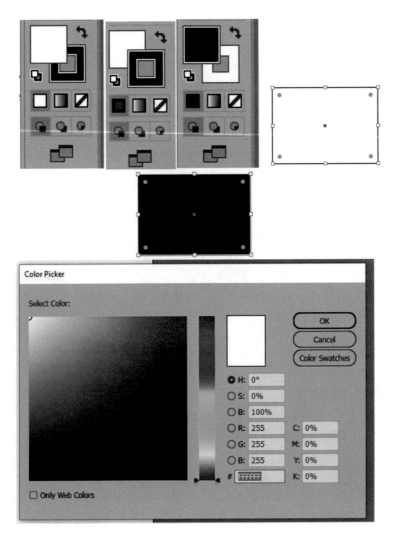

Figure 4-22. *Toolbars panel with Stroke editable with Color Picker default color, Stroke editable with color picker (X), fill and stroke swapped (Shift+X), and the Color Picker dialog box*

The Color panel menu also allows you various ways to view the color (Grayscale, RGB, HSB CMYK, Web Safe RGB), alter color change (Invert and Complement), or create a new swatch. For now, we'll just keep it on the CMYK Color setting, but choose from the menu Show Options if you cannot see all the settings. Refer to Figure 4-23.

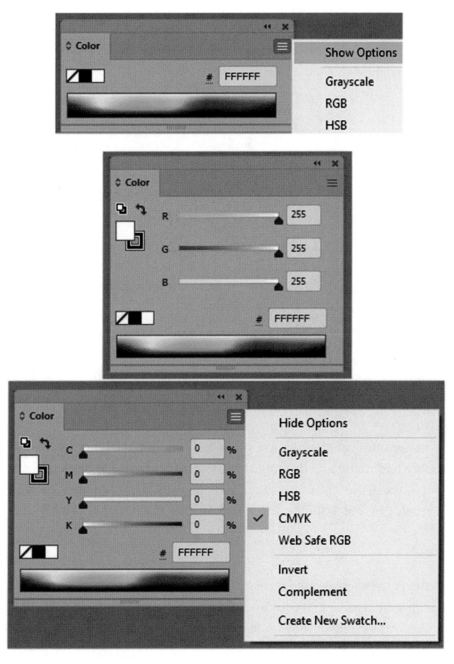

Figure 4-23. *Color panel with its menu for Show and Hide Options*

Use the arrows beside the panel's tab name if you need to show or hide more options.

Color Guide

The Color Guide panel is great along with its dialog box for altering colors on selected shapes. Refer to Figure 4-24.

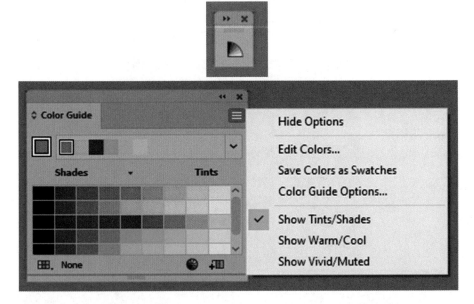

Figure 4-24. *Color Guide panel collapsed and open with its menu*

I've discussed this panel in some of my past books, but in later chapters, you can discover more information on this topic and how it applies to infographics for coloring them. I will be going over the essentials of this panel again in Chapter 8 when we recolor parts of a graphic as well as look at a new feature called Generative Recolor.

Swatches

The Swatches panel allows you to store the color swatches, gradients, and patterns you create that are in folders so that you can save and later share them with others. These swatches that are selected will appear in the Toolbars panel in either the stroke or fill that is currently in the front. Refer to Figure 4-25.

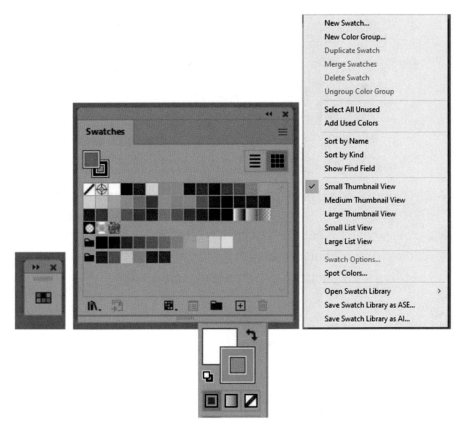

Figure 4-25. *Swatches panel collapsed and open with its menu*

Its menu and the icon on the lower left of the panel have a link to additional Swatch Libraries. You can make the preview swatches bigger if you choose Large Thumbnail view from the menu; currently, it is set to small.

Swatches can be accessed from the Control panel for stroke and fill of selected vector shapes and paths. Refer to Figure 4-26.

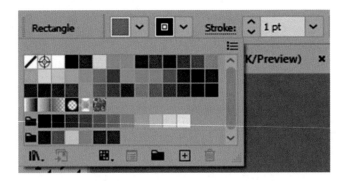

Figure 4-26. *Control panel for path with access to the fill and stroke*

These swatches can also be added to the Libraries panel. For further collaboration, we'll look at that in more detail in Volume 3.

We will be using the Swatches panel throughout the book.

Brushes

The Brushes panel and its library can store a variety of unique vector brushes, and we will look at them briefly in Chapter 8 as we build infographics and see how they can be applied to selected strokes. Refer to Figure 4-27.

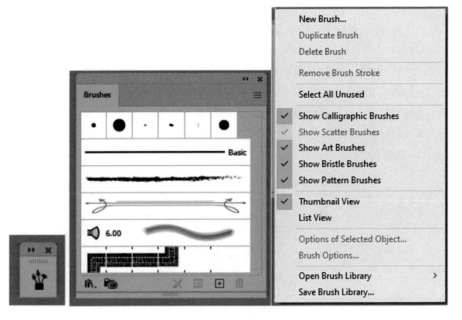

Figure 4-27. *Brushes panel collapsed and open with its menu*

Its menu and the icon on the bottom left of the panel have a link to additional Brush libraries.

Symbols

The Symbols panel can be used to store graphics or parts of your infographics as symbols that can act like a template graphic that you can use many times in your artwork. We will be looking at how it can be used in Chapter 8 and later in Volumes 2 and 3. The menu and the lower left area of the panel also contains a link to additional symbol libraries that you can use for practice. Refer to Figure 4-28.

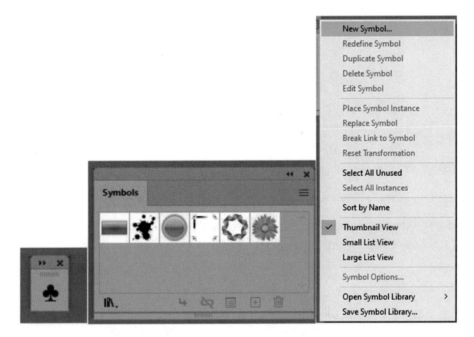

Figure 4-28. *Symbols panel collapsed and open with its menu*

Stroke

The Stroke panel as well as the Control panel and Properties panel can be used to modify the weight of a stroke. We will be exploring more stroke options and their related Width tool in Chapter 6. Refer to Figure 4-29.

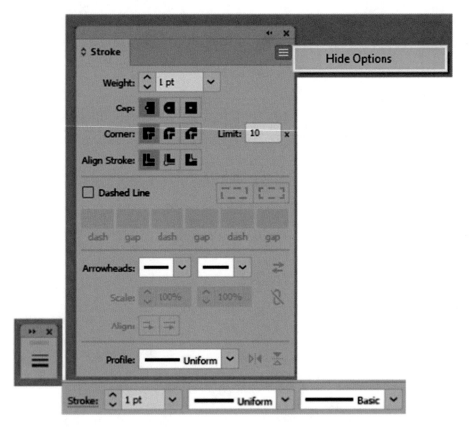

Figure 4-29. *Stroke panel collapsed and open with its menu with Show/Hide Options and the Control panel with its stroke options*

Note   If you cannot see all your stroke options, make sure to use the panel's menu and choose Show Options. Refer to Figure 4-30.

Figure 4-30. *Stroke panel collapsed. Use the menu to access Show Options*

Gradient

The Gradients panel creates gradients. However, they are stored in the Swatches panel and then accessed and altered using the Gradient tool in combination with the Gradients panel. You can easily create your own gradients and store them in the Swatches panel which can later be applied to a fill or stroke of the object. You will see this in Chapter 8 when used with the Gradient tool. Refer to Figure 4-31.

Figure 4-31. *Gradient panel collapsed and open with its menu Show/ Hide Options*

Note   If you cannot see all your Gradient options, make sure to use the panel's menu and choose Show Options. Refer to Figure 4-32.

Figure 4-32. *Gradient panel collapsed and use the menu to show options*

Transparency

The Transparency panel allows you to set the opacity and blending mode of a selected shape as well as an opacity mask as seen in Chapter 8. Refer to Figure 4-33.

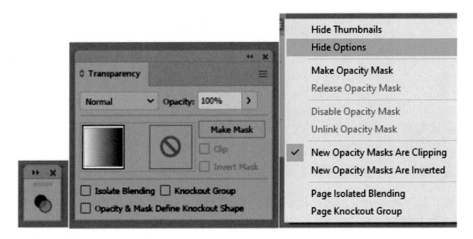

Figure 4-33. *Transparency panel collapsed and open with its menu Show/Hide and other options*

This is a bit different than working in Photoshop where you would set the Layer's opacity by using the Layers panel. However, in Chapter 8, you will see that many of the blending modes are similar to the ones found in Photoshop.

Appearance

The Appearance panel allows you to add multiple strokes and fills with varying opacities and effects. We will look at this more closely in Chapter 8. Refer to Figure 4-34.

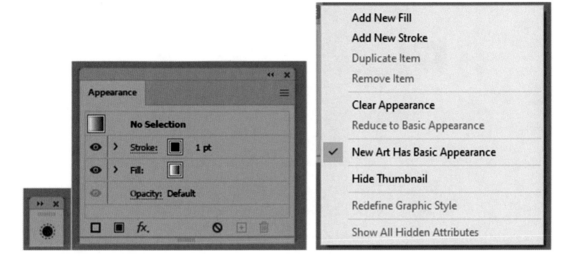

Figure 4-34. *Appearance panel collapsed and open with its menu*

Graphic Styles

With the Graphic Styles panel, once you have created an Appearance, it can be turned into a graphic style. Graphic styles are like the Layer styles in Photoshop, but they do have some slight differences in the way they are created. Refer to Figure 4-35 and Figure 4-36.

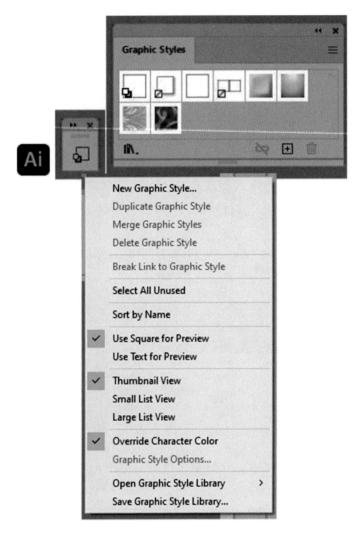

Figure 4-35. *Graphic Styles panel collapsed and open with its menu in Illustrator*

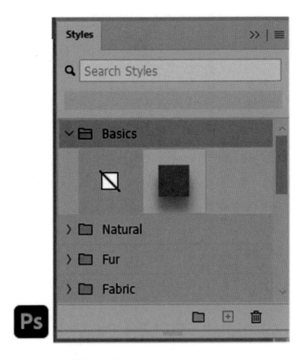

Figure 4-36. *Styles panel in Photoshop*

We will look at this panel in Illustrator more closely in Chapter 8. I will mention styles again in regard to Photoshop in Volume 3. In Illustrator, the panel's menu and the icon on the lower left of the panel also have a link to various Graphic Style libraries that you can modify. Refer to Figure 4-35.

Layers

The Layers panel, along with the Toolbars, Control, and Properties panels, are probably the most important panels in Illustrator. The Layers panel stores all the shapes, objects, and symbols that you can apply graphic styles or live effects to when they are stored on separate layers or sublayers. These layers can be organized and do have some similarities to Photoshop layers, but differences as well. We will see how layers work in the Illustrator Layers panel in Chapters 5 through 9. Refer to Figure 4-37 and Figure 4-38.

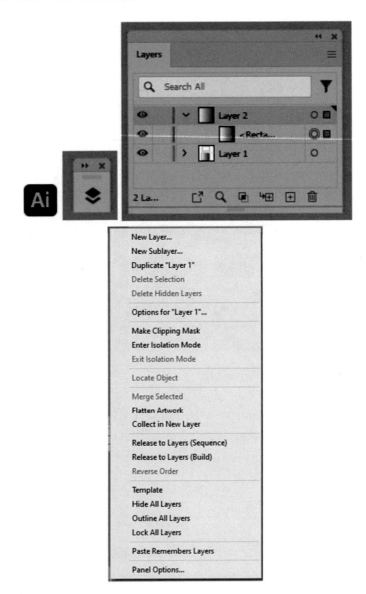

Figure 4-37. *Layers panel collapsed and open with its menu and the Layer Options dialog box in Illustrator*

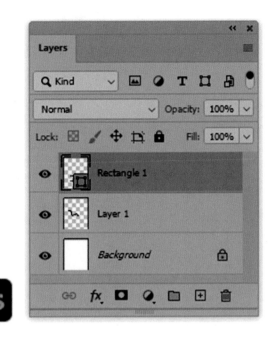

Figure 4-38. *Layers panel in Photoshop*

Similar to Photoshop, the updated Illustrator Layers panel has added a new search feature so that you can find layer or object names easily using various search filters, which is great when working with a lot of layers.

Asset Export

The Asset Export panel is useful for later exporting your design creations in a variety of file formats for the web. We'll talk about those options briefly in Volume 3. Refer to Figure 4-39.

Figure 4-39. *Asset Export panel collapsed and open with its menu*

Artboards

While working with your Artboard tool, you can use the Artboard panel to create and easily find other artboards to store your graphics on. In this book, we will be mainly using a single artboard, but you can create multiple artboards as well, which we will look at later in Chapter 5. Refer to Figure 4-40.

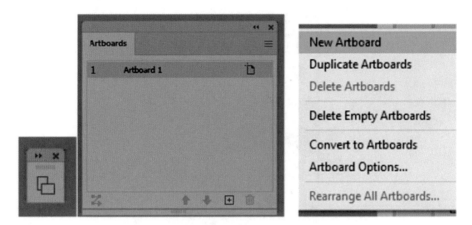

Figure 4-40. *Artboard tool and Artboards panel collapsed and open with its menu*

Working with the Artboard tool will be shown later in Chapter 5. Note that artboard options are also available in Photoshop, but again I prefer to use them one at a time when working on a project.

Comments

The Comments panel, while not important to this book, may be useful if you are sharing comments with other collaborators on your current project. They can be saved as you work in the Creative Cloud for others in your group to view. In this book, we are working alone, so you do not need to work with this panel in any chapter. Refer to Figure 4-41.

Figure 4-41. *Comments panel collapsed and open*

Properties

The Properties panel is in some ways very similar to the Illustrator Controls panel in that it can help you while you are working with a tool as well as with transforming the scale and size of the object, shape, or path. As you will see, starting in Chapter 6, the Properties panel, which is also found in Photoshop, can also advise you with Quick Actions rather than having to remember where in the main menu that command is located. Refer to Figure 4-42 and Figure 4-43.

Figure 4-42. *Properties panel collapsed and open, it changes based on what kind of path or tool is selected in Illustrator*

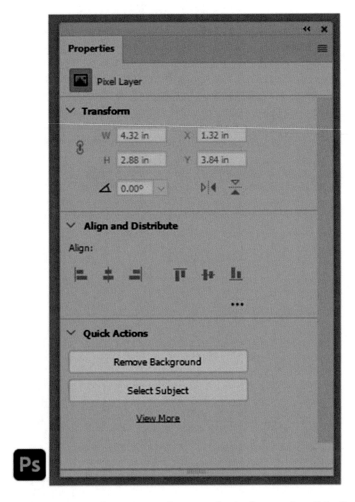

Figure 4-43. *Properties panel open, it changes based on what kind of layer path is selected in Photoshop*

Libraries

The Libraries panel in Illustrator as well as in Photoshop can be used to share your colors, text, patterns, and graphics between Photoshop and Illustrator. We will discuss this more in Volume 3. Refer to Figure 4-44.

Figure 4-44. *Libraries panel collapsed and open with its menu, it has access to Patterns created in Photoshop*

Using Your History Panel

In past versions of Illustrator, you may have noticed that unlike Photoshop, Illustrator did not have a History panel to undo, Manage States, or create a new document from the current state. Now, starting in version 26.4, a History panel has finally been added. If you are familiar with how to use this panel when working in Photoshop, I would encourage you to use it if you need to undo a step by clicking on a previous state. However, you can, as I will mention in my steps in this book, continue to use Edit ➤ Undo (Ctrl/CMD+Z) or Edit ➤ Redo (Shift+Ctrl/CMD+Z) if you are more comfortable with the main menu or key commands. You can locate this panel using the Window menu if you do not see it in your current workspace. Refer to Figure 4-45.

Figure 4-45. *History panel for undoing steps*

For more details on this new panel, make sure to visit the following link:

https://helpx.adobe.com/illustrator/using/recovery-undo-automation.html#history

New Contextual Task Bar

A new item that has recently been added to assist with your workflow and complete your job is the Window ➤ Contextual Task Bar for Photoshop and Illustrator and is very similar to the Quick Actions found in the Properties panel. In Illustrator, it will appear near items when the Selection tool is active. Refer to Figure 4-46.

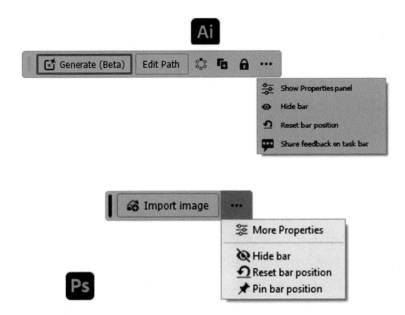

Figure 4-46. *Illustrator and Photoshop Contextual Task Bar with menu*

While we will not be focusing on the Contextual Task Bar in this book, you may find it useful when while working on your projects and want to switch quickly to editing the path or another suggested task.

For how to use it in Illustrator, refer to these pages:

https://helpx.adobe.com/illustrator/using/workspace-basics.
html#contextual-task-bar

https://helpx.adobe.com/photoshop/using/using-tools.html#more-
contextual-taskbars

Other panels found in the Window menu that we will look at later in other chapters in this book, Volume 2 and Volume 3, include

- 3D and Materials (Refer to Volume 2)

- Align (Refer to Chapters 6 and 8)

- Image Trace (Refer to Volume 2)

- Links (Refer to Chapter 5 and Chapter 8)

- Pathfinder (Refer to Chapter 7)

- Pattern Options (Refer to Chapter 8 and Volume 2)

- Transform (Refer to Chapter 6)

- Retype (Beta) (Refer to Chapter 8)

- SVG Interactivity (Refer to Volume 3)

- Type ➤ Character (Refer to Chapter 8)

- Type ➤ Glyphs (Refer to Chapter 8)

- Type➤ OpenType (Refer to Chapter 8)

- Type ➤Paragraph (Refer to Chapter 8)

Note   While not relevant to this book or series, in Volumes 2 and 3, I will mention briefly the newly added Illustrator panels Text to Vector Graphic (Beta) and Mockup (Beta). I will mention how they relate to the other panels and applications as well as provide links to further online resources. For now, refer to your Window menu, Contextual Task Bar, and Properties panel for previewing and access.

If you like, you can open these panels as well and create your own custom New Workspace, but for now we will keep those additional panels closed. Refer to Figure 4-47.

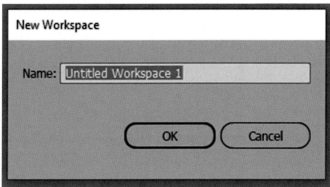

Figure 4-47. *Create a New Workspace that is custom to the tools and panels you use*

Menus

We will be looking at the Object menu and related commands in various chapters throughout the book as well as in Volumes 2 and 3.

In Volume 2, we will be looking in more detail at the Effect menu in regard to adding 2D and 3D effects to an infographic. Refer to Figure 4-48.

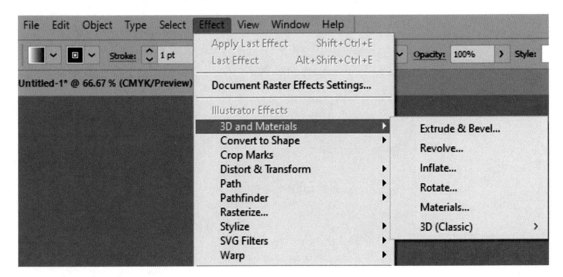

Figure 4-48. *Illustrator main menu*

Summary

This chapter is a starting point for learning about design infographics in Illustrator and how to set up your workspace. Now that you know the basics of some of panels and tools that you will encounter in most chapters, you can begin to work on an actual project and begin the process of altering actual paths and shapes in your artwork.

In the next chapter, you will be reviewing how to create multiple artboards as well as how to save your Illustrator files.

Working with Artboards and Saving Files

In this chapter, I will now describe how to link your digital mock-up to the artboard so that it will display for tracing over should you need to and then conclude with how to save your Illustrator file and other design considerations.

Note This chapter does contain project files that can be found in the Volume 1 Chapter 5 folder, or you can just follow along with the file that you created earlier in Chapter 4.

Working with Artboards

As you work on your single artboard or multiple artboards, it's important to know how to expand your current artboard or add more than one to a page so you can view multiple layouts. Here are some tips to get you started.

Adding Rulers

To begin with, you want to make sure when working with your files that you can add rulers. After you open a file, go to View ➤ Rulers ➤ Show Rulers (Ctrl/CMD+R). You should do this if you need to drag out guides while working on the file and aligning shapes. Selected guides are colored based on the current layer color. You can also adjust increments if you right-click the ruler. Refer to Figure 5-1.

© Jennifer Harder 2023
J. Harder, *Creating Infographics with Adobe Illustrator: Volume 1*,
https://doi.org/10.1007/979-8-8688-0005-4_5

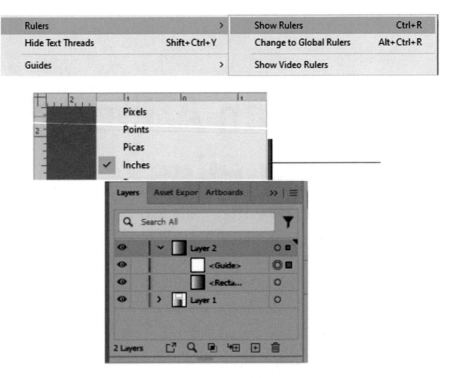

Figure 5-1. *Show your rulers so that you can use guides in Illustrator for lining up paths and objects*

Also make sure that your View ➤ Smart Guides (Ctrl/CMD+U) are activated as well to assist in path alignment. Refer to Figure 5-2.

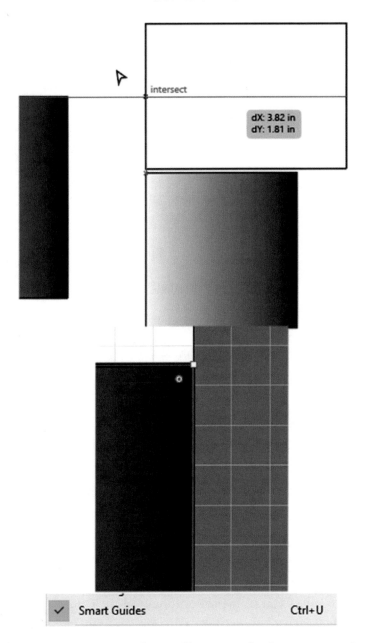

Figure 5-2. *Show your Smart Guides in Illustrator for lining up paths and add grids*

Adding grids can also be useful for certain tasks; use View ➤ Show Grid and then view Hide Grid when you no longer need it. Refer to Figure 5-2.

Editing the Artboard

If you need to work on your artboard or multiple artboards, here are some steps. Currently, you will have a single artboard in your application. If after creating your file you discover that the artboard is too small or large, you can edit it with your Toolbars Artboard tool (Shift I O). This is located just above the Hand tool. Click it to enter the Artboard editing mode as you will see when you look at the Control panel. Refer to Figure 5-3.

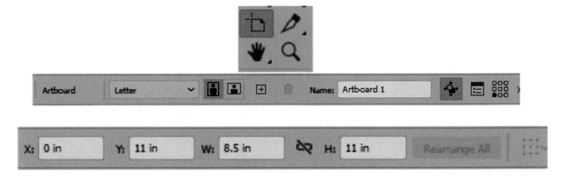

Figure 5-3. *Artboard tool and settings in the Control panel for a single artboard*

A bounding box will appear around the entire artboard and a name label in the upper left. Once selected, you will be able to do the following steps. Refer to Figure 5-4.

Figure 5-4. *Selected Artboard label*

Scale the bounding box using the handles by dragging on the corner or side handles. Hold down the Shift key as you scale proportionally or Alt/Option+Shift if you want to scale proportionally from the center of the artboard. Or drag on the artboard to move it about.

If you want an exact page size, then it is better to use the Control panel. Select a known page size from the drop-down list of presets such as Letter, Legal, and Tabloid. In this case, Letter was selected. If you already scaled, it may show up as Custom. Refer to Figure 5-5.

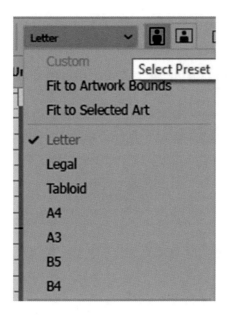

Figure 5-5. *Control panel for Artboard page size settings*

You can then set if you want the layout to be portrait or landscape. Refer to Figure 5-6.

Figure 5-6. *Control panel for Artboard orientation settings*

As you work on your artboard, if it becomes off-center from your rulers (0 no longer for the X and 11 for the y coordinate), then double-click the ruler crosshairs to reset. That only will work for the currently selected artboard. Refer to Figure 5-7.

Figure 5-7. *Artboard page crosshairs*

Likewise, by using the Control panel, you can also do other tasks such as add another New Artboard (plus icon) or delete a selected artboard (trash can icon). You can also rename a selected artboard, type a new name, and click enter to confirm the new name. Refer to Figure 5-8.

Figure 5-8. *Control panel for Artboard new, delete, and name settings*

Then you can Move/Copy Artwork with Artboard (when the icon is enabled) set additional artboard options, as well as a new reference point changing the x or y coordinate value for scaling and moving purposes. Refer to Figure 5-9.

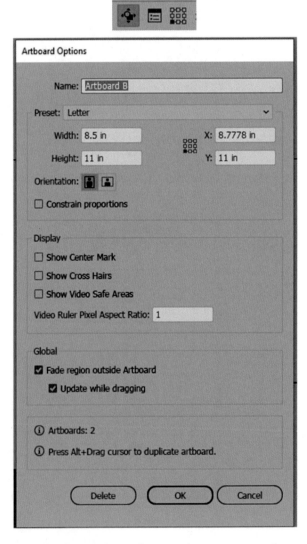

Figure 5-9. *Control panel for Artboard Move/Copy Artwork, options, reference point with dialog box settings*

The next section allows you to adjust the x and y coordinate value for a selected artboard as well as the width and height whose proportions can remain linked or unlinked. Refer to Figure 5-10.

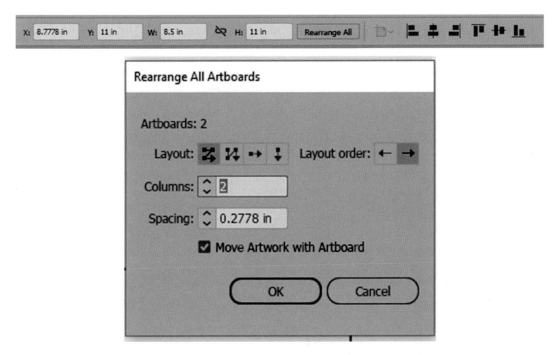

Figure 5-10. Control panel for Artboard settings for x/y coordinate, width/height, and Rearrange All Artboards dialog box

You can rearrange all artboards using the button and dialog box to change the layout. Refer to Figures 5-10 and 5-12. Alternatively, click only one artboard to select it, then Shift+Click selected artboards and use the alignment buttons. You can also use Ctrl/Cmd+A if you want to select all the artboards, such as to then Horizontal Align (Left, Center, Right), Vertical Align (Top, Center, Bottom), or for two, three, or more artboards Vertical Distribute (Top, Center, Bottom), and Horizontal Distribute (Left, Center, Right). During this time, the Align to Artboard icon will be disabled. Refer to Figure 5-11.

Figure 5-11. Control panel for Artboard settings for arranging multiple selected artboards

Multiple artboards are useful when you are working on two or more layouts of the same project, and you want to keep them all in the same file. Later you may want to separate them into their own files if you are planning on only showing one or two to the client.

Be careful that if you already have various objects of artwork on the artboard, do not select them, or you may turn them into an artboard. That is why it is best to set up your artboards first when creating multiple projects. If you do this by accident, click the trash can icon to undo that step, but keep the artwork. You can also see a preview of your artboard in the Artboards panel which has similar settings in its menu as the Control panel. You can also use it to Duplicate Artboards or Delete Empty Artboards as well when you have excess artboards. Refer to Figure 5-12.

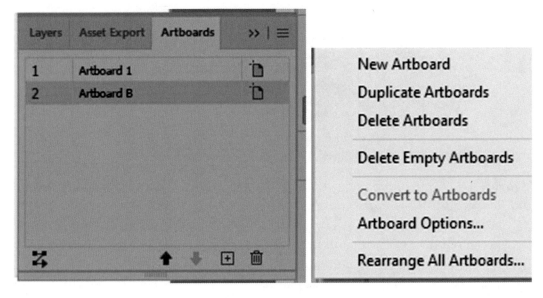

Figure 5-12. *Artboards panel and its menu with two artboards*

You can also use the arrow keys on your keyboard to move or nudge your selected artboard. Refer to Figure 5-13.

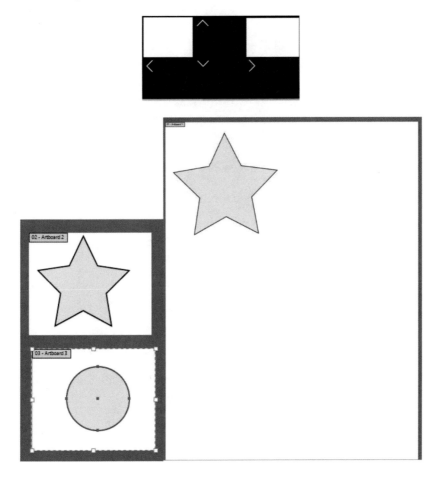

Figure 5-13. *Use the arrow keys to nudge your selected artboards while in Artboard mode*

Once you have created all the artboards you require, you can either click the Hand tool in the Toolbars panel or in the Properties panel click the Exit button to exit the Artboard mode and work on your various projects on the artboard. Note that the Properties panel contains many of the same settings as the Control panel. Refer to Figure 5-14.

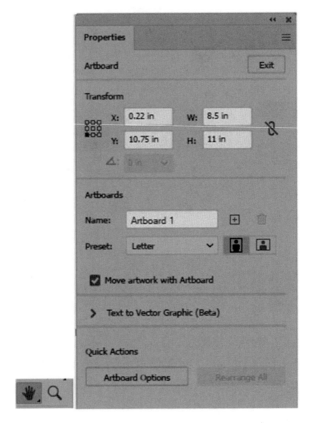

Figure 5-14. *Use the Hand tool or Exit button in the Properties panel to exit Artboard editing mode*

You can learn more details about artboards here:

https://helpx.adobe.com/illustrator/using/introduction-to-artboards.html

Linking Your Digital Mock-Up Image to the Illustrator File

Whether working with single or multiple artboards, it is important to know if you have digitized your sketch, in this case as a JPG file, how to link it with your Illustrator file to the document. Later in Chapter 8, we'll use various tools such as the shape and pen tools to trace over the image.

With your artboard visible, from the menu, choose File ➤ Place.

When the Place dialog box opens, browse your folders, and locate the (.jpg) file that you earlier saved from the scan you created in Photoshop in Chapter 3. Select the file, in my example I am using Mockup_Sketch.jpg. Click the Place button. Refer to Figure 5-15.

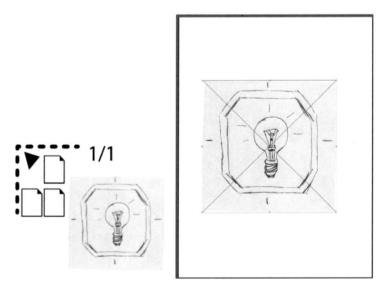

Figure 5-15. *Use the Place dialog box to locate your files*

The thumbnail preview also known as the "Placement Gun" will appear, then click the artboard, and the file has now placed a linked copy on the artboard. Refer to Figure 5-16.

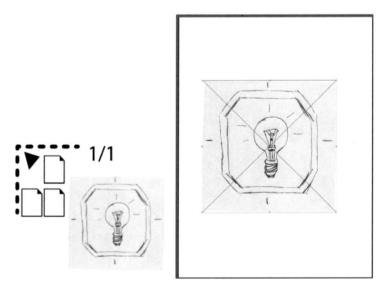

Figure 5-16. *Use the "Placement Gun" to place a linked file on the artboard*

Note   While in the Place dialog box, you can also Shift+Click more than one image before clicking the Place button, and this will load up the "Placement Gun" with multiple images, and then you can click different locations on the artboard until you have released all the linked images. Refer to Figure 5-17.

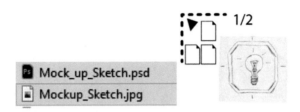

Figure 5-17. *Load multiple file with the "Placement Gun" and place them on the artboard*

To check where your linked images are located, you can review this in the Window ➤ Links panel. The Links panel can hold linked or embedded images. Refer to Figure 5-18.

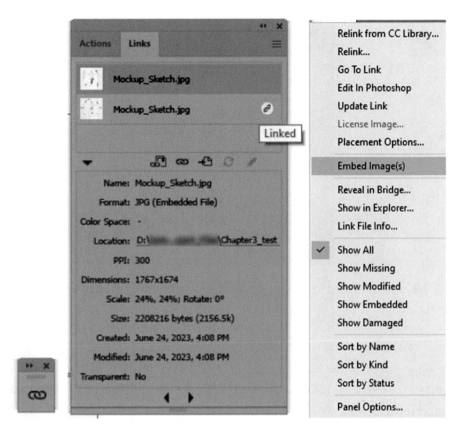

Figure 5-18. *Links panel collapsed and open with menu*

Keep in mind if you embed the images, it will increase the Illustrator file size. However, if you keep it linked, the file's size will stay small, but then you must remember to move the mock-up with the file, or it may become unlinked, resulting in an error message, and you will need to locate the missing file by clicking replace or use the menu to update link. Refer to Figure 5-19.

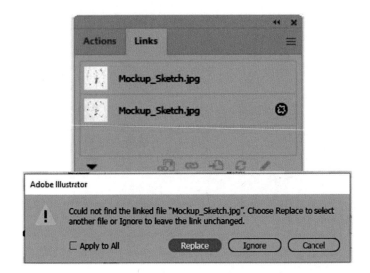

Figure 5-19. *Links panel with one broken link and the warning message to locate the missing file*

The file can be removed if you select it with your Selection tool (black arrow) and press the Backspace/Delete key on your keyboard. You can Edit ➤ Undo this move (Ctrl/CMD+Z) or use your History panel. In this case, we will just leave the linked file on Layer 1, and in Chapter 8, we will look more at layer order and its importance when you need to trace over the mock-up. Refer to Figure 5-20.

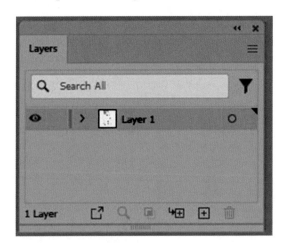

Figure 5-20. *Layers panel with a thumbnail of item on layer*

Next you should save your file.

Project: Saving Your Illustrator File

At this point, if you are working on a project, if you have added a path or object to your new file, you can File ➤ Save the document as an .ai file somewhere on your computer so that you can continue to work with the various tools in Illustrator. An Illustrator file will allow you to use and edit all the features in the Illustrator app. Refer to Figure 5-21.

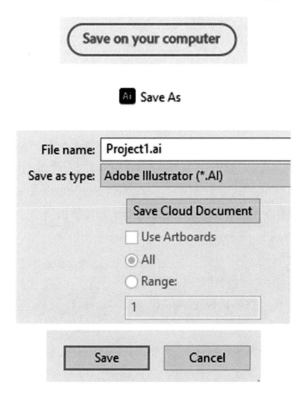

Figure 5-21. *Save your file in the Save As dialog box*

Most files in Chapters 6–9 as well as the chapters in Volumes 2 and 3 will be in the .ai format. But for other clients, for printing projects, you may be asked to save the file as a .eps or .pdf. Refer to Figure 5-22.

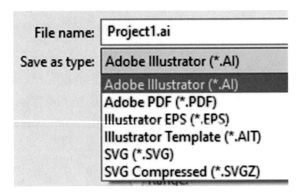

Figure 5-22. *Choose a file format from the Save As dialog box*

Note   If you have more than one artboard in your file, you may have this area in the dialog box active. By default, it is disabled and set to one. But with multiple artboards, when you save as an (.eps), you could then click the Use Artboards settings and set to all or set a range. Refer to Figure 5-23.

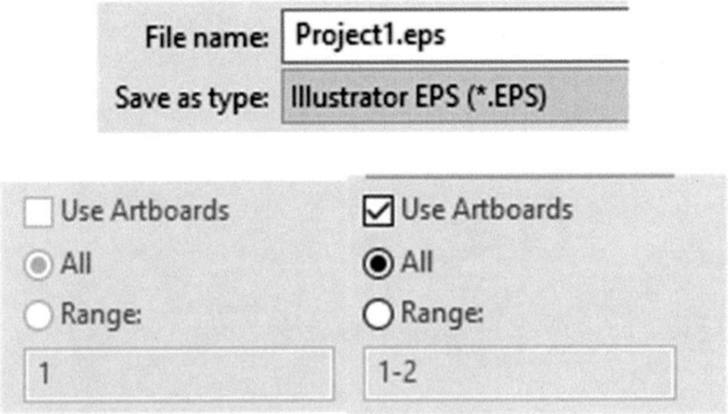

Figure 5-23. *Save as various file types with artboards in the Save As dialog box*

For (.ai) files, after clicking Save in Figure 5-21, make sure to Click OK the following Illustrator Options. Refer to Figure 5-24.

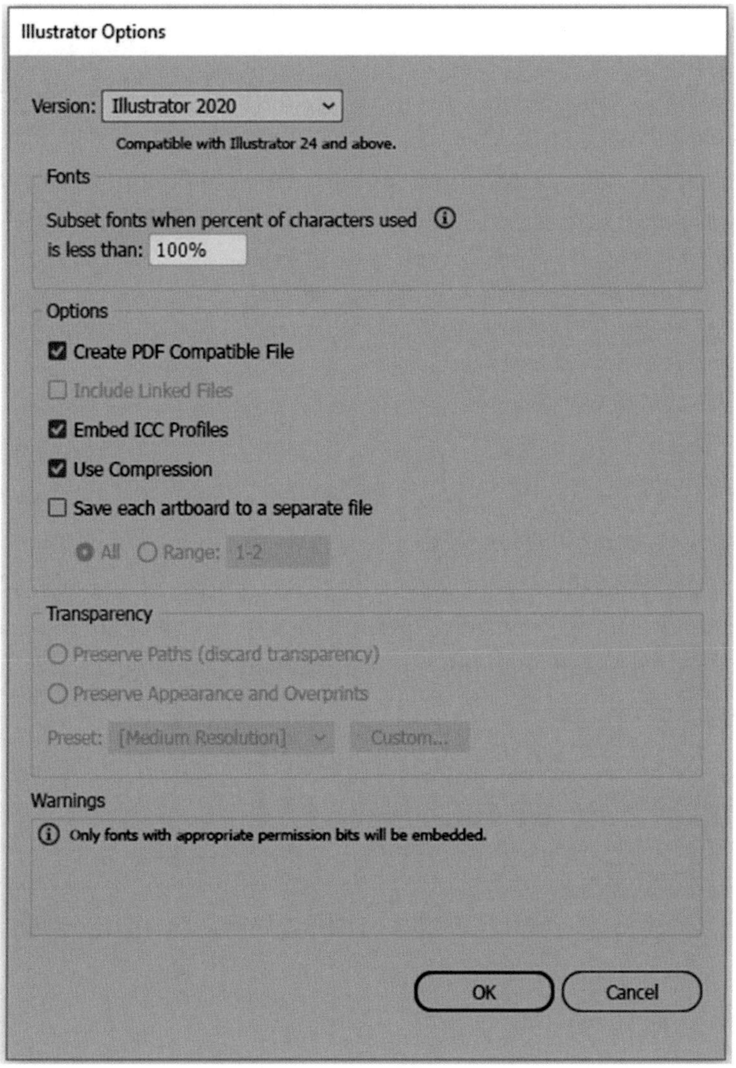

Figure 5-24. *Illustrator Options dialog box*

I make sure that the version is compatible with Illustrator 2020. If I am saving for an older computer, I would lower the version in the drop-down menu, but then the file will not be able to retain the latest features.

For fonts, I will leave the setting for subset fonts when percent of characters used is less than 100%. In this case, only fonts with appropriate permission bits will be embedded. However, if you have the fonts on your computer or are accessing them from the Creative Cloud, this is not an issue. If it is a concern, you can turn a Type into Outlines as you will see in Chapter 8.

Keep the options enabled for Create PDF Compatible File, Embed ICC Profiles for color, and Use Compression. In this case, we do not need to Include Linked files as this would increase the file size, and unless you have multiple artboards, you do not need to save each artboard to a separate file. Also, if we had more, in this case, you would want to keep them together in a single document until you plan to export or save as a copy.

The Transparency options are kept disabled for the following:

- Preserved Paths (discard transparency)

- Preserve Appearance and Overprints

- Preset: [Resolution]

You can ignore the settings as Transparency will be maintained within the file (.ai). These options are only available for older versions like Illustrator 8 or lower.

Then click OK to complete saving the file as an (.ai). Refer to Figure 5-24.

In this example, you can refer to my file Project1_final.ai to review the file with the linked and embedded image examples for file Mockup_Sketch.jpg.

Other project files in will be in the (.psd) format and those you can File ➤ Open in Adobe Photoshop to review.

Saving Duplicates of Your File

Later, if you need to make any duplicates of my open Illustrator files for practice, use File ➤ Save As. To create a copy of the file, in the Save As dialog box, rename your file as required, with your initials on the end so you know which copy you are working on, and click Save and OK to the Illustrator Options dialog box. Refer to Figures 5-24 and 5-25.

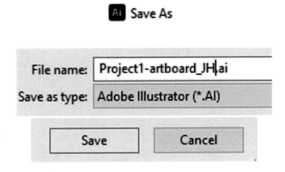

Figure 5-25. *Save As dialog box with initials on the end of file name*

Optionally, you could use this setting in the Illustrator Options dialog box if you needed to save multiple artboards and the composite. Refer to Figure 5-26.

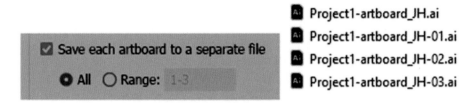

Figure 5-26. *Save as options in Save As dialog box*

After exiting Save As, this will automatically close the original file and just leave your copy open. For separate artboards, you would need to File ➤ Open one at a time. Refer to my Artboards_Example folder.

Working with Your Infographics Between Photoshop and Illustrator

It's important to have color conversion from CMYK to RGB for consistency when working between Photoshop and Illustrator.

In some cases, you may have created an Illustrator file in RGB color mode that you want to convert to CMYK color mode. To convert an Illustrator file from CMYK Color to RGB color mode is important for Photoshop (.psd) files to ensure that there is a consistent color conversion before an Illustration is pasted into a Photoshop RGB file. While not required for this book, nevertheless I always recommend making a copy of your original CMYK Illustrator document using File ➤ Save As and then, on the copy of the file from the menu, go to File ➤ Document color mode and choose RGB Color before pasting the item directly from Illustrator into Photoshop.

Or use this method to convert a copy to CMYK Color from this menu if for Photoshop CMYK document. We'll look at this conversion briefly in Volume 3. Refer to Figure 5-27.

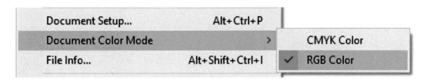

Figure 5-27. *Set the files' document color mode*

When converting to RGB, there may be a slight color shift, but that is OK because you are working on a copy of your file. Then File ➤ Save to commit the change. You can then select your paths, shape, or object with the Selection tool. Refer to Figure 5-28.

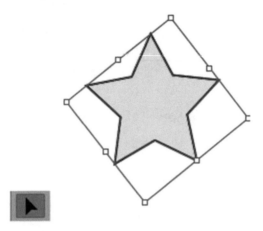

Figure 5-28. *Select a path or shape with the Selection tool*

Choose Edit ➤ Copy (Ctrl/CMD+C) and then return to Photoshop and Edit ➤ Paste (Ctrl/CMD +V) and paste as a Smart Object layer into your own (.psd) document which is in RGB color mode. Click OK and then make sure to click the Check in the Options panel to commit and complete the paste of the layer. Refer to Figure 5-29.

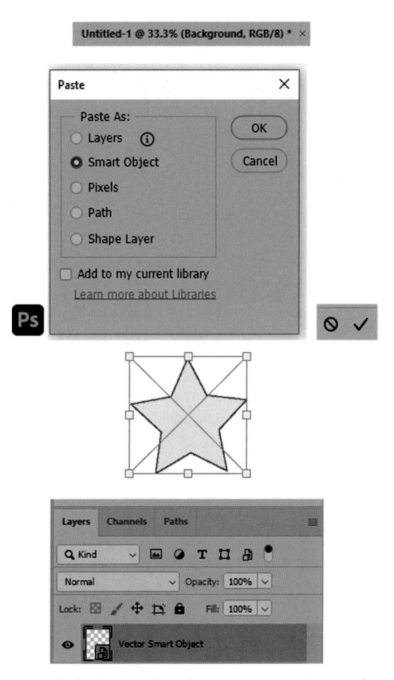

Figure 5-29. *Paste dialog box in Photoshop set to Smart Object and confirm Option settings in the Layers panel*

This is one way you can ensure that your Illustrator Smart Object layer will be in the same RGB color mode as the Photoshop document.

The Illustrator Vector Smart Object layer in Photoshop is a great type of layer to use when you still want to have access to editing colors and shapes in Illustrator during a project. I also recommend that when you initially create the Photoshop document, make it at least 300–600 pixels/inch resolution to ensure that your infographic appears at its best. See the folder Smart_object for example files.

I will discuss more about this Photoshop option as well as the importance of Flattening layers (Layer ➤ Flatten Image) or use of Layers panel menu and what direction you could take infographics in Volume 3.

Summary

In this chapter, we reviewed how to work with artboards, how to link files to the artboard, as well as how to save your file. Later we looked at how to work between Photoshop and Illustrator and change color modes.

In the next chapter, you will be reviewing shape tools as well as looking more closely at the three selection tools and how they can be used in conjunction with the Layers panel, as well as the Control, Properties, Align, and Transform panels.

CHAPTER 6

A Basic Review of Illustrator's Shape Tools

This chapter is an overview of Illustrator's basic shape tools and related panels that you would use to start creating infographic rudimentary shapes.

Once you have created and scanned your logos in a digital format, you will want to start using Illustrator to trace over your drawing. Or maybe you just want to start drawing some basic shapes or edit your Illustration. You will explore some tools that may already be familiar to you and new and updated tools in later chapters. Later in Chapter 9, based on what you have learned here, you will create and review a few project ideas that can be created with basic shapes, custom shapes, and text.

Note   This chapter contains reference examples that can be found in the Volume 1 Chapter 6 folder. Some of the text in this chapter on shapes has been adapted and updated from my earlier books *Accurate Layer Selections Using Photoshop's Selection Tool* and *Perspective Warps and Distorts with Adobe Tools: Volume 2*.

In this chapter, we are now going to cover some of the tools that can be found in the Toolbars panel, as well as some of the main panels that we can use to assist us in infographic creation. I will only be focusing on the basic features of each of these tools, but I will also provide an Adobe help link if you would like more details on that tool. For now, if you would like to practice along, create a new document as you did in Chapter 4 so that you have an artboard to practice with the following tools and panels.

© Jennifer Harder 2023
J. Harder, *Creating Infographics with Adobe Illustrator: Volume 1*,
https://doi.org/10.1007/979-8-8688-0005-4_6

Drawing Tools Overview

When starting to draw an infographic or logo, there are several basic tools such as Rectangle, Rounded Rectangle, Ellipse, Polygon, Star, and related panels we can use to build our shapes. These basic shapes are found in the Toolbars panel. Refer to Figure 6-1.

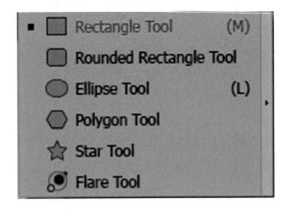

Figure 6-1. *Drawing tools found in the Toolbars panel*

As you select and use the following tools, make sure that your Toolbar setting is set to Draw Normal as you want to draw your shapes, in this case, in front of one another. In other situations, you may want to use one of the other two settings of Draw Behind or Draw Inside. Refer to Figure 6-2.

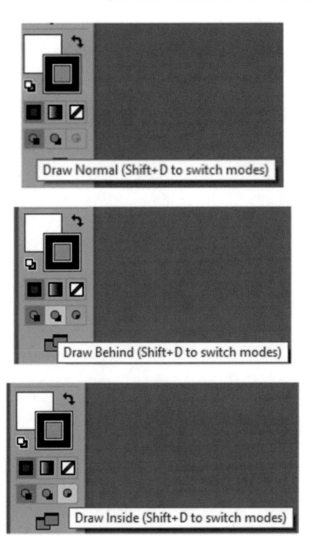

Figure 6-2. Drawing settings in the Toolbars panel

However, for this book, our focus is to draw the shapes one at a time in Draw Normal mode. You can use the keyboard shortcut Shift+D if you need to switch or cycle back to this setting. Later, I will mention how you can arrange shapes if they are not in the order you want when they overlap. See the section "Arranging Shape and Path Order."

Also, this book will not be focused on the Flare tool as this is a specialized tool and not often associated with infographic creation.

You can explore the basics of that tool on your own here:

```
https://helpx.adobe.com/illustrator/using/tool-techniques/flare-
tool.html
```

Now we will do a basic overview of each of the five main tools. These tools for initial shape building can be used in conjunction with the Control, Properties, and Transform panels. Refer to Figure 6-3.

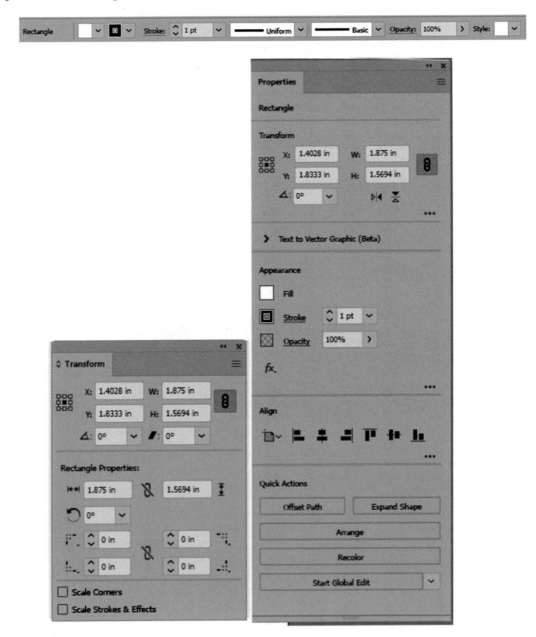

Figure 6-3. *Use the Control, Transform, or Properties panel to edit your shapes and paths*

Later in Chapter 7, I will mention the Pathfinder panel as well. See the section "Combining Shapes with the Pathfinder Panel."

With nothing selected on your artboard, make sure in your Properties panel that Scale Strokes & Effects is unchecked so your stroke does not change should you decide to scale the shape later on while you practice. For these examples, I also left Scale Corners unchecked as well. Refer to Figure 6-4.

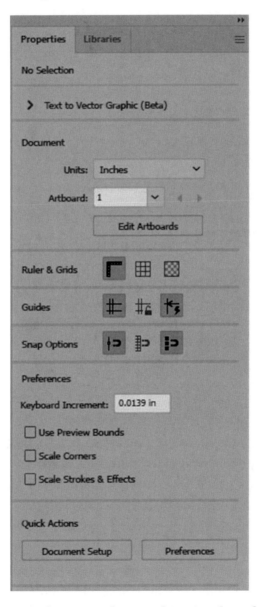

Figure 6-4. *Properties panel setting when nothing is selected on the artboard*

In these steps, make sure that you press the D key to ensure that your colors for fill and stroke in the Toolbars panel are reset to white fill and black stroke. Refer to Figure 6-2.

Rectangle Tool (M)

The Rectangle tool is used for creating rectangles and squares. Once this tool is selected from the Toolbars panel, you can draw a rectangle by dragging out the shape to the size and length you want as you hold down the mouse key and then release. You will now have a rectangle on the artboard. Using the same tool, you can continue to draw out more rectangles. Refer to Figure 6-5.

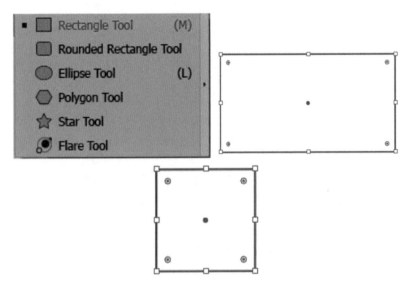

Figure 6-5. *Use the Toolbars' Rectangle tool selected to draw rectangles and squares*

If you want a square, hold down the Shift key as you drag out the shape like before and release the Shift key and mouse at the same time. If you want to drag out the shape from the center as you drag, hold down the Alt/Option key or Alt/Option+Shift keys. You can apply this option to the other tools later as well as you use them.

If you want to set some settings for an exact size, rather than drag out a shape, while the Rectangle tool is selected, click once the artboard to bring up the dialog box and enter your width and height. You can also constrain width and height proportions using the link icon should you want to type the same setting ratio while the link is active. Once you have entered your settings, click OK. Refer to Figure 6-6.

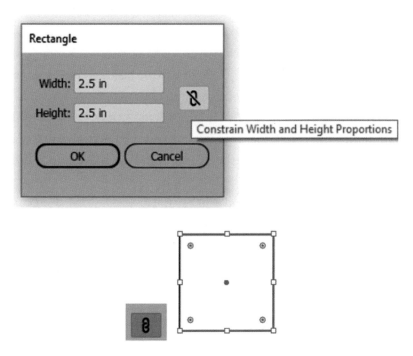

Figure 6-6. *The Rectangle dialog box with Constrain Width and Height Proportions link inactive and active and a square on the artboard*

The currently selected rectangle can have its corners rounded by dragging on the live corner widgets, or you can use the next tool to do that automatically. In this example, all four sides will be round. Refer to Figure 6-7.

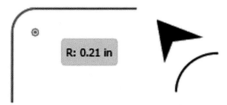

Figure 6-7. *Drag on the rectangles live corner widget to round all sides at the same time*

If you cannot see the widgets check that you have, set your View ➤ Show Corner Widget as active. You can toggle between show and hide. Rectangles are often good for containers for surrounding a graph's legend or surrounding another shape or art that is being focused on or contained.

Rounded Rectangle Tool

The Rounded Rectangle tool is very similar to the Rectangle tool. Just drag out the shape while the tool is selected, and you can use all of the same key commands to create rounded rectangles and squares. Remember to hold down the Shift key when you want to make a rounded square. Refer to the Rectangle tool for more details on other key commands. As you drag out the shape, you can use your up and down arrow keys on your keyboard to adjust the corner radius. Left and right keys will turn your edges from rounded to cornered.

If you want to enter the dialog box and enter some exact settings, then click the artboard while the tool is selected. In this dialog box, beside the earlier rectangle settings (width, height, and constrain width and height proportions link) is a setting for all four-corner radius. However, you can later adjust each corner individually as we will look at that in more detail later when we review the Transform panel. For now, click OK to commit your settings. Refer to Figure 6-8.

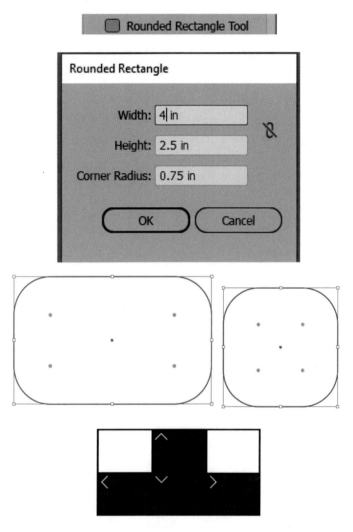

Figure 6-8. *Toolbars' Rounded Rectangle tool, Rounded Rectangle dialog box, and rounded rectangles on the artboard. Use arrows when you drag out a shape without the dialog box*

Again, with this shape, while selected, you can use the live corner widgets to continue to adjust the shape. Rounded rectangles are often good for containers for surrounding legend or another shape and are gentler in appearance than the angled rectangle.

Ellipse Tool (L)

The Ellipse tool is good for drawing ovals and circles while the tool is selected. Just drag out the shape of an oval, or while dragging, hold down the Shift key for a circle. You can also use your Alt or Alt/Option+Shift combination as you did with the Rectangle tool. If you want a precise shape, then click the artboard. Like the square, you can set the width, height, and constrain width and height proportions using the link. Refer to Figure 6-9.

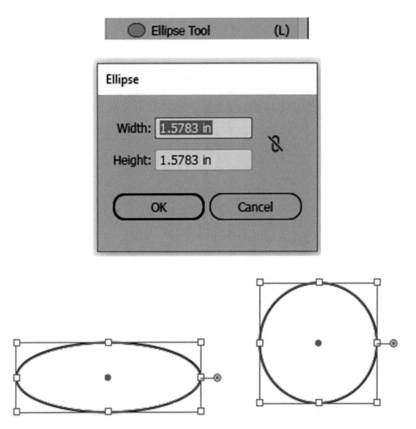

Figure 6-9. *Toolbar's Ellipse tool, Ellipse dialog box, and ellipses on the artboard*

The ellipse can be divided into a wedge or segment by dragging on pie widgets start or end angle circle handles. This is a great way to create parts of a rudimentary pie chart design, but it is not an actual graph in which data can be adjusted. We will look at some more detail on this pie shape later in Chapter 9 in the infographic resume example and on the topic of pie graphs in Volume 2. Refer to Figure 6-10.

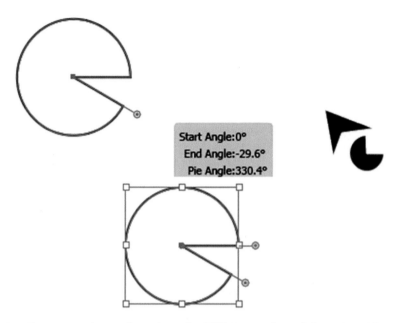

Figure 6-10. *Create a pie angle using the Ellipse tool and the pie widgets*

Polygon Tool

The Polygon tool is useful for creating sided shapes from 3 (triangle) to 1000 sides, which at that point would resemble a circle. While this tool is selected, you can drag out an equally sided shape. Hold down the Shift key as you drag if you want one of the sides to remain horizontal and Alt/Option+Shift drag from the center. As you drag, you can also use the up and down arrow keys on your keyboard to add more or fewer sides to your shape. Refer to Figure 6-11.

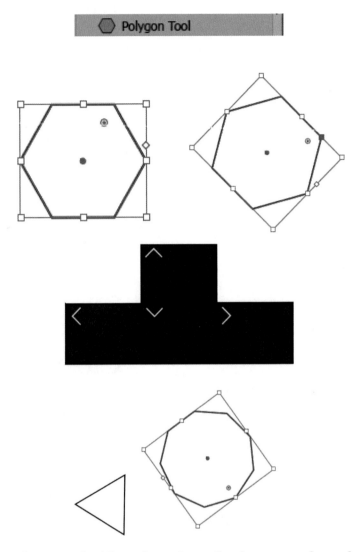

Figure 6-11. *Polygon tool with various shaped polygons on the artboard that can be modified during drawing with the arrow keys*

Once you release your shape, if it is still selected, you can increase or decrease the number of sides between 3 and 11 using the side diamond widget and dragging it up and down. Refer to Figure 6-12.

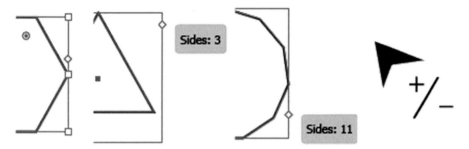

Figure 6-12. *Use the polygon side widget to add more or less sides to a polygon on the artboard*

You can even use the single live corner widget while the shape is selected to round all the corners of your shape. Refer to Figure 6-13.

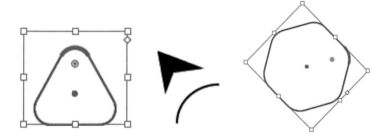

Figure 6-13. *Round the sides of a polygon with the corner widget*

If you want a precise size, while the Polygon tool is selected, click the artboard, and you can use the dialog box to set the radius and number of sides. Refer to Figure 6-14.

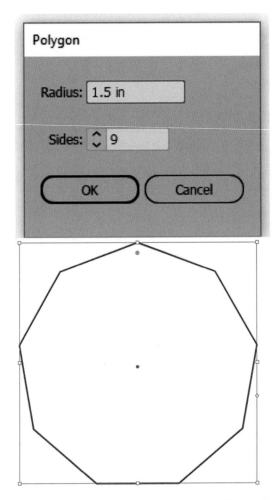

Figure 6-14. *Polygon dialog box for adding a set number of sides*

Note   There is no constrain link. Later you can use your Selection tool to make the polygon disproportionate.

Polygons can add interest to a logo design or infographic.

We will look at some more options for this tool later in the chapter when we review the Control and Transform panels.

Star Tool

The Star tool, like the Polygon tool, will create a multisided shape, but this time as a star. While the tool is selected, you can drag out an equal-sided star. Hold down the Shift key if you want the two bottom points to be horizontal. Refer to Figure 6-15.

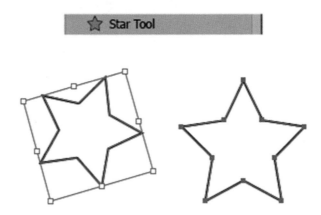

Figure 6-15. *Toolbars' Star tool and a star on the artboard*

Alt/Option or Alt/Option+Shift drag from the center, and this will cause the second inner radius to alter slightly, making the star more pointy. Again, as you drag out the shape, you can use the up and down arrow keys on your keyboard to add more or less points to the star. Refer to Figure 6-16.

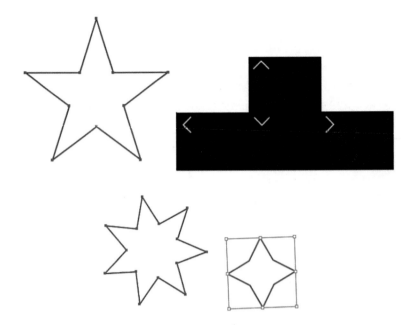

Figure 6-16. *While dragging out a star, use the arrow keys to add more or less sides*

If you need precise settings, then, while the tool is selected, click the artboard and use the dialog box to set Radius 1, Radius 2, and then number of points (3–1000), and click OK to commit the shape. Refer to Figure 6-17.

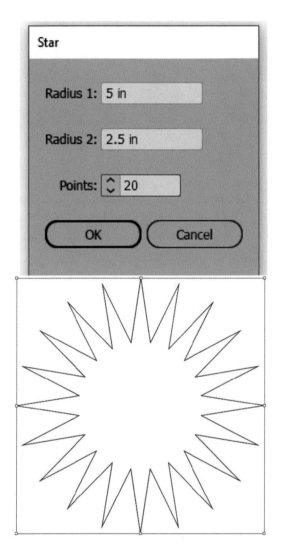

Figure 6-17. *The Star dialog box and a star on the artboard*

Note   Unlike the Polygon tool, you will not be able to use the live corner widgets directly for the round cornering of the star; I will show you how to do that later. Also, if you need to make the star disproportionate, you can scale it later with the Selection tool which we will review shortly. Stars can add interest, often for children's designs or added to something sale related when you want specific text to stand out. Refer to Figure 6-18.

Figure 6-18. *Children's artwork and advertisement for a sale are good uses of the Star tool*

You can learn more about the basic shapes from this page.

`https://helpx.adobe.com/illustrator/how-to/draw-basic-shapes.html`

Line Segment, Arc, and Spiral Tools

There are three other tools that you may want to use as well for your infographic creation which though not actual shapes, can be very useful in adding creative detail to your logo or infographic. They are the Line Segment tool (\), Arc tool, and Spiral tool. These tools follow basically the same drawing process as the other aforementioned shape tools, and you can use your mouse while the tool is selected to drag out, for example, an individual line, arc, or spiral. However, they are for single-stroke lines only but are very useful for details or hair creation. Like the basic shape tools, if you need to access their dialog boxes, click the artboard first. Refer to Figure 6-19.

Figure 6-19. *Toolbars' panel with various line drawing options*

For the Line Segment Tool Options dialog box, you can set length, angle (0–360) degrees, and fill line though this is disabled by default. Click OK to confirm settings. Refer to Figure 6-20.

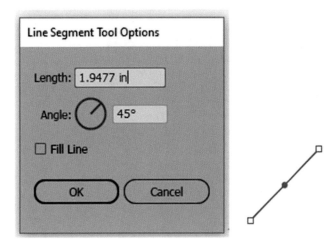

Figure 6-20. *Line Segment Tool Options panel and a line on the artboard*

As you drag out a line segment, hold down the Shift key to constrain to 45 degree angles.

For the Arc Segment Tool Options dialog box, you can set the length of x and y axis, reference point, type (open or closed), base along (x axis or y axis), slope (concave -100 to convex 100), and to fill arc though this is disabled by default. Click OK to confirm settings. Refer to Figure 6-21.

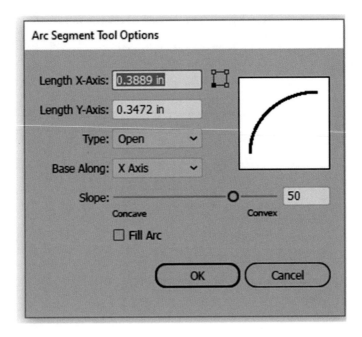

Figure 6-21. *Arc Segment Tool dialog box with Preview and the arc on the artboard*

Note   For the Preview setting in the Arc Segment tool, this will only appear if you double-click the tool in the Toolbars panel first before you draw. When you click the artboard, the preview will not be in the dialog box. When you drag out an arc, you can use the up and down arrow keys on your keyboard to adjust the slope.

For the Spiral dialog box, you can set a radius, a decay rate (5%–150%), number of segments (2–1000), and a style of either clockwise or counterclockwise. Click OK to confirm settings. Refer to Figure 6-22.

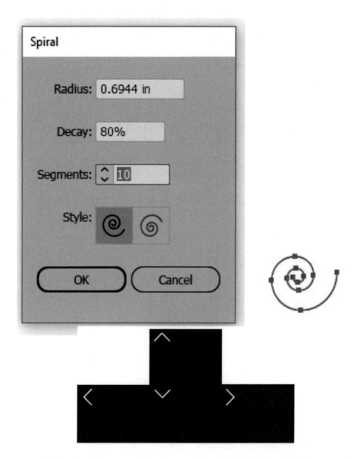

Figure 6-22. *Spiral dialog box and a spiral on the artboard. Use the arrow keys when not in the dialog box while drawing out a spiral*

If you drag out a spiral, use the up and down arrow keys on your keyboard to add or remove segments.

Drawing Tools That Can Be Used to Create Basic Graphs

With the Line Segment tools are two other tools that can be used to create graph-like shapes. These are the Rectangular Grid tool and the Polar Grid tool which you can use to emulate other types of graphs. Refer to Figure 6-23.

Figure 6-23. *Toolbars' panel with various line drawing options*

The Rectangular Grid tool could be used to create a waffle graph/chart. The Polar Grid tool could be used to create a type of unique pie chart, radar graph, or org chart. If you use either of these tools just for design, you can drag out a shape while holding down the Shift key to create a proportionate shape or click the artboard first or double-click the tool to access the dialog box. Make sure to press your D key if you need to reset your stroke and fill. Refer to Figure 6-24.

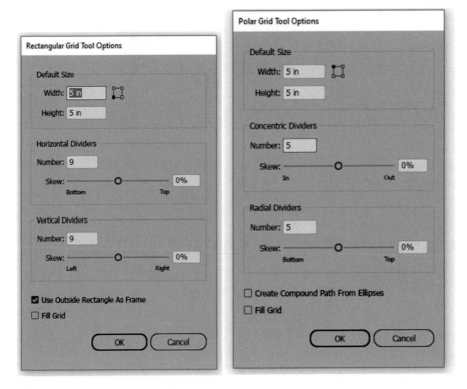

Figure 6-24. *Rectangular Grid Tool Options and Polar Grid Tool Options panel*

The rectangular grid by default is a series of grouped lines. Refer to Figure 6-25.

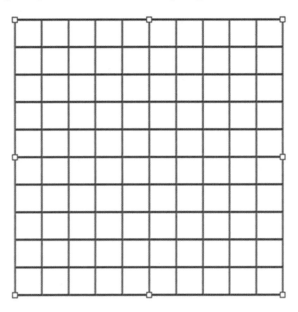

Figure 6-25. *A rectangular grid on the artboard*

Using the dialog box, you can set the default width, height, and the reference point from which it is dragged out. You can also set the number of horizontal and vertical dividers (0–999) as well as the skew percentage (-500, 0, 500%). For horizontal, set the range from bottom to top or vertical, left to right using the sliders. You can also enable the setting Use Outside Rectangle As Frame and the option to fill the grid though you can leave this setting disabled. Refer to Figure 6-26.

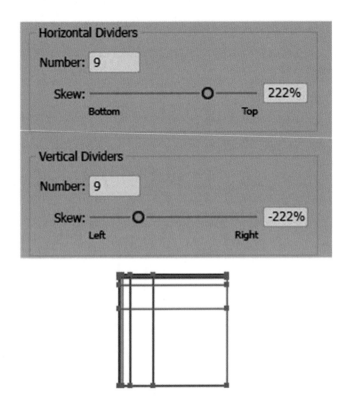

Figure 6-26. *Rectangular Grid Tool Options dialog box settings and the grid skewed on the artboard*

In the case of the waffle graph/chart, you would need to set your shape as a square, for example, 5 inches for both width and height, if you consider each block to be 1%. To create a 10 by 10 to create 100%, you would need to set the number dividers to 9 each and skew to 0% and the "Use Outside Rectangle As Frame" enabled and leave "Fill Grid" disabled. Upon clicking OK, this would create the grid or the chart you require. However, I would not fill in the squares themselves using the "Fill Grid" option as that would fill all the squares or create 100%. Later in Chapter 8, you will look at the Live Paint tool which will help you complete the waffle chart. Refer to Figure 6-24.

For the Polar Grid Tool dialog box, you can also enter similar settings, but this time for arc lines. Refer to Figure 6-24 and Figure 6-27.

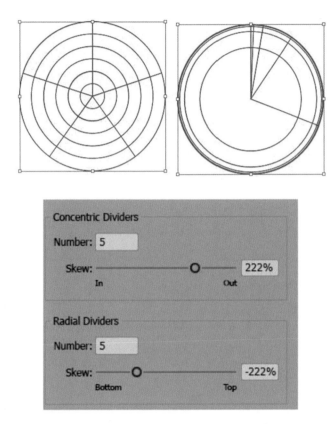

Figure 6-27. *Polar Grid normal and skewed with Polar Grid Tool Option dialog box settings*

This includes the width, height, and the reference point from which it is dragged out. You can also set the number of concentric and radial dividers (0–999), as well as the skew percent (-500, 0, 500%). For concentric dividers, set the range from in to out or radial dividers, bottom to top using the sliders. You can also enable the settings Create Compound path from ellipses and the option to fill the grid though you can leave these settings disabled for now. As you will see later in Chapter 8, a Polar Grid can also be used with the Live Paint tool.

Moving and Selecting Your Shapes on the Artboard

After creating your basic shapes, at this point, it is helpful to be able to move them around on the artboard board on the current layer.

Selection Tool (V)

As mentioned in Chapter 4, you can use the Selection tool (V) from the Toolbars panel to select a shape or object on the artboard and then drag it around and move it to a new location on or off the artboard. You can also use the bounding box handles around the shape to scalc or rotate a shape and make it disproportionate, such as the examples of the polygon and star. Refer to Figure 6-28.

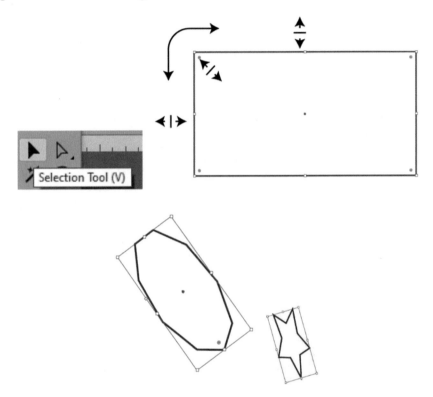

Figure 6-28. *Use the Selection tool to move, scale proportionally and disproportionately, and rotate various paths and shapes on the artboard*

The Selection tool can also be used to duplicate a shape when you select the shape and hold down the Alt/Option key and drag the new shape away. Refer to Figure 6-29.

Figure 6-29. *Use the Selection tool to duplicate shapes and paths*

While a shape is selected, you can press the Backspace/Delete button to remove it from the board. Use the menu Edit ➤ Undo (Ctrl/CMD+Z) or your History panel, as mentioned in Chapter 4, if you want to undo these steps. Refer to Figure 6-30.

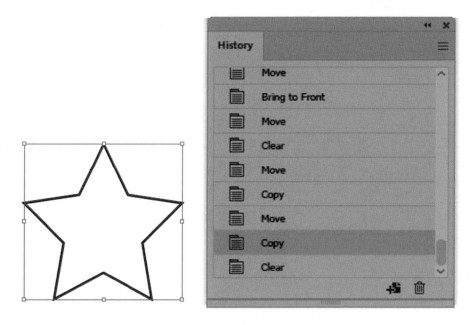

Figure 6-30. *Use the History panel if you delete selected a path or shape by accident*

Tip: Shift+Click multiple shapes if you want to select and move them at the same time. Refer to Figure 6-31.

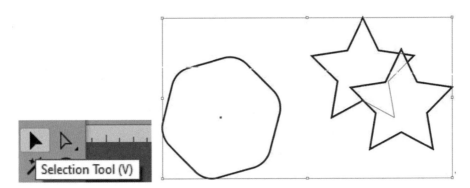

Figure 6-31. *Use the Selection too to select multiple shapes*

Direct Selection Tool (A)

The Direct Selection tool as mentioned before is used for the selection of individual points on any path, and you can then drag a point to move it. Or with a star, use it to round a corner point or Shift+Click more points if you want to round them with the live corner widgets. Refer to Figure 6-32.

Figure 6-32. *Use the Direct Selection tool to select point or multiple points and round corners*

Group Selection Tool

The other tool found with the Direct Selection tool is the Group Selection tool. It's used on group paths to select individual paths, and multiple clicking will select more paths until all the paths are selected with a grouped object. Refer to Figure 6-33.

Figure 6-33. *Use the Group Selection tool to select one or more paths in a group*

To create a grouped object, you need to Shift+Click on each path first or use your Selection tool to drag a marquee around several paths and then, from the main menu, choose Object ➤ Group (Ctrl/CMD+G). This will make the paths all one unit so that with the Selection tool, you can move them together. To ungroup paths, choose Object ➤ Ungroup (Shift +Ctrl/CMD+G). Refer to Figure 6-34.

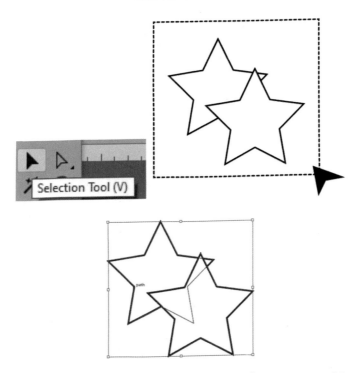

Figure 6-34. *Use the Selection tool to select shapes that you want to group*

Basic Modification to Shapes

If you want to do some custom adjustments/modifications to a selected shape or path, you can use the Object ➤ Transform menu or one of the corresponding tools in the Toolbars panel to do such precise things like rotation, reflection, scaling, and shearing. You can access these options by double-clicking the tool to access the dialog box for precise settings as well, and create a copy if you do not want to edit the original. Use the preview check in each dialog box, turning it off and on, to check the settings against the original.

- Selection Tool, Direct Selection, Group Selection Tools: For the dialog box, use Object ➤ Transform ➤ Move. Adjust position (horizontal and vertical) positive or negative, distance, and angle (0–360) degrees. In the Options by default, the object is transformed, and if patterns were present, they could be transformed as well. The object or copy is moved around the reference point. Click Copy rather than OK when you need to create a moved copy leaving the original in place. Refer to Figure 6-35.

241

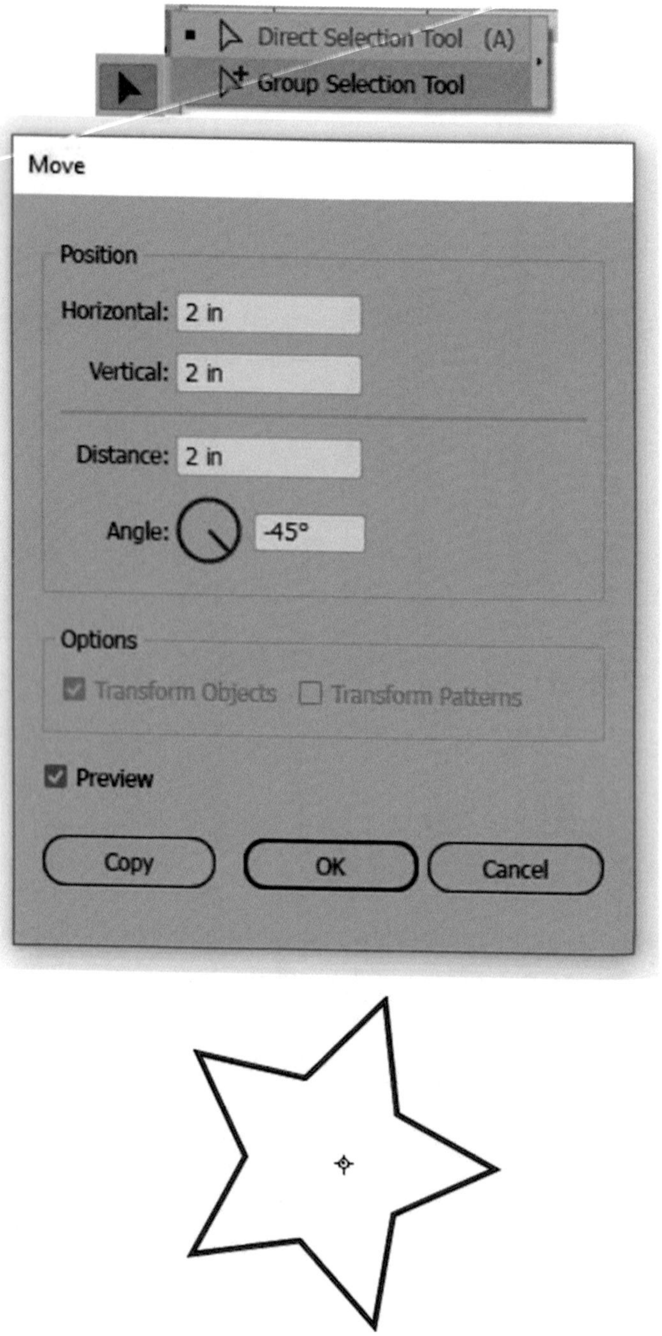

Figure 6-35. *The Selection, Direct Selection, and Group Selection tools all have access to the Move dialog box when you double-click them in the Toolbars panel*

- Rotate Tool (R): For the dialog box, use Object ➤ Transform ➤
  Rotate. You can set a rotation angle (0–360) degrees; you can enter
  positive and negative numbers. In the Options, by default, the
  object is transformed, and if patterns were present, they could
  be transformed as well. The object or copy is rotated around the
  reference point which can be adjusted outside the dialog box if you
  want to do a manual rotation. Click Copy rather than OK when you
  need to create a rotated copy leaving the original in place. Refer to
  Figure 6-36.

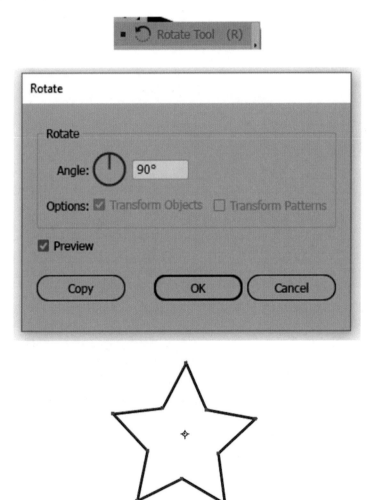

Figure 6-36. *Use the Rotate tool or Rotate dialog box to rotate a shape or copy*

- Reflect Tool (O): For the dialog box, use Object ➤ Transform ➤ Reflect. You can do a reflection on the object's horizontal or vertical axis, at an angle (0–360) degrees. In the Options, by default, the object is transformed, and if patterns were present, they could be transformed as well. The object or copy is reflected around the reference point which can be adjusted outside the dialog box if you want to do a manual reflection. Click Copy rather than OK when you need to create a reflected copy leaving the original in place. Some shapes, if they are symmetrical on one axis, may show little or no reflection. Refer to Figure 6-37.

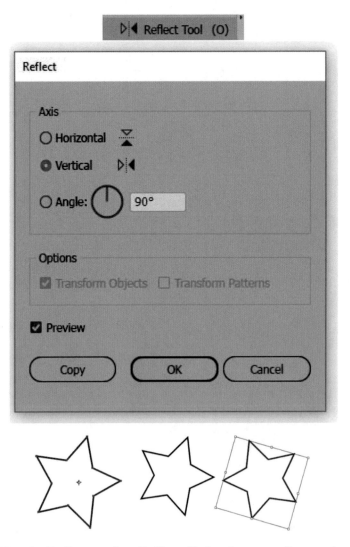

Figure 6-37. *Use the Reflect tool or Reflect dialog box to reflect a shape or copy*

- Scale Tool (S): For the dialog box, use Object ➤ Transform ➤ Scale. Scaling can be uniform or non-uniform on the horizontal or vertical, up to positive or negative of 20000%. In the Options, by default, the object is transformed, and if patterns were present, they could be transformed as well. However, you can also choose to scale corners and scale strokes and effects if present. The object or copy is scaled around the reference point which can be adjusted outside the dialog box if you want to do a manual scale. Click Copy rather than OK when you need to create a scaled copy leaving the original in place. Refer to Figure 6-38.

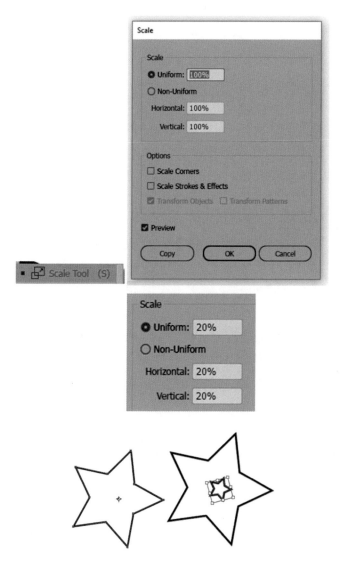

Figure 6-38. *Use the Scale tool or Scale dialog box to scale a shape or copy*

- Shear Tool: For the dialog box, use Object ➤ Transform ➤ Shear. You can set a Shear Angle (0–360) degrees. Set the axis as horizontal, vertical, or an angle (0–360) degrees. In the Options, by default, the object is transformed, and if patterns were present, they could be transformed as well. This will cause a distortion in the object or path. The object or copy is sheared around the reference point which can be adjusted outside the dialog box if you want to do a manual shear. Click Copy rather than OK when you need to create a sheared copy leaving the original in place. Refer to Figure 6-39.

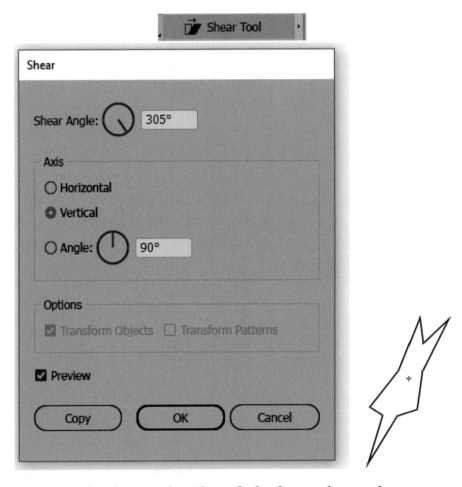

Figure 6-39. *Use the Shear tool or Shear dialog box to shear a shape or copy*

Tip   Outside the dialog box, create a copy for any of these tools (Rotate, Reflect, Scale, Shear). While using the tool, set the reference point to a new location, then hold down the Alt/Option key and drag out a new copy based on the setting of the reference point. Refer to Figure 6-40.

Figure 6-40.   *Outside the dialog box, you can manually use the reference point and the Alt/Option key with a Rotate, Reflect, Scale, or Shear tool to create a copy of a path*

After using the dialog box, you can repeat any of these steps with Object ➤ Transform again. Use the Reset Bounding Box setting when you want to reset the bounding box after a transformation. Refer to Figure 6-41.

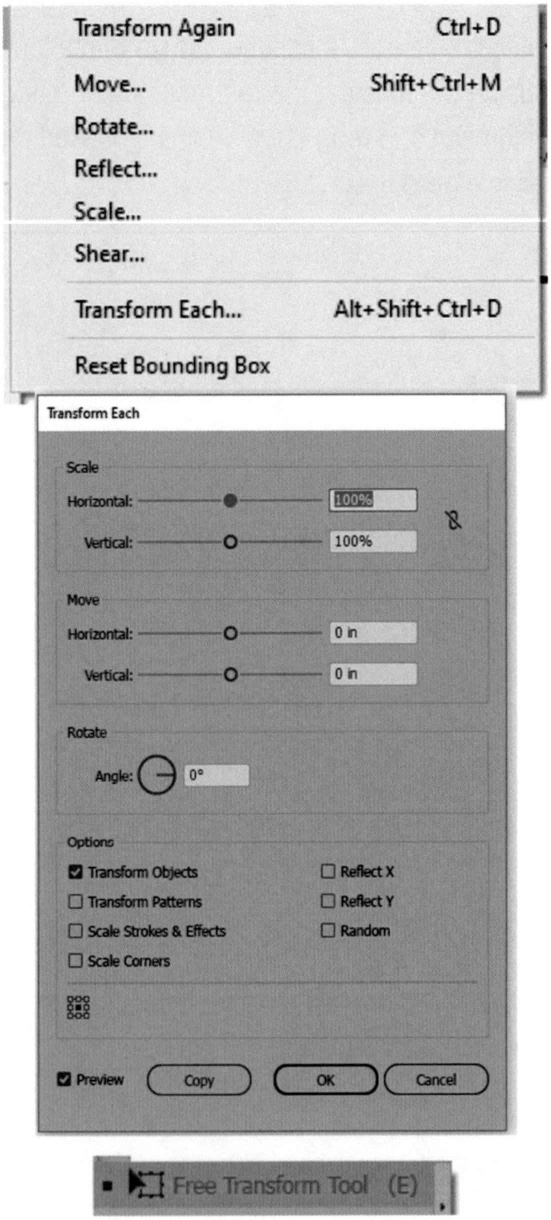

Figure 6-41. *Object ➤ Transform Options, Transform Each dialog box and the Free Transform tool*

Tip   While not a topic of this book, Object ➤ Transform Each has its own dialog box and will allow you to do multiple transformations such as Scale, Move, Rotate, and Reflect all at once. This can affect both objects and their patterns. You can also use the Free Transform Tool (E) if you want to do these transformations of Free transform (rotate, reflect, scale, skew), perspective, and free distort manually. Refer to Figure 6-41.

Here are some pages for more details on the topics of using tools and related dialog boxes for distortion:

https://helpx.adobe.com/illustrator/using/rotating-reflecting-objects.html

https://helpx.adobe.com/illustrator/using/scaling-shearing-distorting-objects.html

Arranging Shape and Path Order

After you have edited your basic shapes, you can then make further modifications, as mentioned, if any of the shapes are in the wrong order above or below an overlapping shape. You can use the Object ➤ Arrange options of

- Bring to Front: Brings the selected shape to the front of the layer.

- Bring Forward: Moves the selected shape one sublayer forward.

- Send Backward: Sends the selected shape one sublayer backward.

- Send to Back: Sends the selected shape to the very back of the layer. Refer to Figure 6-42.

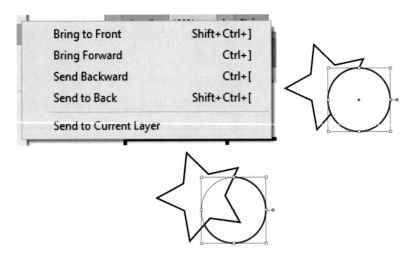

Figure 6-42. *Object ➤ Arrange submenu with selected object set using Bring to Front and then Send to Back*

Using the key commands such as Ctrl/CMD +] or Ctrl/CMD+[multiple times, when a shape is selected, can assist you in moving the selected shape to the exact location in the sublayer order.

Note   This will only work on the current layer and its sublayers. I will explain how to move the shape to another layer in Chapter 8. See the section "Working with Layers." However, the Object ➤ Arrange ➤ Send to Current Layer option will work if you need to move a shape to another layer selected in your Layers panel.

To create an exact copy of a shape on or below another, you can also use Edit ➤ Copy and then Edit ➤ Paste in Front (Ctrl/CMD+F) or Paste in Back (Ctrl/CMD+B).

Working with the Control, Transform, and Properties Panel

Once one of your basic shapes is selected with the Selection tool, you can make many modifications to basic shapes using the following panels: Transform, Control, and Properties. Refer to Figure 6-43.

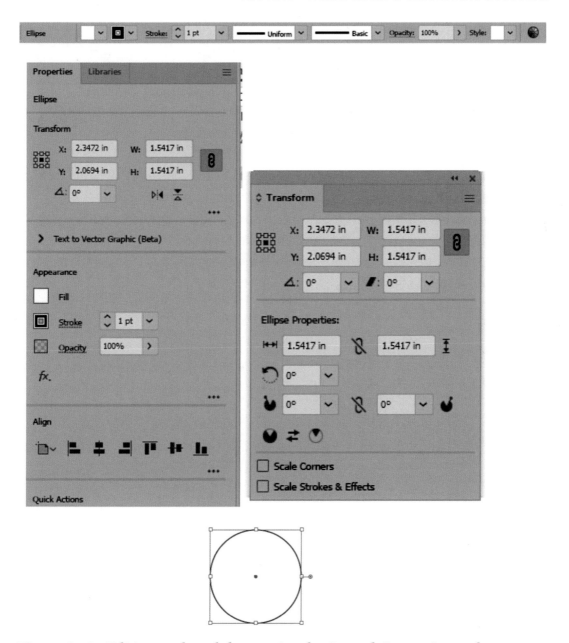

Figure 6-43. *Editing a selected shape using the Control, Properties, and Transform panels*

These panels, as you will see in a moment, are often interconnected to each other and will change based on the type of basic shape or path that is chosen, as we will see later when you work with the pen tool in Chapter 7.

For the moment, click some of the basic shapes you have drawn, and observe how these panels change. In some cases, you may prefer working with only the Control or only the Properties panel. In these examples, I prefer to use the Control panel for basic adjustments to the selected shape to alter the fill or stroke color.

However, as you may notice, the Properties panel or Transform panel may display more detailed options. Likewise, you can access some of these hidden options for specific panels via the Control or Properties panel rather than having many panels open at once. In the Properties panel, click the ellipsis (…) in each subsection (Transform, Appearance, Align) for access to more options as well you can click the underlined names. Refer to Figure 6-44.

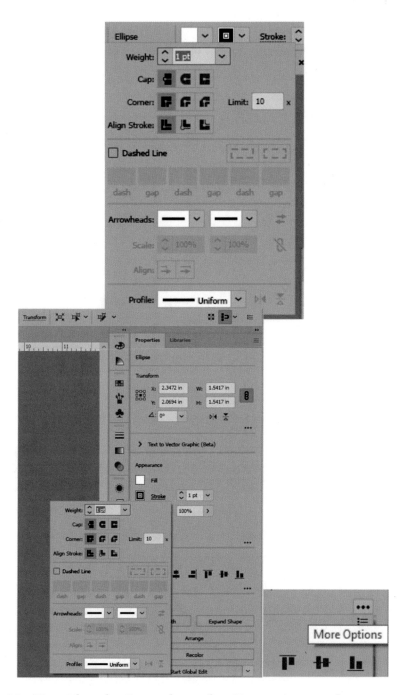

Figure 6-44. *Use either the Control panel or Properties panel to access additional panels*

For now, let's focus on the Control panel.

For example, a shape created with the Rectangle tool is selected with the Selection tool. Refer to Figure 6-45.

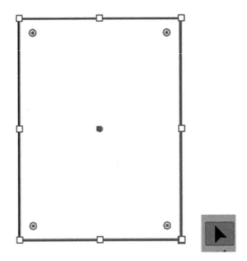

Figure 6-45. *Selecting a path with the Selection tool*

You will see the following layout for the Control panel. For the panel, some of these options we will discuss in more detail later in the chapter, but let's start looking from left to right. Refer to Figure 6-46.

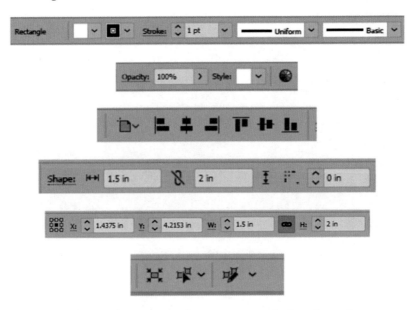

Figure 6-46. *Control panel options when a rectangle is selected*

In relation to the following selected shapes, rectangle, rounded rectangle, square, ellipse, polygon, and star, this area of the Control panel will remain mostly the same. Refer to Figure 6-47.

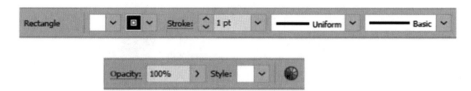

Figure 6-47. *Control panel options for altering the rectangles or path's appearance*

The first item is the identifier of the shape; a rectangle or rounded rectangle, if created by one of those tools, is always identified as a rectangle. An ellipse is identified with the word ellipse and polygon by the word polygon. However, star, being a more modified shape, is identified by the word path. We will look at custom shapes in more detail later in Chapter 7. If you have a grouped path, then the word group will appear.

Note: If you alter/move any of the points with the Direct Selection tool on one of the named shapes, it will automatically convert to an expanded shape or path, which you will discover when you select the path again when you select the Section tool. Use Edi ➤ Undo (Ctrl/CMD+Z) of the History panel if you want to undo that change. Refer to Figure 6-48.

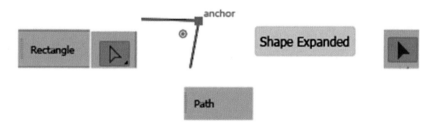

Figure 6-48. *Shapes become regular paths if they are altered using the Direct Selection tool*

The next section, when the shape is selected with the Selection tool, allows you to alter the fill color and stroke color of the shape. These swatches correspond with items found in the Swatches panel. They can be solid colors, gradients, or patterns. In this case, if you want to change the color of either the fill or stroke, you can use the drop-down panel and choose a new swatch. Do this color change one at a time. Refer to Figure 6-49.

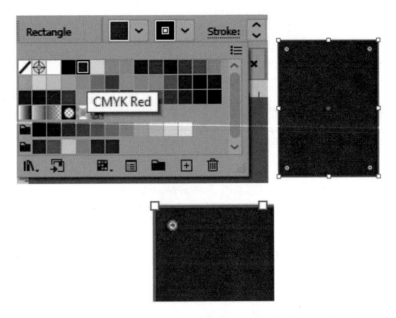

Figure 6-49. *Swatches panel options for fill and stroke from the Control panel*

The next section allows you to adjust the weight of the stroke. Use the up and down arrows on the text box or type the number in yourself, or select a preset from the drop-down panel. However, if you want to access the Stroke panel for more precise options, click the underlined word "Stroke," and you will be able to access all of the features in the Stroke panel. From here, you can set the stroke weight. You can also set the following using the icon buttons and text box: cap (butt, round, projecting), corner (miter join, round join, bevel join), and miter limit (1–500) which will make the corner more angled and pointy or flat and smooth, as well as align strokes based on options of center, inside, or outside. By default, it is kept to center. Refer to Figure 6-50.

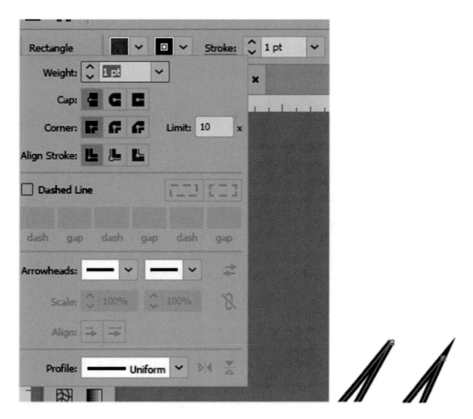

Figure 6-50. *Stroke panel options from the Control panel and an adjusted miter limit*

Next, you can make the line dashed and add a dash and gap in point size, and using the two icon buttons, you can "preserve exact dash and gap lengths" or "align dashes to corners and path ends, adjusting the lengths to fit." Depending on the settings, this will cause the dashed stroke to adjust to corners and gaps differently. Refer to Figure 6-51.

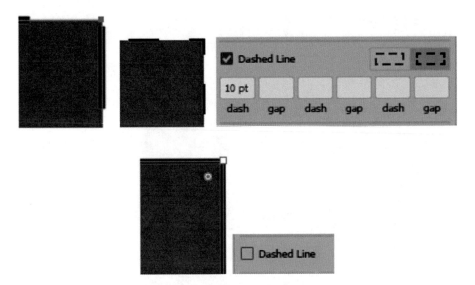

Figure 6-51. *Stroked panel options for setting a solid or dashed line*

You can uncheck this option if you want the line to be solid again.

The next area in this stroke section allows you to add arrowheads to both the start and end of the stroke with 39 options (the default is none or a solid line). You can reverse the order of the arrowheads and scale the arrowheads up to 1000% for both start and end. Refer to Figure 6-52.

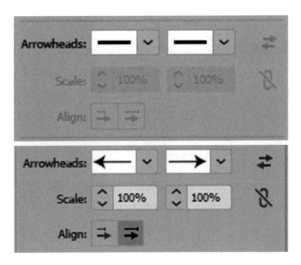

Figure 6-52. *Stroke Arrowhead options of none or a selected arrow from the drop-down list*

Use the link icon if you want both start and end arrowheads to scale at the same time with a similar ratio or percentage. Align the arrowhead to extend the arrow tip beyond end of path or place the arrow tip at end of path. The arrowheads work best for open paths but can be used on closed paths as well along with dashed lines. Set the arrowheads back to none in the drop-down list if you do not want them. Refer to Figure 6-53.

Figure 6-53. *Arrowheads on a closed and open path with a dashed line*

The last area in the Stroke panel and drop-down is Profile which can also be found in the main Control panel area. This allows you to set one of the variable width profiles for your line. Uniform is the default, but there are six other options. You can create your own custom options using the Width tool and its Width Point Options dialog box when you double-click a point or click to create a new point. Upon exiting the dialog box, you can then add the profile. While in the Stroke panel or drop-down list from the Control panel, you can flip certain profiles, along, across, or both ways depending on the profile chosen. Refer to Figure 6-54.

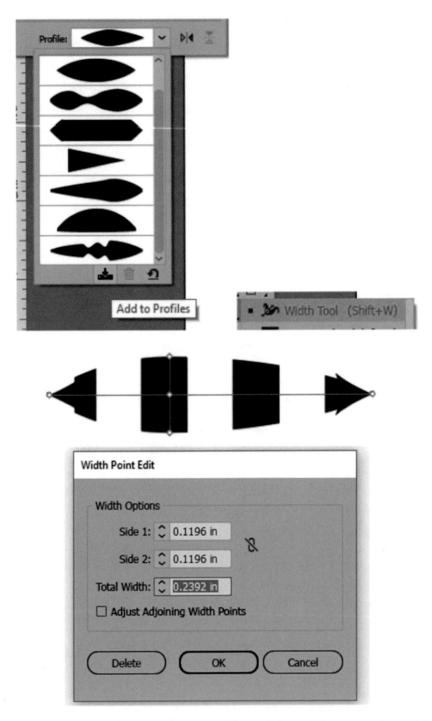

Figure 6-54. *Control panel setting a variable width profile, using the Width tool and Width Point Edit dialog box to adjust settings*

More details can be found on the Width tool at this page:

`https://helpx.adobe.com/illustrator/using/tool-techniques/width-tool.html`

Besides the variable width profile, in the Control panel is the brush definition. This connects to the same area as the Brushes panel. By default, it is set to the setting of Uniform and Basic for brush definition, but you can use other settings from the list as well as access more options from the Brush libraries. Refer to Figure 6-55.

Figure 6-55. *Use the Control panel to set various brush definitions from the Brushes panel*

Next in the Control panel is opacity which can be set from 0% to 100%. For more options, click the word "Opacity," and this will bring up the same options found in the Transparency panel. This area allows you to control the blending mode opacity and opacity mask setting and make the mask, link, clip, and invert based on the options chosen. The lower section has more advanced options for Isolate Blending, Knockout Group, and Opacity & Mask Define Knockout Shape. Refer to Figure 6-56.

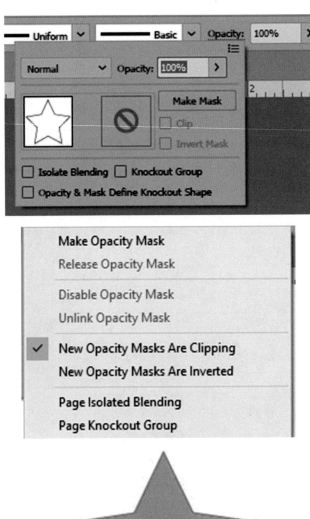

Figure 6-56. *Use the Control panel to access Opacity/ Transparency settings*

More advanced options can be found in the menu in the upper right corner of the panel or drop-down list.

The next area allows you to set the style from the drop-down, you can select the option from the list, and this is the same as the Graphic Styles panel. Refer to Figure 6-57.

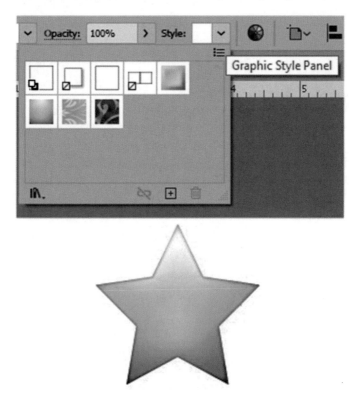

Figure 6-57. *Use the Control panel to access graphic styles*

At the moment, you can use any one of the preset graphic styles found in the list; look for more using the lower left library icon.

However, to create your own graphic styles, you first need to create an appearance, which we will look at briefly along with styles and symbols later in Chapter 8. See the section "Creating Graphic Styles" in Chapter 8.

The next section, which I will mention in more detail later, is the Recolor Artwork and its new feature Generative Recolor. Refer to Figure 6-58.

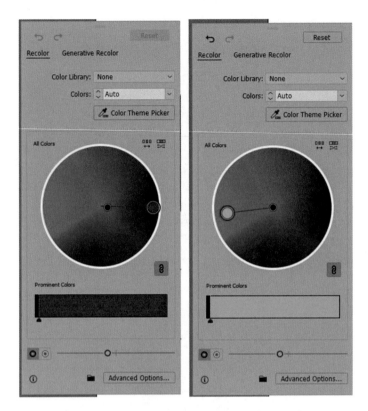

Figure 6-58. *Recolor panel settings from the Control panel*

This pop-out panel allows you to recolor your shape quickly even if it only has two colors and is connected to the Color Guide panel, whose similar dialog box can be accessed via the Advanced Options button. Refer to the section "Color Guide Panel" in Chapter 8. Refer to Figure 6-59.

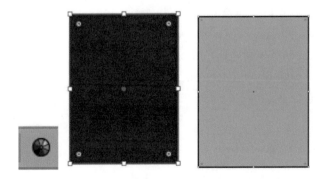

Figure 6-59. *Before and after Recolor of a selected rectangle*

The next section in the Control panel allows you to align multiple shapes when Shift+Click on them and then click an icon to align them. This has many of the similar settings as the Align panel mentioned in Chapter 4. You can also use Object ➤ Align and Object ➤ Distribute options from the main menu. Refer to Figure 6-60.

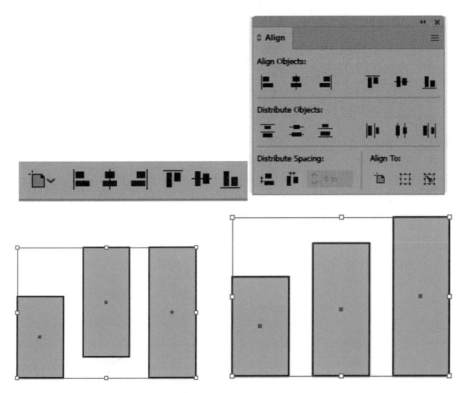

Figure 6-60. *Control panel and Align Panel Options for aligning paths, shapes, and objects*

When only one item is selected, it can be aligned to the artboard or to a selection. Refer to Figure 6-61.

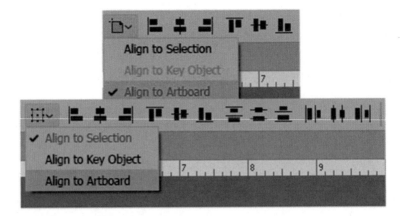

Figure 6-61. *Control panel align and Distribute Options*

However, when two or more items are selected, more options are available as seen in the Align panel such as Align to Selection and Align to Key Object. You can then see all the alignment options such as for Horizontal Alignment (Left, Center, Right), Vertical Alignment (Top, Center, Bottom), Vertical Distribute (Top, Center, Bottom), and Horizontal Distribute (Left, Center, Right). Refer to Figure 6-62.

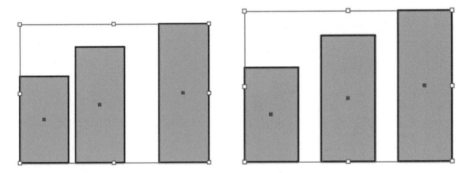

Figure 6-62. *Use the Control panel to distribute selected objects such as horizontal distribute center*

Use the Align panel to do additional distribution of spacing vertically and horizontally by a set value. Refer to Figure 6-60.

When a single shape is selected, the Shape or Transform panel choices will vary. You can see this when you click the shape name and additional items, and you will also see this in the Transform panel, also appearing at the same time. Similar options are available for the Rectangle and Rounded Rectangle. Refer to Figure 6-63.

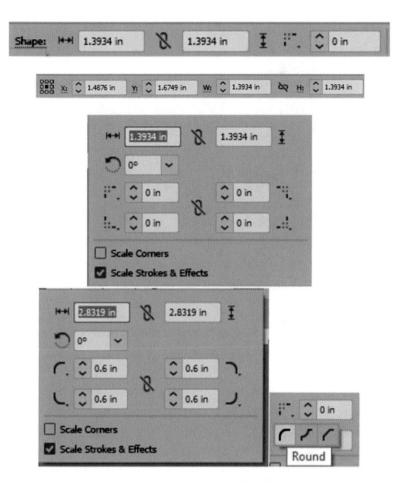

Figure 6-63. *Use the Control panel to edit using Shape options found in the Transform panel as well*

Width and height can be constrained proportionately and disproportionately by setting the link.

Here you can set rectangle angle (0–360) degrees. Then set individual corner strokes if they are not linked to the options of round, inverted round, or chamfer as well as a different corner radius for each of the four sides. Here you also have the option to scale corners as well as scale strokes and effects which is useful when you need to shrink or enlarge a shape. In some situations, however, you may just want the stroke to remain consistent when you scale so you can in those situations uncheck that option. Refer to Figure 6-64.

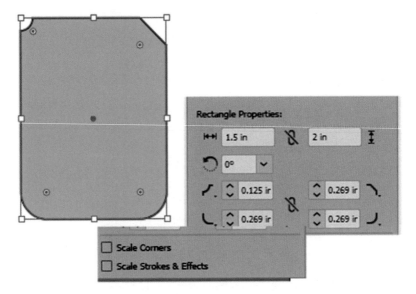

Figure 6-64. *Alter the corner and radius for each side and uncheck from the Control panel Shape options Scale Corners and Scale Strokes and Effects when you do not want these options for your paths*

These same settings will appear in the Transform panel in the related text box area.

The Control panel and Transform panel will also allow you to set your x and y coordinates and shear your shape. Some advanced options are found in the Transform menu for vertical and horizontal flipping. Refer to Figure 6-65.

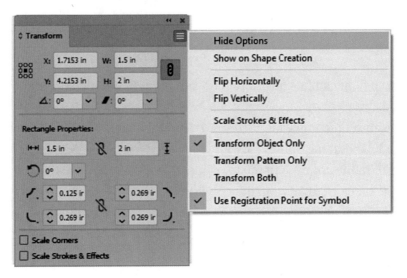

Figure 6-65. *Transform panel has advanced options for scaling and transformation*

Notice, however, if you switch and select an ellipse, polygon, or star path, the Shape area and Transform panel area vary this section. Refer to Figure 6-66.

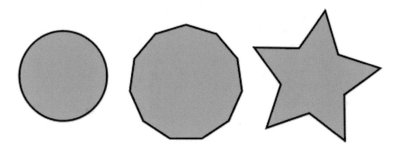

Figure 6-66. *Ellipses, polygons, and star (path) have slightly different shape settings in the Control panel*

Ellipses will allow us to change the width and height, constrain proportionately and disproportionately, rotate, change the pie angle start and end, constrain pie angles, and invert the pie. Refer to Figure 6-67.

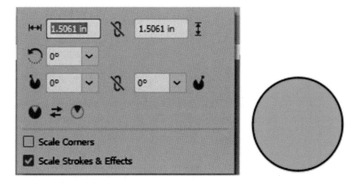

Figure 6-67. *Use the Control panel to set Shape options for the ellipse*

For the polygon, you can set the number of sides to 3–20 unless you enter a custom number. You can also set polygon angle (0–360) degrees, corner type (round, inverted round, or chamfer), and corner radius for all sides. Then you can set the polygon radius and polygon side length. Refer to Figure 6-68.

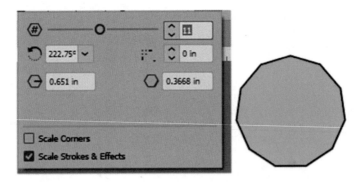

Figure 6-68. *Use the Control panel to set Shape options for the polygon*

The star, as noted earlier, comes in as a path. There is no Shape word link, but you can access this area from the x and y coordinates, w (width) and h (height) underlined letter links in the Control panel. Here you can see that you can still rotate or shear the star. However, when checked with the Transform panel, it will reveal that there are no shape properties. Refer to Figure 6-69.

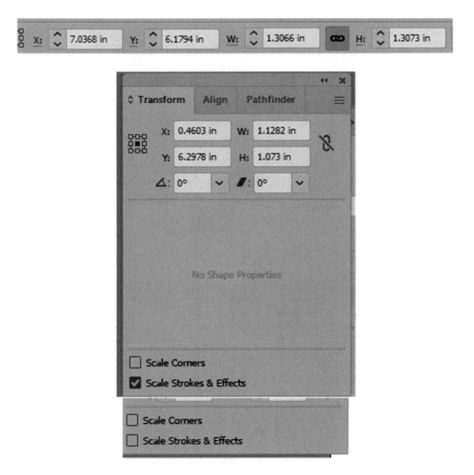

Figure 6-69. *The Control panel has no Shape options for a star (path), and you must use one of the letters (X, Y, W, or H) to access more options or the Transform panel*

Note   The option to "scale corners" and "scale strokes and effects" remains consistent for all the mentioned shapes and paths, and you can check or uncheck this setting as required. Refer to Figure 6-69.

Remember: In the case of a star or polygon shape, when you want to round a select corner or several corners, you need to use the Direct Selection tool and select those points. I will talk about these options in the Control panel in more detail in a moment, but I just want to point out here the one section called corners. Refer to Figure 6-70.

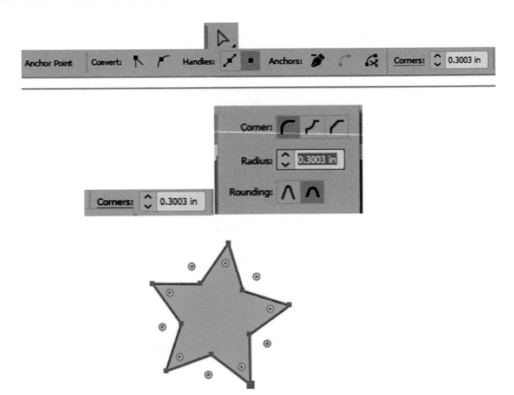

Figure 6-70. *Use the Direct Selection tool and the Control panel to edit the sides of the star path*

This will allow you to set the same individual corner option you looked at earlier, as well as the radius for rounding and the type of rounding which can be relative or absolute.

Coming back to the Selection tool, when the object is selected, in the Control panel, you can set the reference point of the shape from the center or one of the eight outer points for scaling, use the x and y coordinates value as well as the width (W) and height (H), and constrain the proportions using the link if you do not want to use the Transform panel. These settings are common for all closed paths and shapes. Refer to Figure 6-71.

Figure 6-71. *While a shape is selected with the Section tool, you have access to (X, Y, width, and height settings)*

The last section of the Control panel allows you to isolate the selected object, select similar objects, and edit similar shapes together for the purpose of global editing when working on multiple artboards. Refer to Figure 6-72.

Figure 6-72. *Additional shape editing options in the Control panel*

The Control panel also allows you to align selected art to the pixel grid, on creation and transformation, as well as additional menu settings as to what options should appear in the Control panel; in this case, all options are enabled with a check. Refer to Figure 6-73.

Figure 6-73. *Control panel settings and menu options*

Line segments, arcs, spirals, and grids can use the Control panel as well as having anchor points. They have many similar Control panel features. Line segments are identified as lines and arcs and spirals as a path, and the grids are known as grouped objects. However, the line does have some basic options in the Transform panel that appear in the Shape drop-down. Refer to Figure 6-74.

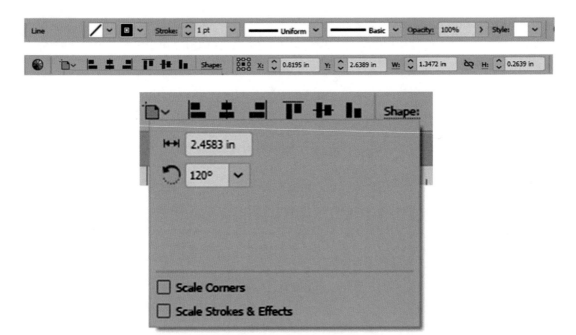

Figure 6-74. *The Line Tool Options in the Control panel and shape editing options*

You can adjust the line length and the line angle (0–360) degrees.

Lines and all paths, with their anchor points, as mentioned earlier, can be further adjusted using the Direct Selection tool. When an anchor point is selected, this brings up slightly different Control panel settings where besides corner adjustments, you can also control the selected points by converting them to corner or round (smooth). You can then show/hide handles for the multiple selected anchor points, but this does not alter the point. Next, there are anchor editing options to remove, connect, or cut selected anchor points, which we will look at more closely in Chapter 7. Refer to Figure 6-75.

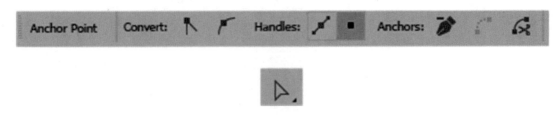

Figure 6-75. *Control panel options when a path is selected with the Direct Selection tool*

You can then align selected points and set the x and y coordinates for a specific point by entering a new number in the text box or using the up and down options in the text box. Width and height options are not available for anchor points. Refer to Figure 6-76.

Figure 6-76. *More Control panel options when a path is selected with the Direct Selection tool*

Refer to my file Shapes.ai if you need to review some examples of these paths.

In the next chapter, let's look at how custom shapes are drawn with the pen tool and other related Pen editing tools when working with anchor points.

Summary

In this chapter, we reviewed the following topics regarding basic shape drawing tools, moving, selecting, and arranging shapes on the artboard.

In the next chapter, you will be focusing on a set of tools that are for drawing custom shapes known as the pen tools.

CHAPTER 7

A Basic Review of Illustrator's Pen Tools

In this chapter, you will be looking at an overview of basic pen tools and related panels that you would use to start creating an infographic's custom shapes and paths.

As mentioned in Chapter 6, once you have created and scanned your logos in a digital format, you will want to start using Illustrator to trace over your drawing. In this chapter, the focus will be on using the pen tools as well as how to combine shapes and adjust colors for fill and stroke. Later in Chapters 8 and 9, based on the knowledge you have gained in this chapter, you will create and review a few project ideas that can be created with basic shapes, custom shapes, and text.

Note   This chapter contains reference examples that can be found in the Volume 1 Chapter 7 folder. Some of the text in this chapter on pen tools has been adapted and updated from my earlier books *Accurate Layer Selections Using Photoshop's Selection Tools* and *Perspective Warps and Distorts with Adobe Tools: Volume 2*.

In this chapter, we are now going to cover some of the tools that can be found in the Toolbars panel, as well as some of the main panels that we can use to assist us in infographic creation. I will only be focusing on the basic features of each of these pen tools, but I will also provide an Adobe help link if you would like more details on that tool. For now, if you would like to practice along, create a new document as you did in Chapter 4 so that you have an artboard to practice with the following tools and panels.

© Jennifer Harder 2023
J. Harder, *Creating Infographics with Adobe Illustrator: Volume 1*,
https://doi.org/10.1007/979-8-8688-0005-4_7

Drawing Custom Shapes with the Pen Tool

While it is helpful to be able to draw basic shapes quickly using Illustrator's shape tools, oftentimes you will be constructing custom shapes or paths that the client requires as part of the illustration of the infographic. Create a File ➤ New Document if you want to practice along.

You can do this easily with the pen tool set. Refer to Figure 7-1.

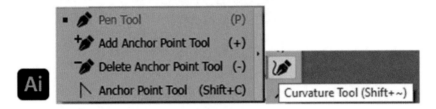

Figure 7-1. *Illustrator Toolbar's Pen Tool Options*

While not required for this book and merely as a reference note, if you are familiar with working in Photoshop for creating vector shapes and selections, you will find these similar tools as well. However, Photoshop currently has a lot more specialized pen tools that can assist you in creating selections, which can be adapted to create vector shape layers. Refer to Figure 7-2.

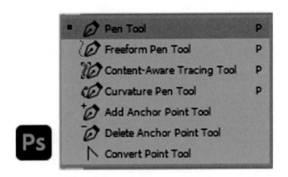

Figure 7-2. *Photoshop Toolbar's Pen Tool Options*

However, if you are not familiar with working with the pen tools in Photoshop but want to know how to work with them in Illustrator, here is a review of those steps.

Pen Tool (P) and Curvature Tool (Shift+~) Basics

The pen tool can be used for either creating a custom shape or tracing over a custom shape which we will look at as we work with layers.

Currently, if you are on Layer 1 or any layer, you can begin to create your shape using the Pen Tool (P). Refer to Figure 7-3.

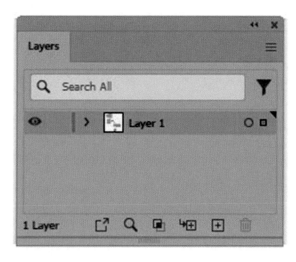

Figure 7-3. *Use the Layers panel and your artboard to begin practicing with the Pen Tool*

Here are a few things you need to know about this tool and its related subtools: Add Anchor Point Tool (+), Delete Anchor Point Tool (-), Anchor Point Tool (Shift+C), and the more specialized tool, the Curvature Tool (Shift +~).

Select from the Toolbars panel the Pen Tool. The Pen Tool relies on the current path's stroke and fill color in the Toolbars panel. Press D on your keyboard if you want the same default colors of white fill and black stroke. Refer to Figure 7-4.

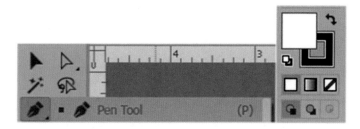

Figure 7-4. *Pen tool with Toolbars fill set to default white and stroke black*

With the Pen Tool, you can click a point. Before you click, you will see an asterisk by the pen icon. Then click another point somewhere on your artboard to continue to create a path. Each end of the path has an anchor point. Refer to Figure 7-5.

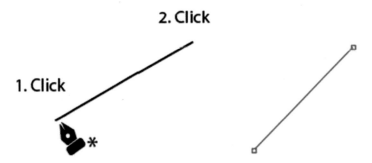

Figure 7-5. *Use the pen tool to create a path*

If you want the path to be straight, vertical, horizontal, or at 45°, then hold down the Shift key on the next click. Refer to Figure 7-6.

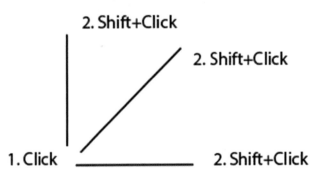

Figure 7-6. *Use the pen tool with the Shift key to create a straight path*

Click another point in your path if you want to continue with straight sides. Refer to Figure 7-7.

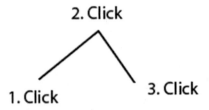

Figure 7-7. *Use the Pen Tool to continue to create more points on the path*

Or if you want a curved side, then as you create the next point, hold down the mouse key and click and drag in a direction to create a curve, revealing your anchor point handles. Refer to Figure 7-8.

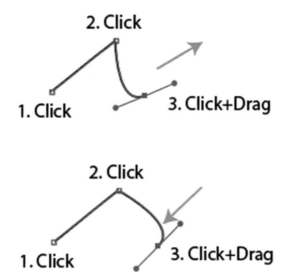

Figure 7-8. *Use the Pen Tool to create a path with a curve*

Tips   On your first click, you can drag to start a curve right away. Holding down the Ctrl/CMD key while dragging can make the handles unequal lengths. Refer to Figure 7-9.

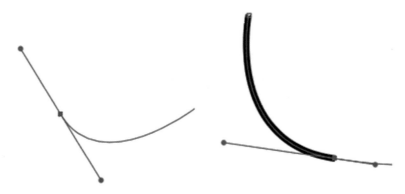

Figure 7-9. *Use the pen tool to create a path with a curve*

Release the mouse key to move your pen tool to a new location and click to create the next anchor point. Refer to Figure 7-10.

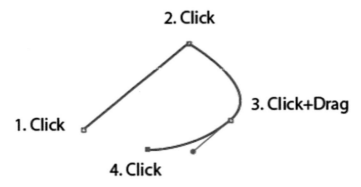

Figure 7-10. *Use the Pen Tool to add more points to the path after creating a curve*

Or click and drag to continue to round the next curve. Refer to Figure 7-11.

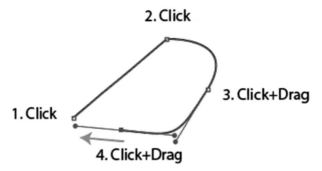

Figure 7-11. *Use the Pen Tool to add more points to the path after creating a curve and curve again*

Or if you want to return to a straight edge after the curve on point 3, release the mouse, then right away hold down the Alt/Option key, and click the same point again. Notice that the Pen Tool icon will change to have an angled path beside it. Then, when you click to create point 4, the path is now straight. Refer to Figure 7-12.

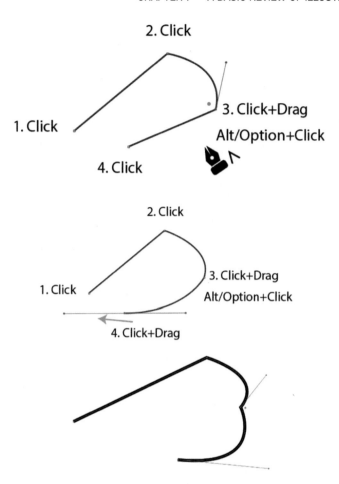

Figure 7-12. *Use the Pen Tool to change a curved line back to a straight corner with Alt/Option+Click or curve the line on the next click and drag*

Or you can click and drag for point 4 to create a curve again, but that point will be angled. This will be more obvious on more pronounced curves. Refer to Figure 7-12.

To close a path, click the original point 1. To know that it is joined correctly, as you hover over the point, you should see the Pen Tool icon add a zero or O icon next to it. Then click to close the path. Refer to Figure 7-13.

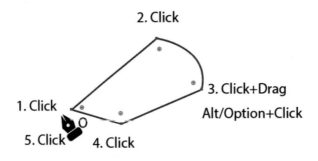

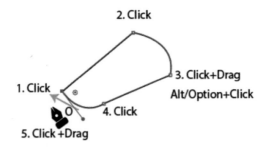

Figure 7-13. *Close the path as either a straight or curved path with the Pen Tool*

Or click and drag to close the path with a curve. Then release the mouse, and you should have a closed path. Refer to Figure 7-13.

Tip   Adding the Shift key while you click and drag can also assist in your path adjustment.

If, while using the Pen Tool, you want to keep the path open and deselect the path to create a new one, then on the last point, you click hold down the Ctrl/CMD key. This changes the pen temporarily to the Direct Selection tool, and click elsewhere on the artboard, and this will allow you to deselect the path and keep it open. Refer to Figure 7-14.

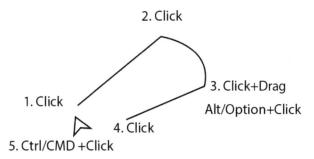

Figure 7-14. *Leave the path open using the Pen Tool when you Ctrl/CMD+Click*

Join Points on an Open Path

With the Pen Tool, you can click an open anchor point, and the pen icon adds a line to it, and then click on that point, and then on the point, you want to connect to and close the path when you see the O near the pen. Refer to Figure 7-15.

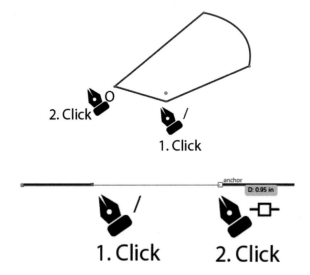

Figure 7-15. *Join two points in for a closed path or connect two open paths with the Pen Tool*

Or if you are joining two open paths but not closing a path, you will see a pen cursor icon connection point between the two points. Refer to Figure 7-15.

Tip   Use your zoom key commands (Ctrl/CMD ++ and Ctrl/CMD+ -) and Hand tool (spacebar) when you need to navigate while using the Pen Tool so you don't deselect the path while you work.

Add Anchor Point Tool (+) Review

Likewise, as in Photoshop, with Illustrator, points can be added to a path with the Add Anchor Point Tool. This is useful when you need to edit or correct part of the path. Refer to Figure 7-16.

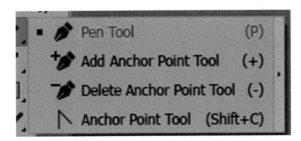

Figure 7-16.   *Toolbars panel Add Anchor Point Tool*

Once your path is complete, to edit further, use this tool to click somewhere on the path to add a new anchor point. Refer to Figure 7-17.

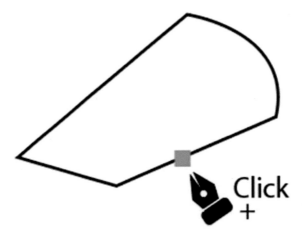

Figure 7-17.   *Add a point with the Add Anchor Point Tool*

Note   If you do not want to switch tools, you can also use the Pen Tool and hover over part of a selected path with the pen cursor, and a plus symbol is added, then just click to add a point. We looked at how to select paths and shapes earlier, see the section "Moving and Selecting your Shapes on the Artboard" in Chapter 6.

If you click a point and not a path, you may get the following warning message. In this case, click OK and use your Zoom tool if you need to get closer to the path before using the Add Anchor Point Tool. Refer to Figure 7-18.

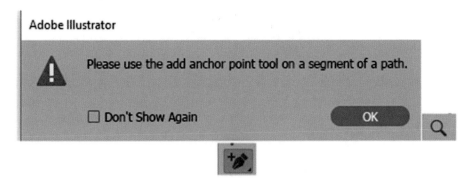

Figure 7-18. *When you click another point with the Add Anchor Point Tool, you will get a warning message to add the point to a segment of a path*

Delete Anchor Point Tool (-) Review

To remove points from a path, use the Delete Anchor Point Tool. Click a selected point. Note that in doing so, you may alter the path, and then you may need to move the handles later with the Direct Selection tool or add another anchor point elsewhere to make adjustments. Refer to Figure 7-19.

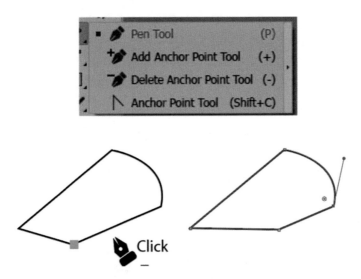

Figure 7-19. *Toolbars panel Delete Anchor Point Tool. Click a point to delete the point*

Note   If you do not want to switch tools, you can also use the Pen Tool and hover over a selected point with the pen cursor, and a minus symbol is added, then just click to remove a point. Earlier in Chapter 6, we looked at how to select paths with your Selection and Direct Selection tools.

Tip   Hold down the Alt/Option key when you want to switch between the Add Anchor Point Tool and Delete Anchor Point Tool while either tool is in use.

If you don't click directly on a point, you may get the following warning message. In this case, click OK and use your Zoom tool if you need to get closer to the point before using the Delete Anchor Point Tool. Refer to Figure 7-20.

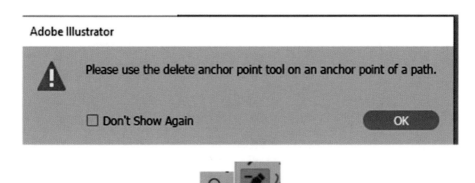

Figure 7-20. *When you click a path with the Delete Anchor Point Tool, you will get a warning message to use the tool on an anchor point of a path*

Anchor Point Tool (Shift +C) Review

The Anchor Point Tool is used to convert points from straight to curved or a combination of both. This is useful after you have created a closed path and need to edit and correct the path. Refer to Figure 7-21.

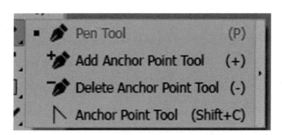

Figure 7-21. *Toolbars panel Anchor Point Tool*

Click a straight point with the Anchor Point Tool and drag to curve the path. Refer to Figure 7-22.

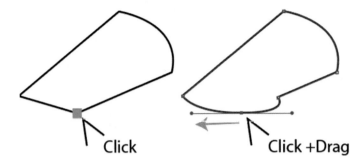

Figure 7-22. *Convert a point from corner to smooth with the Anchor Point Tool*

Or click a curved path to cause it to become straight on both sides of the point. Refer to Figure 7-23.

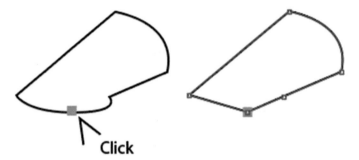

Figure 7-23. *Convert a point from smooth to corner with the Anchor Point Tool*

If the point next to it is curved, that side may remain curved.

For a combination of straight and curved sides: After you click and drag out your curve with the Anchor Point Tool, click one of the handles to straighten that part of the path. Refer to Figure 7-24.

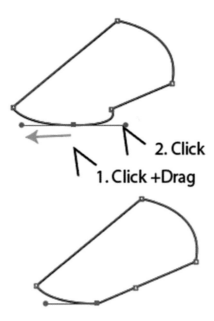

2. Click

1. Click +Drag

Figure 7-24. *Create a point that is both smooth and corner with the Anchor Point Tool*

Or click and drag on the handle to cause the path to remain curved but alter the direction of the curve. Refer to Figure 7-25.

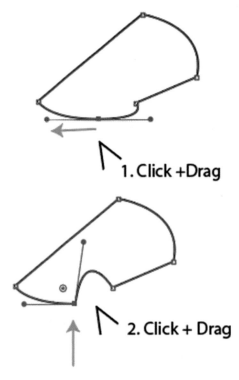

Figure 7-25. *Create a point that changes the path's direction with the Anchor Point Tool*

You can also use the tool to click and drag on the path itself if you need to scale part of the path. Refer to Figure 7-26.

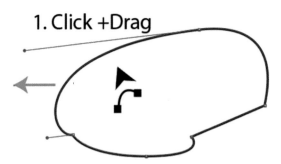

Figure 7-26. *Adjust the path with the Anchor Point Tool*

Tip   The Anchor Point Tool is good for untangling twisted points as well that you may have created while using the Pen Tool. Click and drag in the opposite direction to untangle. Refer to Figure 7-27.

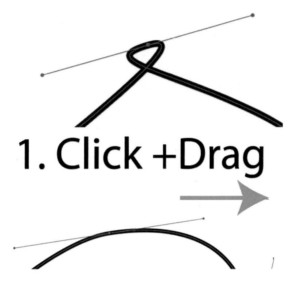

Figure 7-27. *Untangle a path with the Anchor Point Tool*

Remember you can always go back to Photoshop and apply what you learned here about the pen tools to your own Photoshop projects.

Hold down the Alt/Option key when you want to switch between the Pen tool and Anchor Point Tool.

You can review these notes in the file pen_practice_diagram.ai.

Curvature Tool (Shift +~) Review

Next to the pen tool in the Toolbars panel, you will find another similar pen tool known as the Curvature Tool. Refer to Figure 7-28.

Figure 7-28. *Toolbars panel Curvature Tool*

I investigated this tool in my book *Accurate Layer Selections Using Photoshop's Selection Tools*. However, this tool is not required for this book.

While I will not be going into any detail in this book as it is not part of the later project in Chapter 9, I will just note a few tips about the tool you can use on your own.

1. It is like the Photoshop Curvature Pen Tool. Refer to Figure 7-29.

Figure 7-29. *Photoshop's Curvature Pen Tool*

2. The Curvature Tool can be used to create a curved path as you click and drag and observe the rubber band preview of the path. Refer to Figure 7-30.

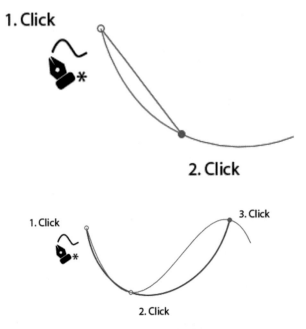

Figure 7-30. *Creating a path with the Curvature Tool and the preview of the path*

3. You can close the path when you click the original point. Refer to Figure 7-31.

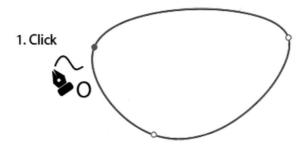

Figure 7-31. *Closing the path with the Curvature Tool*

4. Once the path is closed, you can select points on the path if you need to move them to scale the path.

5. You can also add points to the selected path by clicking a part of the path. Refer to Figure 7-32.

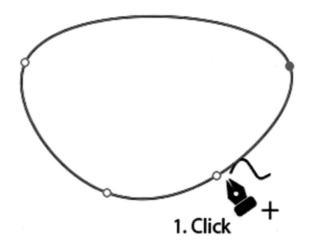

Figure 7-32. *Adding points to the path with the Curvature Tool*

6. As with the Pen Tool, you can hold down the Ctrl/CMD key to release on the next click and keep the path open.

7. You can also use the Shift key while clicking to keep the anchor points level.

8. Hold down the Alt/Option key or double-click as you click to create a straight path. Refer to Figure 7-33.

1. Click + Alt/Option

Figure 7-33. *Creating straight paths and corner points with the Curvature Tool*

9. While a point is selected, press the Backspace/Delete key to remove the point but not the path. Refer to Figure 7-34.

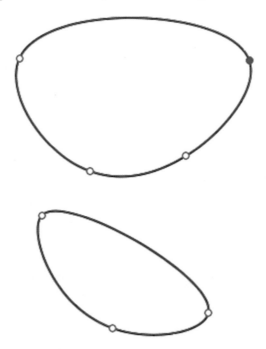

Figure 7-34. *Deleting points from the path with the Curvature Tool*

10. Double-click a point when you want to make it cornered or
     curved. Refer to Figure 7-35.

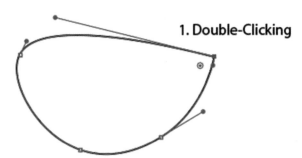

Figure 7-35. *Change the point of a path from corner to smooth and curved by double-clicking with the Curvature Tool*

Likewise, you can switch to the Pen Tool at any time to complete or edit the path. You can refer to my file curve_practice_diagram.ai.

Swapping Fill and Stroke Colors with the Pen Tool

Paths or shapes, as mentioned, will often have a stroke or fill that is applied when the selected path is being drawn with the Pen Tool. You can see the current colors in the Toolbars panel. Refer to Figure 7-36.

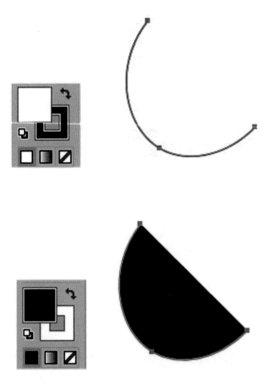

Figure 7-36. *Swapping the fill and stroke for an open path using the Toolbars panel while the path is selected*

While drawing, you can switch or swap the stroke and fill colors by pressing Shift+ X.

In other situations, while you are using the Pen Tool or before you start, you may want to set your fill to none. I find this is best when you are tracing over a placed graphic image on a locked layer or a template layer as you will see locked layers later in the project in Chapter 8 as we talk about layer order. Refer to Figure 7-36 and Figure 7-37.

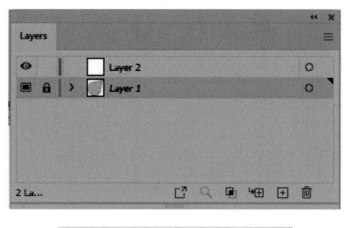

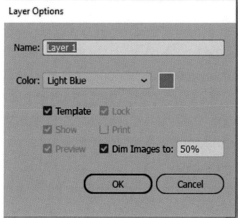

Figure 7-37. *Creating a template layer to trace over for practice*

While using the Pen Tool, you can easily click your Toolbars panel and switch the fill to none. Do so by clicking the square with the red slash through it while the fill is in front of the stroke. Refer to Figure 7-38.

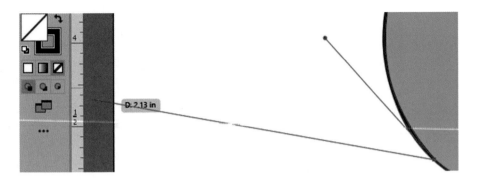

Figure 7-38. *Setting the fill to none while using the pen tool for tracing*

This will make it easier to trace over the template or underlying graphic.

Note   Besides having a path with no fill, you can also have no stroke while tracing over another path though doing so does make it difficult to locate the path afterward. Paths with no fill or stroke are used for the purpose of text on a path, clipping masks or envelope meshes to partly cover a path or shape. I will mention clipping masks briefly in the section "Combining Shapes with the Pathfinder Panel" and the section on "Clipping Masks and Compound Paths."

Control Panel Anchor Point Options and How They Relate to Related Tools

While working with the Pen Tool, be aware that after a path is complete, you can still continue to edit the points with your Direct Selection tool using the Control panel as well as some related tools found in the Toolbars panel.

When a point is selected on a path, you can, as mentioned earlier, return and convert the point from straight to curved. Refer to Figure 7-39.

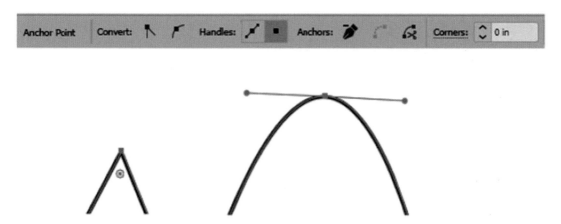

Figure 7-39. *Convert a point from straight to curved using the Control panel*

Rather than using the Delete Anchor Point Tool, instead, from the Control panel's "Anchors" section, you can choose the "Remove selected anchor points" icon but keep the path closed. This will work if several points have been Shift-clicked. Refer to Figure 7-40.

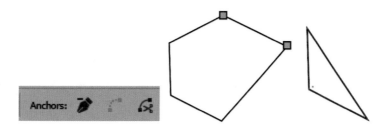

Figure 7-40. *Use the control panel to remove selected anchor points*

If two points of an open path are selected, you can use the "Connect selected end points" icon. Refer to Figure 7-41.

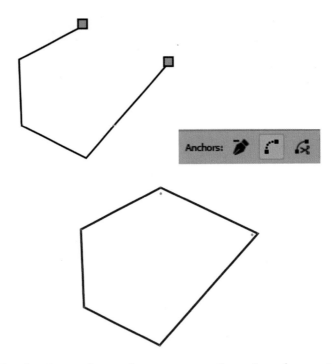

Figure 7-41. *Use the Control panel to connect selected anchor points*

Or use from the menu Object ➤ Path ➤ Join (Ctrl/CMD+J). This is also similar to using the Toolbars panel Join tool. However, the Join tool requires that you paint over the path, and the points need to be fairly close together. Refer to Figure 7-42.

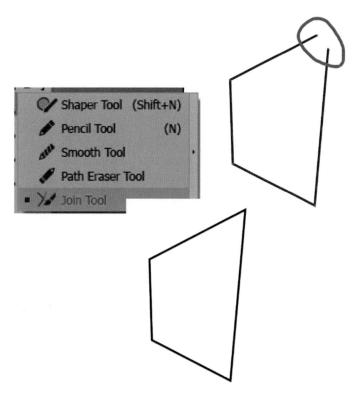

Figure 7-42. *Toolbars panel Join tool used to connect a path on the artboard*

The other icon option in the Control panel is the "Cut path at selected anchor points." When two points are Shift + Click selected with the Direct Selection tool, you can click this icon to remove that part of the path from the rest of the path. Refer to Figure 7-43.

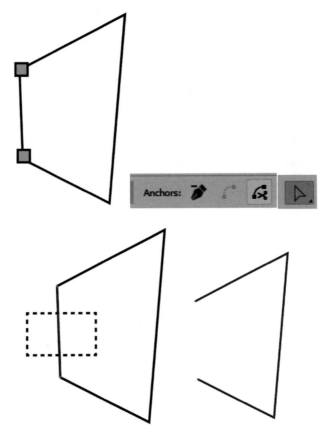

Figure 7-43. *Use the Control panel to cut a path selected anchor points*

Then with the Direct Selection tool, drag a marquee to select it, and press the Backspace/Delete key twice to remove the line segment and points entirely.

Another similar tool that you can use is the Path Eraser tool which you can use to split or erase parts of a path when you paint from point to point so that part of the path is removed. Refer to Figure 7-44.

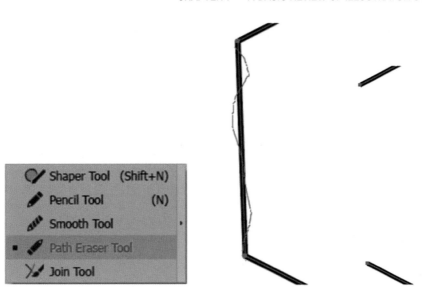

Figure 7-44. *Use the Toolbars panel Path Eraser tool when you want to erase part of a path*

Though not required for this book, you should explore on your own other tools within this collection. This includes the Shaper tool (Shift+N) which allows you to create basic shapes such as square, circle, and triangle quickly using your freehand drawing skill. The Pencil tool (N) also can be used for freehand drawing of a path that can be closed or opened. The Smooth tool can later be used when dragged over the selected path to remove extra anchor points and make the path less complex. Refer to the menu Object ➤ Path submenu in Illustrator if you need to make any further edits to anchor points on a path.

For more details on these tools, you can refer to these pages:

https://helpx.adobe.com/illustrator/using/building-new-shapes-using-shape.html

https://helpx.adobe.com/illustrator/using/drawing-pen-curvature-or-pencil.html

---

Tip   Instead of using the Smooth tool, you can also use the newly updated Object ➤ Path ➤ Smooth slider to adjust your paths. It has more control on the path overall rather than just sections of the path for maximum smoothing and auto smooth.

Combining Shapes with the Pathfinder Panel

Another useful panel in the construction of logos and infographics is the Pathfinder panel, which you can use to construct and merge shapes and paths. Refer to Figure 7-45.

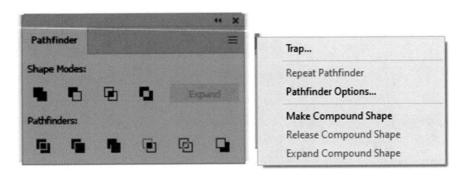

Figure 7-45. *Pathfinder panel and its menu options*

This panel is divided into two sections. The first is the upper section or Shape Modes that can be used in an editable mode, known as Make Compound Shape, when two shapes or paths are selected and you hold down the Alt/Option key and you click the icon. Refer to Figure 7-46.

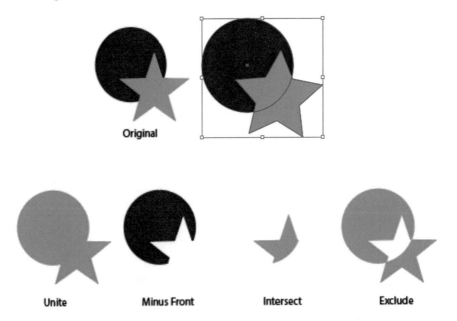

Figure 7-46. *Combine and divide various selected shapes using the Pathfinder panel Shape Modes*

These include the options of

- Unite: A compound added shape

- Minus Front: A compound shape that subtracts from the front of the shape area

- Intersect: A compound shape, which leaves the intersection of the two shapes

- Exclude: A compound shape that removes the overlapping area and only leaves the surrounding shapes

When using these Shape Modes, if you do not hold down the Alt/Option key or afterward click the Expand button while the compound shape is selected, this will cause the shape to be destructive, and the setting of the paths will be permanent unless you choose Edit ➤ Undo (Ctrl/CMD+Z) right away or use your History panel. You can use the Pathfinder panel's menu to make, release, and expand compound shapes.

The second Pathfinders section is in the same panel. However, it has no editable compound shape option, and the effects that are applied are permanent to the combining of the grouped shape or remaining path. Refer to Figure 7-47.

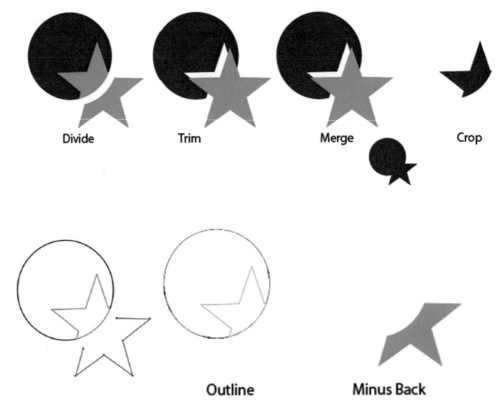

Figure 7-47. *Combine and divide various selected shapes using the Pathfinder panel Pathfinders options with some paths altered using selection tools*

These include

- Divide: Divides the shape in multiple segments which you can later drag away from the shape using the Direct Selection tool while grouped.

- Trim: Separates the two different colored shapes and deletes the part of the shape behind the upper shape.

- Merge: This can act just like trim, but if the shape's colors are the same, then it is similar to unite.

- Crop: Changes the color of the upper shape that was originally the lower shape color and leaves only that part of the upper shape that was within the lower shape.

- Outline: Leaves the surrounding stroke where the two shapes touched. In example Figure 7-47 part of the lower stroke of the star was then be selected with the Direct Selection tool and deleted. To see the complete outline path that is created refer to the similar example in Figure 7-48.

- Minus Back: Leaves only the part of the upper shape outside of the lower shape.

Note   Alternatively, you can also use the Effect ➤ Pathfinder menu on grouped paths to create a similar effect. In this case, the effects will appear similar and remain editable. As well as additional options for Hard and Soft mix of colors. To complete the transformation, use Object ➤ Expand Appearance. Refer to Figure 7-48.

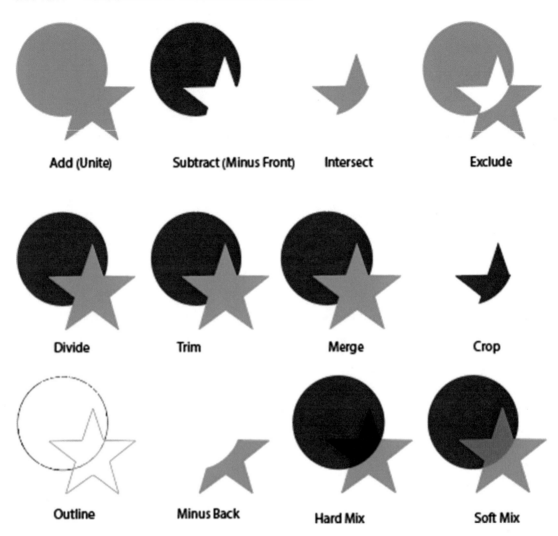

Figure 7-48. *Various kinds of effects you can create with grouped paths and Pathfinder effects*

For Photoshop users, you can also find for live Shape Modes Pathfinder options for working with vector layers in the Properties panel. However, there are only four options available. You can refer to my file pathfinder_examples.ai to review this.

Clipping Masks and Compound Paths

Other types of useful paths you may want to create, at this point, include clipping masks and compound paths. You can use your basic shapes to hide and show parts of infographics. With a clipping mask, for example, if you create a shape and then overlap it with another shape and then use the Selection tool, drag a marquee around both shapes, while both are selected, then choose Object ➤ Clipping Mask ➤ Make. The uppermost path becomes the invisible mask that hides parts of the lower shape. Refer to Figure 7-49.

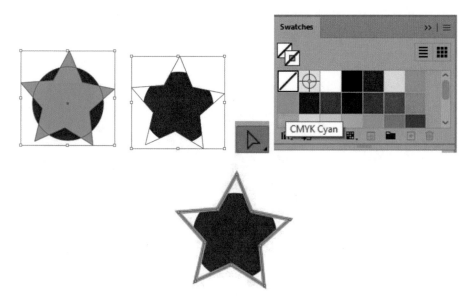

Figure 7-49. *Use a shape to create a clipping mask and edit with the Swatches panel*

You can with the Direct Selection tool select the mask and then use the Swatches panel to apply a color to the stroke. From the main menu, you can release the path using Object>Clipping Mask ➤ Release. Note that the Control panel and Properties panel will allow you to edit the content of the clipping mask. While selected with the Selection tool, use the toggle icons of Edit Clipping path and Edit Contents. Refer to Figure 7-50.

Figure 7-50. *Selected Clipping Groups can be edited with either the Control or Properties panel*

The compound path is similar to the compound shape, and you can use it to create a hole or holes in the lower shape using the upper shape or shapes. When you have selected all shapes or closed paths, including the overlapping ones, choose Object ➤ Compound Path ➤ Make. The upper shapes create a hole, and now anything later placed behind the compound path will show through. You can release the path by choosing Object ➤ Compound Path ➤ Release. Refer to Figure 7-51.

Figure 7-51. *Create a compound path and edit the color using the Direct Selection tool*

Tip   The parts of a compound path shape can have a stroke added when you select the edge with the Direct Selection tool and use the Swatches panel to select a swatch. Refer to file clipping_mask_compound_path.ai for examples.

Summary

In this chapter, we reviewed the following topics regarding drawing with the pen tool, moving, selecting, and arranging paths on the artboard. As you edited the custom shapes with other tools and panels, you looked at how to combine shapes using the Pathfinder panel as well as how to create clipping masks and compound paths.

In the next chapter, you will be focusing on how to work with the Layers panel and other coloring tools as well as type tools and symbols.

CHAPTER 8

Working with Illustrator's Layers and Additional Drawing and Type Tools

In this chapter, we will be focusing on working with layers. Next, we will work with different tools and panels to color the fill and stroke of an object. Then we will look at the Type tools and various brush tools and work with symbols. Some of the tools in this chapter may be familiar to you already, but we will also look at some new and updated panels as well. Later in Chapter 9, based on the knowledge you have gained in this chapter, you will create and review a few project ideas that can be created with basic shapes, custom shapes, and text.

Note   This chapter contains projects that can be found in the Volume 1 Chapter 8 folder. Some of the text in this chapter related to type tools has been adapted and updated from my earlier books *Accurate Layer Selections Using Photoshop's Selection Tools* and *Perspective Warps and Distorts with Adobe Tools: Volume 2.*

In this chapter, we are now going to cover some of the tools that can be found in the Toolbars panel, as well as some of the main panels that we can use to assist us in infographic creation. I will only be focusing on the basic features of each of these tools, but I will also provide an Adobe help link if you would like more details on that tool. For now, if you would like to practice along, create a new document as you did in Chapter 4 so that you have an artboard to practice with the following tools and panels.

© Jennifer Harder 2023
J. Harder, *Creating Infographics with Adobe Illustrator: Volume 1*,
https://doi.org/10.1007/979-8-8688-0005-4_8

Working with Layers

The Layers panel with its recent updates is now more useful with its search and filter options, and you can now find your layers and sublayers much faster. However, when organizing items from layer to layer for better layer order, the Object ➤ Arrange options from the menu don't allow you to move to a new layer only within the sublayers of a single layer.

In those situations, you have to use Edit ➤ Copy and Edit ➤ Paste when a new layer is selected or select a new layer and choose Object ➤ Arrange ➤ Send to Current Layer while that item is selected. Or you can work with the Layers panel itself to move items to another layer as I will point out here. Refer to Figure 8-1.

Figure 8-1. *Layers panel and its menu options*

Here are a few tips to help you get started when working with multiple layers using the Layers panel.

In the Layers panel, by default, you will start with Layer 1; to add another layer, you can then click the Create New Layer icon. Refer to Figure 8-2.

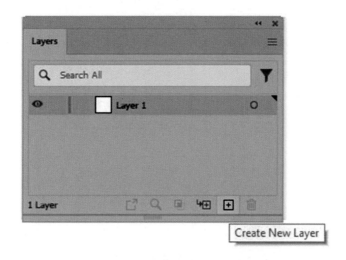

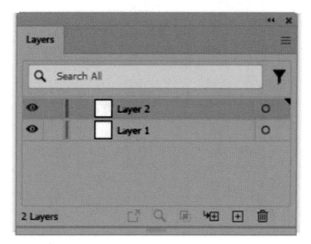

Figure 8-2. *Create a New Layer in the Layers panel*

As you add paths or shapes to each layer, sublayers are created. These are indicated by an arrow that can be collapsed and expanded so that you can view the sublayers which may have a name based on the type of shape. Refer to Figure 8-3.

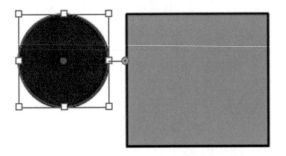

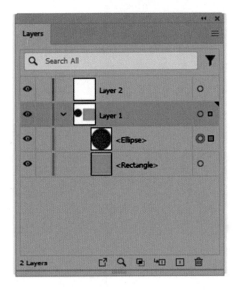

Figure 8-3. *Art on the artboard and how it appears in the Layers panel*

You can also add blank sublayers if required by clicking the Create New Sublayer icon. Refer to Figure 8-4.

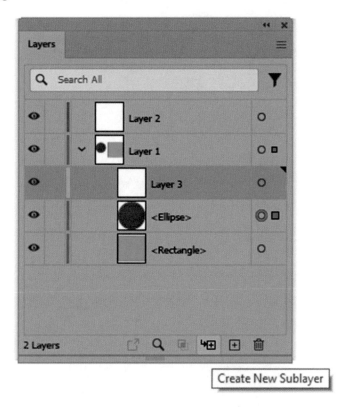

Create New Sublayer

Figure 8-4.   *Create a New Sublayer in the Layers panel*

To remove a selected layer or sublayer, you can select it and press the Delete Selection trash can icon. The layer or sublayer is then removed. If the layer contains artwork, you may get a warning message. Select Yes if you want to delete the layer or No to cancel the deletion. Refer to Figure 8-5.

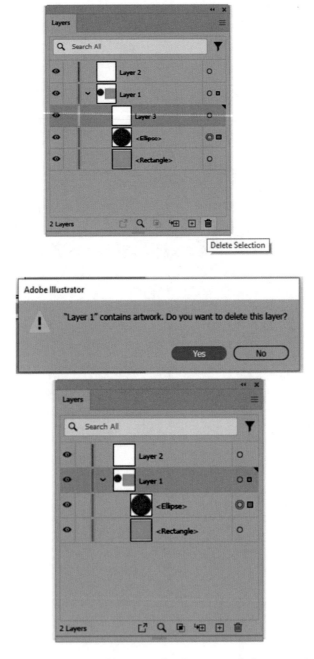

Figure 8-5. *Delete a layer or sublayer in the layer and the warning message*

Select the layer you want to draw your paths or shapes on. Anything on top will be above the other layers. Refer to Figure 8-6.

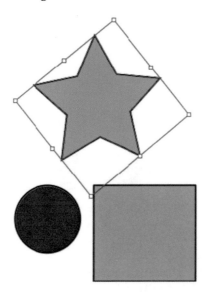

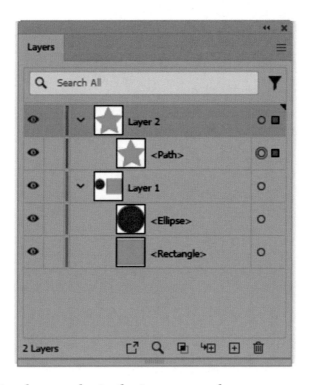

Figure 8-6. *Review layer order in the Layers panel*

Layers can be moved above or below each other if you drag them in the Layers panel up or down. As well, sublayers can be dragged out of one layer into another. Refer to Figure 8-7.

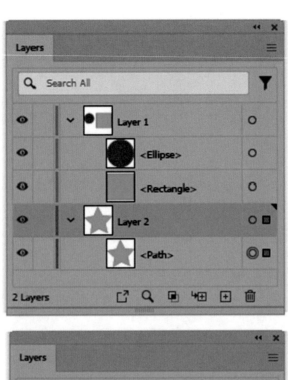

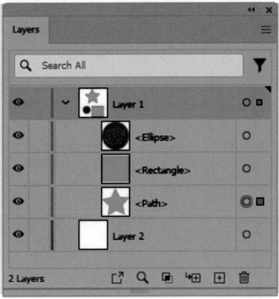

Figure 8-7. *Move layers or sublayers up or down in the Layers panel*

Another way to move shapes from layer to layer is to, while the item is selected, drag on the colored square on the layer which indicates the selected art. This can then be dragged above the sublayer or out of the current layer into another. Refer to Figure 8-8.

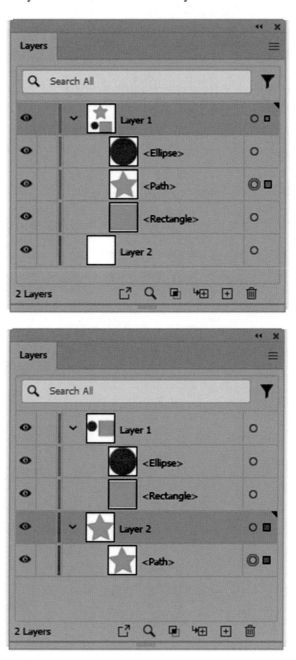

Figure 8-8. *Use the square in the Layers panel to move sublayers to other layers*

Note   The circle beside each layer (the targeted path), when it is a double circle or filled double circle, indicates the appearance of that shape or path. In this case, a cyan star has a cyan fill and a black stroke. You can move the appearance of the shape to another shape by dragging the double circle dot onto a single-dot-filled or hollow form to alter the appearance of another shape in the Layers panel.

Or Alt/Option+Drag when you want the original shape to keep its appearance as well. We will look at altering appearance and graphic styles later in this chapter. Here I Alt/Option dragged the dot from the star up on the rectangle layer sublayer, and now the rectangle has the same appearance colors as the star. Refer to Figure 8-9.

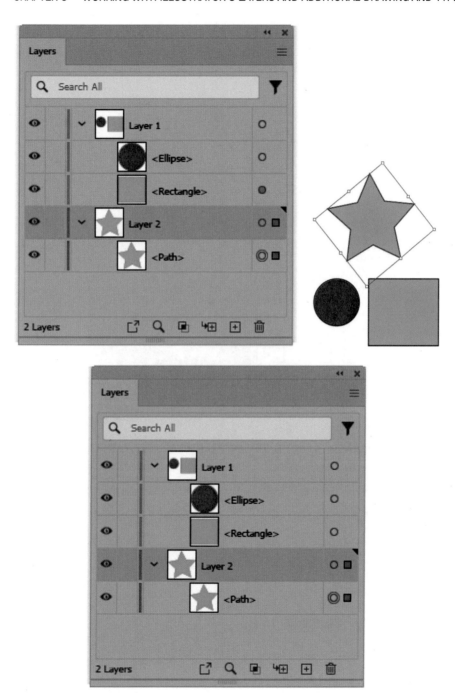

Figure 8-9. *Change the appearance of a path or shape using the target to add the appearance to another path in the Layers panel*

A sublayer or layer can also be duplicated; if you drag it over the Create New Layer icon, it will appear directly below the current selected path. This is good when you need to make a copy of a shape without destroying the original. Refer to Figure 8-10.

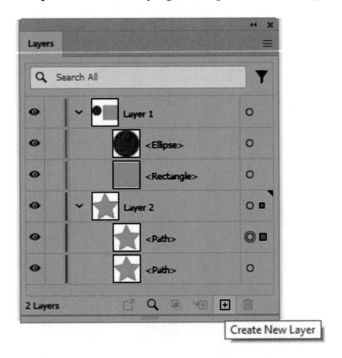

Figure 8-10. *Duplicate a layer or sublayer using the Layers panel*

When you need to locate a selected item, you can use the search to filter layer, By Object or By Layer type. Click the X in the search area to clear the search and reveal all layers. Refer to Figure 8-11.

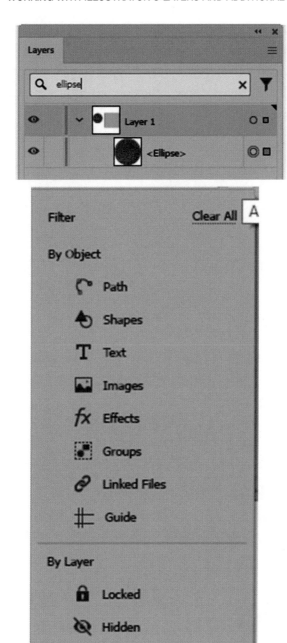

Figure 8-11. *Use the new filter options in the Layers panel*

If a layer is selected with a specific sublayer that has a path selected with a square, you can also use the menu to locate an object on the artboard, and you will move to that sublayer in the Layers panel. Or if the object sublayer is not selected on the artboard, click beside the circle on the layer to make the colored square appear to reveal it on the artboard. Refer to Figure 8-12.

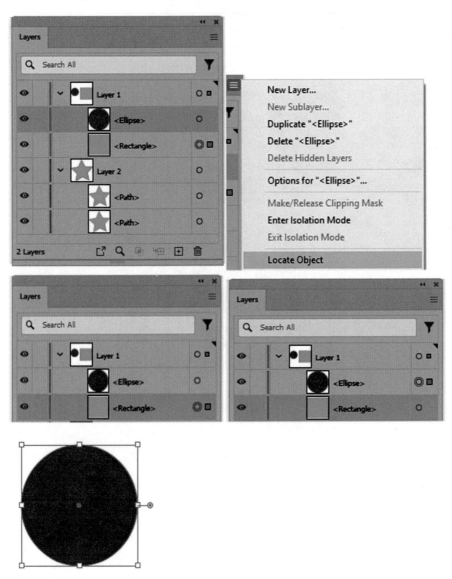

Figure 8-12. *Use the Layers panel to locate a path or sublayer on a specific layer that has a square on the right in the Layers panel and is on the artboard*

Note   The Locate Object menu item is the same as the magnifying glass at the bottom of the Layers panel. Refer to Figure 8-13.

Figure 8-13. *Layers panel lower bar Locate Object icon*

If you need to change the layer's color or other settings, the current layer color is assigned when you create a new layer on the layer and sublayers. It appears as a vertical bar in the same color and as the square when a path is selected. Refer to Figure 8-12. You may need to change the layer color if it clashes with your artwork and makes the anchor points difficult to see. You can edit this as well as other layer settings when you double-click the Layer thumbnail.

Here you can see the Layer Options dialog box. Refer to Figure 8-14.

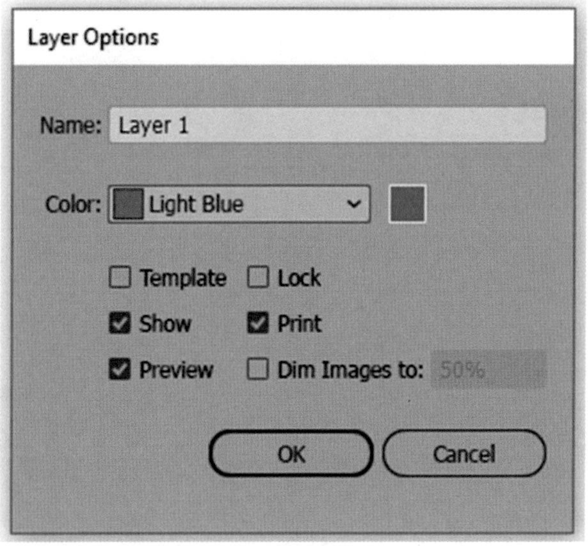

Figure 8-14. *Layers panel Options dialog box*

Here you can change the name; alternatively, you can double-click the name outside of the box and type it in and then click another layer to set the name. Refer to Figure 8-15.

Figure 8-15. *Rename a layer in the Layers panel*

While in the dialog box, use the drop-down list in the dialog box to change the color or the color picker. Additional settings, when enabled, allow you to make the layer a template, lock/unlock the layer, show/hide the layer, print, preview, or dim the images. Click OK to exit the dialog box and commit your changes. Refer to Figure 8-16.

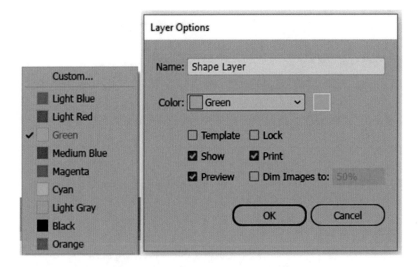

Figure 8-16. *Layer Options dialog box for color settings*

Layers can also be locked by adding the lock icon by clicking in the blank square or shown and hidden by turning on and off the eye icon. Refer to Figure 8-17.

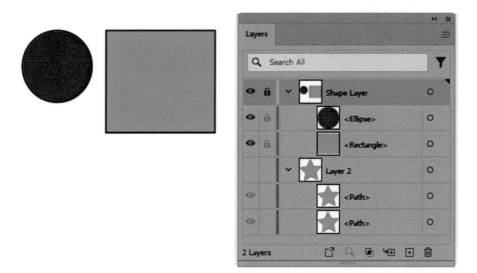

Figure 8-17. *Locking and hiding layers using the Layers panel*

Clicking the lock to lock the layer or eye to hide the layer will cause the sublayers to lock or hide as well.

A template layer will show up with a different square icon, not an eye, and will be locked. Sublayers will also be part of the template. Refer to Figure 8-18.

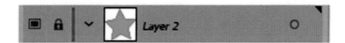

Figure 8-18. *The eye is replaced by a square for a template layer*

Sublayers such as for a <path> can also be renamed, but they will only have show and lock options, while blank sublayers that you create will have the same Layer Options settings. This will be useful to know when you work with your layers to create interactive infographics in Volume 3.

Working in Outline Mode (Preview)

You can work in outline or preview mode using the main menu View ➤ Outline/Preview (Ctrl/CMD+Y). This makes it easier to select items behind other items.

Or for a single layer, uncheck the preview in the Layers dialog box or from the Layers panel; Ctrl/CMD+Click the eye to toggle the visibility and outline. Refer to Figure 8-16 and Figure 8-19.

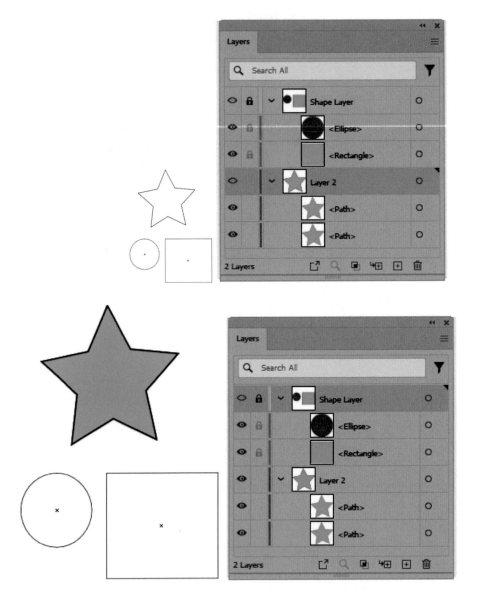

Figure 8-19. *View all or selected layers in Outline mode and how they appear on the artboard and Layers panel*

If you want the top layer or sublayer to be the clipping mask or path for a sublayer in the following, while the top layer and object sublayer <path> are selected, use the make/release clipping mask icon to make the mask/path. Refer to Figure 8-20 and Figure 8-21.

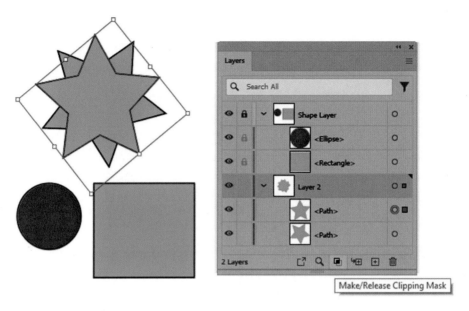

Figure 8-20. *Select a path and use the Layers panel to turn it into a clipping mask*

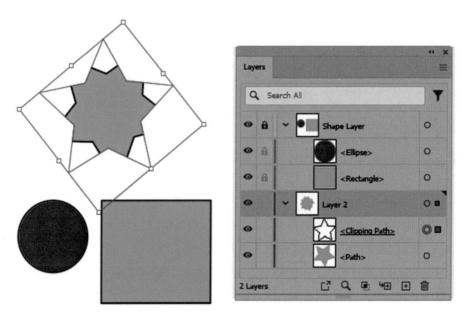

Figure 8-21. *Clipping mask/path settings as they appear on the artboard and in the Layers panel*

However, if you click the icon again to release the clipping mask path, it will not change back to its past blue color, only a path with no fill or stroke. So, Edit➤Undo Ctrl/CMD+Z or use the History panel if that was not your intent. Refer to Figure 8-22.

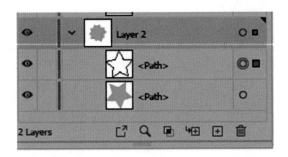

Figure 8-22. *Clipping mask/path does not return to the original color fill if released*

If your object upon becoming a clipping path/mask does not have the same name as mine <Clipping path>, another indication that it is a clipping path/mask is that the name becomes underlined. Refer to Figure 8-21.

The other icon on the lower left is Collect for Export which works with the Asset Export panel, and we will explore this further in Volume 3. Refer to Figure 8-23.

Figure 8-23. *Lower Layers panel button icon Collect for Export*

Note   While we will not go through all the options in the Layers panel menu, I will just point out that it does contain additional options for entering and exiting isolation mode, flattening artwork to a single layer, and collecting artwork in a new layer, as well as more hide/show and lock layers options. Refer to Figure 8-24.

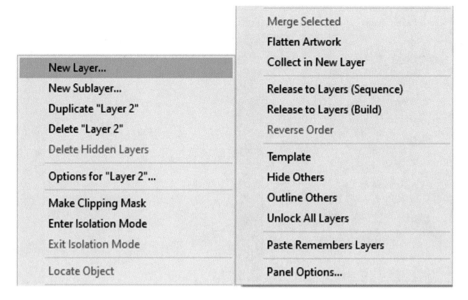

Figure 8-24. *Additional options found in the Layers Panel menu*

Tip   Use the Layers Menu Panel Options dialog box if you need to enlarge the size of your Row Size "Layer" in the panel by changing it from the default Medium to Large and click OK. Refer to Figure 8-25.

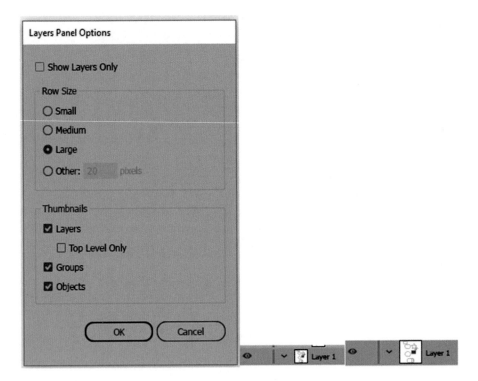

Figure 8-25. *Layers Panel Options dialog box you can decrease or increase the layer size*

Project: Trace over a Linked File

You should now have a better idea of how to navigate layers and work with your basic shapes and pen tools, so at this point, you can begin to trace over a mock-up on another layer.

In this example, File ➤ Open the file project light_bulb_trace_start.ai. Make a copy of the file with your initials if you want to follow along. This is a similar file to the one you saw and started in Chapter 5. Refer to Figure 8-26.

Figure 8-26. *Mock-up of light bulb sketch*

Make sure to also refer to your Window ➤ Links panel if you are getting any warning messages about a missing image and you may need to relink. If required to relink then locate the file Mockup_Sketch.jpg.

The layers have been arranged, and you can see three layers in the Layers panel. The lower one is the placed graphic and that layer is locked, and the other layers are blank which we will use for basic tracing. I have changed their names. Refer to Figure 8-27.

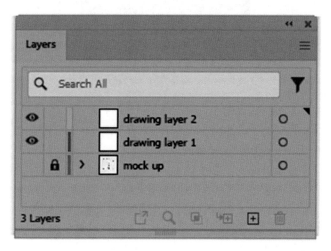

Figure 8-27. *Layout of multiple layers in the Layers panel*

In the Properties panel Preferences, make sure that Scale Stroke & Effects is turned off before you start to draw. Also make sure that your View ➤ Rulers ➤ Show Rulers and View ➤ Smart Guides are on. Refer to Figure 8-28.

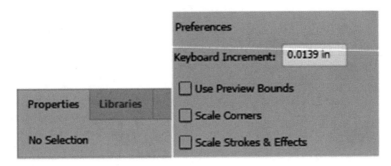

Figure 8-28. *Use the Properties panel to uncheck Scale Strokes & Effects when no selection is made*

An easier way to trace over an image is to set the pen or basic shape to a fill of none with a stroke in the Control panel. You do not want the fill to cover the drawing as you trace over it. Refer to Figure 8-29.

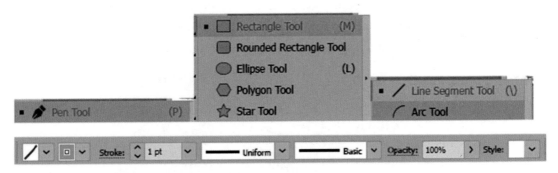

Figure 8-29. *Various pen, shape, and line tools you can use to edit your paths while using the Control panel*

Set the stroke color in the Control panel before you start drawing. I usually make it into a bright blue cyan color and about 1pt or 0.5pt stroke so that it is very thin so that I can see part of my initial drawing underneath. Do this now. You can always change and adjust the stroke color weight or fill color as you will see later on.

At this point, depending on the sketch on the locked lower "mock-up layer," now start working on "drawing layer 1." Begin to trace out parts of the drawing with either the Pen tool or use a combination of basic shapes as we looked in the earlier chapter. You will notice that many of today's logos or components of an infographic have parts of the design that are rounded and simplified. Refer to Figure 8-30.

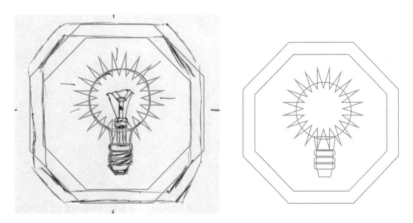

Figure 8-30. *Tracing your logo over the mock-up sketch*

The design need not be overly realistic but more of an abstract representation with simple colors. Your own drawing or mock-up does not have to be the same. In my case, to get inspiration, I drew a real light bulb. However, one does not have to draw or retrace all the parts of a light bulb to know that is what it is. Generally, just the glass bulb, the filament, the base cap, and maybe some indication that it is glowing are all that are needed. However, if this were an infographic about the parts of a light bulb, then a more detailed sketch might be required.

In this example, let's look at some of the simple shapes I drew. To create parts of the bulb, I used the Ellipse tool holding the Shift key down and the Rectangle tool and modified the points on the rectangle using the Direct Selection tool. I can also use the arrow keys on my keyboard to nudge individual points left and right. Refer to Figure 8-31.

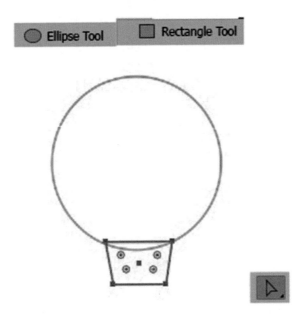

Figure 8-31. *Use the Ellipse, Rectangle, and Direct Selection tools to modify various shapes of a bulb*

I also used the Rounded Rectangle tool to create three screw elements on a rectangle, above the base contact cap which is a rectangle. I could then use either the Pen tool or the Rectangle tool again to create the cap's electrical foot contact. Refer to Figure 8-32.

Figure 8-32. *Create other parts of the bulb using the Rounded Rectangle tool*

The stem/glass support was drawn with the Rectangle tool, and parts of the filament were drawn with the Ellipse tool, Line Segment tool, and Pen tool for wires. Some of these lines were drawn on "drawing layer 2" while I hid and locked the "drawing layer 1." Refer to Figure 8-33.

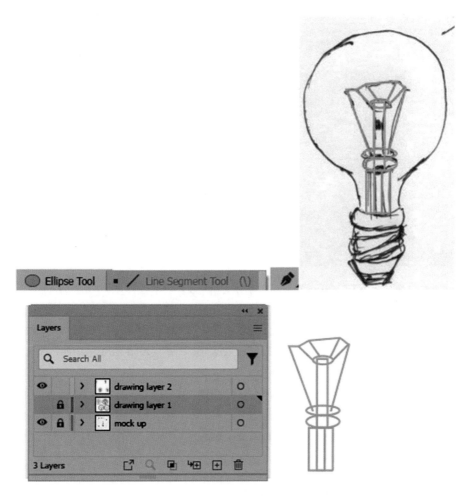

Figure 8-33. *Drawing parts of the filament using the Ellipse, Line, and Pen tools while locking and hiding other some layers in the Layers panel to get a more accurate trace*

The light source was drawn with the Star tool on drawing layer 1 and set to Radius 1: 1.1528 in and Radius 2: 0.5278 in and 20 points. Refer to Figure 8-34.

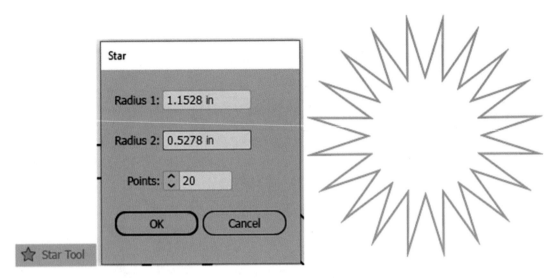

Figure 8-34. *Using the Star tool and Star dialog box to create light rays*

I also used the Polygon tool while holding down the Shift key to create two eight-sided octagons. The outer is about 4.3291 inches for width and height, and the inner is about 3.6763 inches for width and height. First is the outer shape then the inner. Remember to use your Shape options in the Control panel if your polygon is not eight sided. You can scale using the Selection tool and then arrange these behind the other shapes if they are not in the correct order. Try using various the Object ➤ Arrange settings as required. Refer to Figure 8-35.

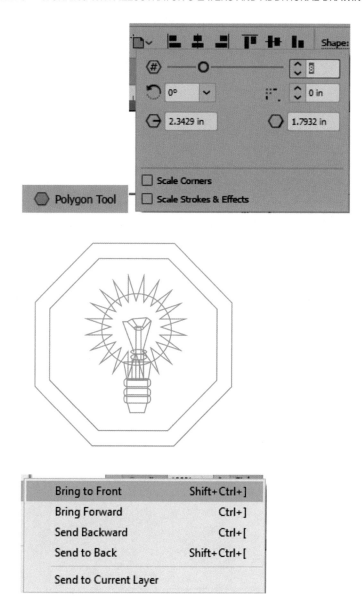

Figure 8-35. *Using the Polygon tool and the Control panel to create and edit the octagons and using the Object>Arrange menu to move some layers behind others*

When both polygons are selected, use your Align options in the Control Panel to center vertically and horizontally. Refer to Figure 8-36.

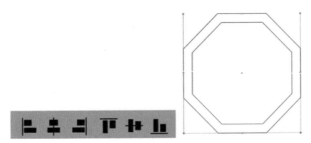

Figure 8-36. *Use the Align options in the Control panel to align the hexagons horizontally and vertically centered*

As you learned in Layer basics, as you draw in complicated areas, you may want to move some parts of the shape to other layers and temporarily hide and show layers so that you can focus on one section at a time. Once you have drawn all the parts that you think you need from your "mock-up" layer, you can turn that layer off and begin to color some areas. Refer to Figure 8-37.

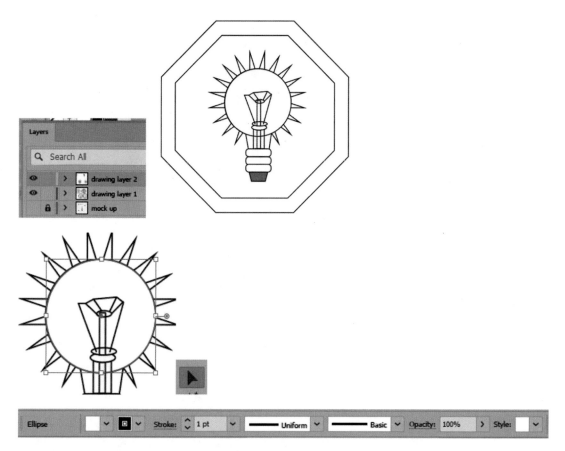

Figure 8-37. *Unlock the drawing layers and hide the mock-up layer in the Layers panel. Use the Control panel and Selection tool to select paths and color parts of the bulb in white and gray colors for now so that you can hide parts of your images or lower paths*

I usually will, with my Selection tool, select paths and give them a white or gray fill and a black stroke. I can do this using my Control panel. At this point, exact colors do not matter. Refer to Figure 8-38.

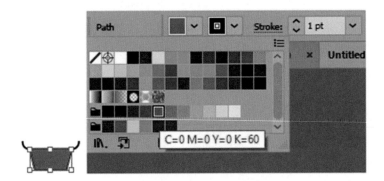

Figure 8-38. *Use the Control panel swatches to color parts of the design*

I may then at this point continue to reorder my sublayers and layers and then Shift+Click select, for example, the bulb ellipse and the altered rectangular bulb base, and then combine them using the Pathfinder panel by just clicking the Unite icon key. Refer to Figure 8-39 and Figure 8-40.

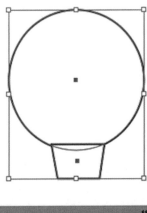

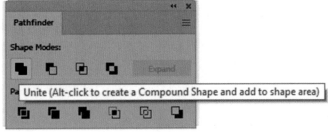

Figure 8-39. *When two paths are selected, use the Pathfinder panel to unite the shapes*

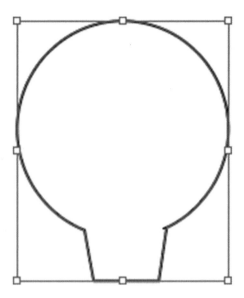

Figure 8-40. *The result of the two united paths as one path*

In this case, the result was permanent. You may in some cases want to, before clicking Unite in the Pathfinder, Alt/Option+Drag copies of your selected shapes off to the side in case you need to reuse them later. Refer to Figure 8-41.

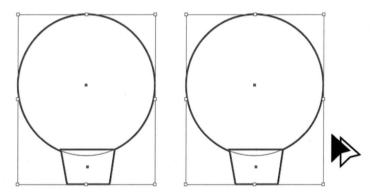

Figure 8-41. *Create copies using Alt/Option+Drag with the Selection tool if you don't want to destroy your original shape*

For your own project, you may wish to unite other shapes or use other Pathfinder options which you can review from earlier in Chapter 7. See section "Combining Shapes with the Pathfinder Panel."

However, as mentioned, the mock-up is only a starting point for your own design. Continue to use Illustrator to refine or remove parts of the light bulb to simplify it. In my example, I decided that the light source did not look that great as a star, but I could use some rounded rectangles to create the rays, and I used the star as my rough placement guide with a fill and stroke both set to none. You can always select the star afterward with the Selection tool and press Backspace/Delete to remove it from the design. Refer to Figure 8-42.

Figure 8-42. *Use the star path as your guide for placing other shapes or modifying and simplifying your design*

I also modified and simplified other parts of my bulb such as the filament, stem, and wires, so that they were less busy, and tapering the cap screw and tapering and rounding the electrical foot contact. The actual base contact cap stem itself is hidden behind, or it can be removed. For the glass bulb, I adjusted the path using the Direct Selection tool and tried to smooth out my corner points using the Control panel. However, doing so may not make both sides as symmetrical as you need them to be, and you may need to adjust the handles of the anchor points on the path further on to suit your needs. You may also need to add points if required. Refer to Figure 8-43.

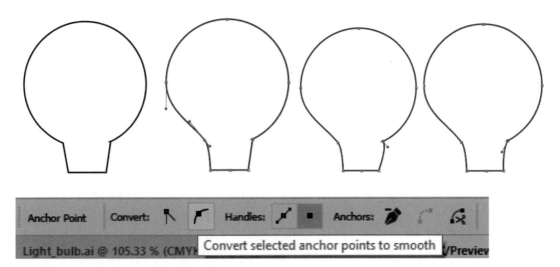

Figure 8-43. *Use your Control panel to make modifications to your bulb shape*

In your case, you may need to select and remove some points and even delete half the shape using the Direct Selection tool. Shift+Click select points and then press Backspace/Delete. Then with the half-open path selected with the Selection tool, use Object ➤ Transform ➤ Reflect—in this case, the axis is vertical—and make a copy rather than clicking OK. Now Shift+Drag and align the new path with the old, and Shift+Click to select both so you can merge the two sides together using the Pathfinder Unite to get a more perfect bulb. Refer to Figure 8-44.

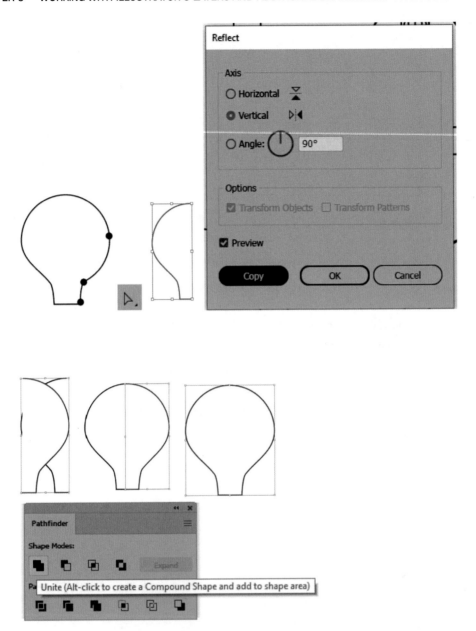

Figure 8-44. *Use the Reflect dialog box to reflect and open path and make a copy of the path and then unite the two paths using the Pathfinder panel*

Note   Some additional points may need to be clicked and deleted afterward using your Delete Anchor Point tool. Use the Anchor Point tool if you need to make further adjustments to the selected point. But for the bulb you want, maintain a symmetrical shape. Refer to Figure 8-45.

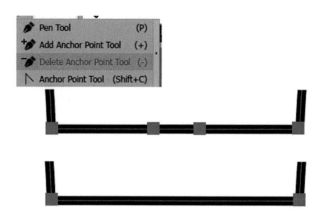

Figure 8-45. *Use the Delete Anchor Point tool to move extra points on the path*

Remember, you can use your Direct Selection tool and your arrow keys on the keyboard if you need to nudge a point or selected points up or down on the artboard to adjust the shape.

Your final results may have more or less points than mine or be slightly different in shape. Take your time and do not rush if you want smooth symmetrical results. You can also use guides that you drag from your rulers if you need to align your points. Here are the points that I used to create the bulb in View ➤ Outline mode (Ctrl/CMD+Y). Use View ➤ Preview to switch back afterward. Refer to Figure 8-46.

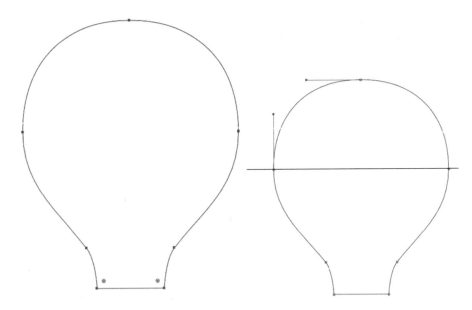

Figure 8-46. *Current points on the bulb path, then use guides to adjust and align points on a path further*

Remember to Use View ➤ Preview to switch back afterward.

Select the guide and press Backspace/Delete when you want to remove it.

I also added a line to make the bulb appear a bit 3D with a highlight using the Arc tool. Refer to Figure 8-47.

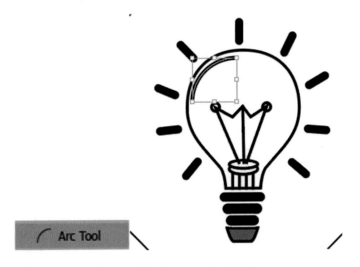

Figure 8-47. *Use the Arc tool to add a line to the bulb*

To finish my design, I colored it with black, orange, yellow, and gray colors. I also made some of the strokes thicker or thinner between 2 and 3 points in weight. The arc can be further adjusted using the Stroke panel with a round cap. Remember you can do this when you select a shape or path with the Selection tool and then use the Control panel to adjust that path or shape to suit your design or color scheme. Refer to Figure 8-48.

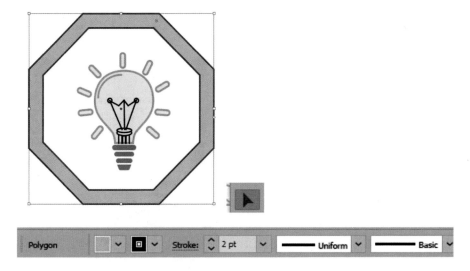

Figure 8-48. *Add color to the paths fill and stroke and adjust stroke weight using the Selection tool and Control panel*

In your own practice, some or all of the steps I point out here. Use the Internet and Google images if you need to look at how other people have drawn light bulb icons and you will discover a variety of ideas. You will see you don't need a lot of lines or paths to represent a light bulb. You can make it as simple or complex as you like; though keep in mind that if the icon is small, you need enough detail so that it will be recognizable, but not so much detail that parts of the design become lost and blurred. Try to design your icon with some similar paths, but at the same time, make it slightly different than the designs you see.

Yours will be slightly different than mine, but you can view my file and the final result in this file light_bulb_final.ai.

Then I will File ➤ Save my sketch in a location on my computer. This chapter will continue with other ways you can modify artwork further for your own logo or infographic project.

Additional Ways of Adding Color to an Object's Fill and Stroke

We saw how we can use the Control panel to color a selected object. However, when you want to recolor shapes or paths, there are various recoloring options you can use. These include using the tools Eyedropper, Live Paint, and the Color Guide panel with some new features. Let's look at some of the features of each of these.

Eyedropper Tool (I)

When a shape or path is selected, you can transfer the basic appearance setting from one shape to another.

Select with your Selection tool the shape you want to add your new stroke and fill to. Refer to Figure 8-49.

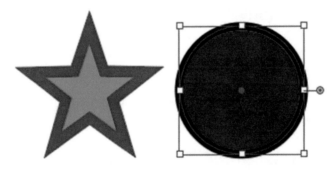

Figure 8-49. *Select a path that you want to alter the appearance such as the fill and stroke*

Then select the Eyedropper tool and click the shape you want to extract the appearance setting from, and they will be applied to the selected shape. Refer to Figure 8-50.

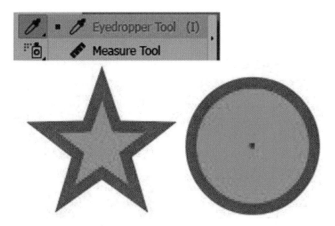

Figure 8-50. *Use the Eyedropper tool and click another path or shape and add that appearance to the selected object*

If you double-click the Eyedropper tool in the Toolbars panel, you can see what appearance settings it picks up and what it applies. Refer to Figure 8-51.

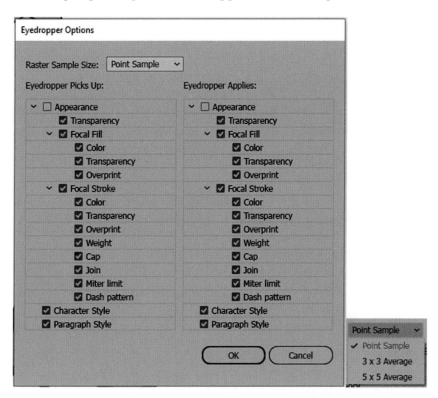

Figure 8-51. *Eyedropper Options dialog box with Raster Sample Size settings of point sample*

This includes transparency overall, focal fill (color, transparency, and overprint), focal stroke (color, transparency, overprint, weight, cap, join, miter limit, and dash pattern), character style, and paragraph style. Note that color also includes gradients and patterns. However, more advanced features like effects and multiple styles can only be transferred when you create a graphic style which I will talk about later in the chapter. Use this dialog box to set your sample range; the default is point sample.

Gradient, Pattern Options, and Transparency (Opacity) Panels

While we will not be going into these panels in depth, keep in mind that if you want to add a gradient or two or more graduated colors to a shape, use the Gradient panel and the Gradient tool to adjust the gradient. The Gradient panel has three types of gradients, two of which can be stored as swatches in the Swatches panel with other default gradients that have been created; these can be accessed directly from the Gradient panel. Refer to Figure 8-52.

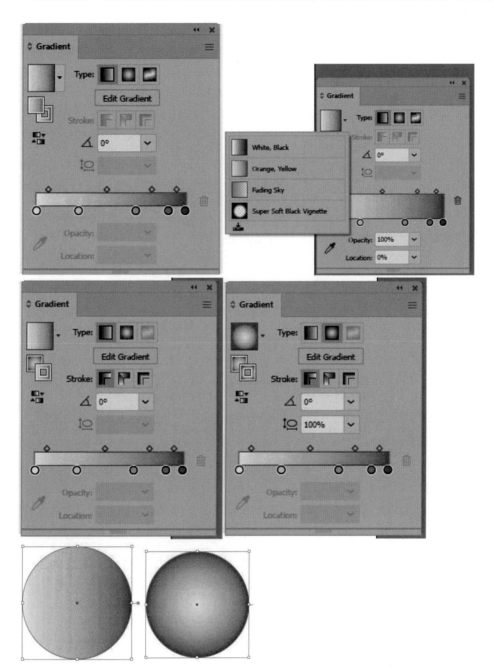

Figure 8-52. *Gradient panel selecting and applying a gradient linear or radial*

Linear is a line gradient, and radial is a circular gradient. They can have two or more round color swatch color stops and midpoint transition diamond sliders that can be adjusted on the gradient annotator.

They can be applied to fills and strokes in gradient editing mode. When on the selected shape, click the Edit Gradient button to start and select the fill or stroke to edit. Refer to Figure 8-52. Strokes containing gradients (linear or radial) can be applied within, along, or across the stroke. Refer to Figure 8-53.

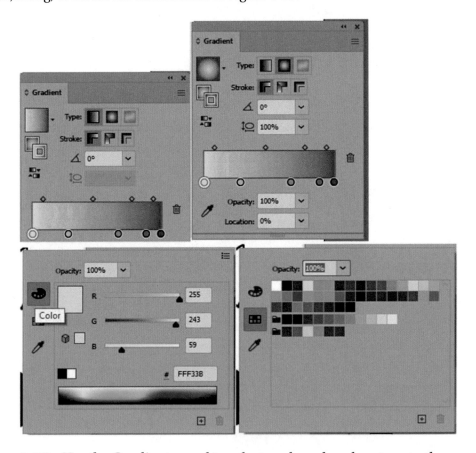

Figure 8-53. *Use the Gradient panel to select and apply color stops to the annotator using color or solid swatches*

Set each gradient you create, which can be set to an angle (-180, 0, 180) degrees by typing, or from the list and each color, stop swatch to a different color when you double-click the stop and select a color or swatch color from the pop-up panel.

Use the eyedropper color picker inside the stop or outside the panel to select a color from another shape or path. Click Esc to exit the color picker. Color Stops can be added by clicking a location on the annotator slider as well as selected and deleted using the trash can icon delete stop on the right of the annotator. Or drag the stop off the annotator. However, at least two color stops must always remain. Refer to Figure 8-53.

For a gradient, you can then set an opacity (0%–100%) for each stop and its location (0%–100%) on the annotator using the lower area of the panel. The midpoint slider location can also be adjusted as well. A gradient can be different for the fill and stroke. Strokes as mentioned earlier can be set linear and radial gradient. The gradient order can be reversed on a fill or stroke, and for radial gradients, you can set the aspect ratio (ellipse icon) using the drop-down list to be more ellipse-like (10%–800%). The round default is 100%. Lower numbers can be set down to 0.5% up to 32767% if you type them in the text area. Refer to Figure 8-54.

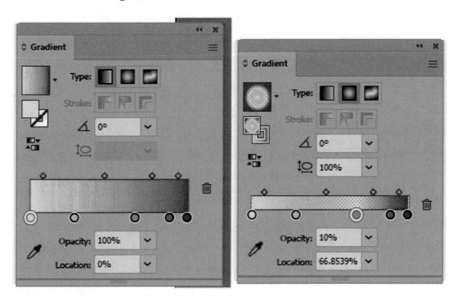

Figure 8-54. *Use the Gradient panel to apply transparency to the selected color stop*

Once your gradient is created, you can click the Add to Swatches icon found from the drop-down list of the active/previously used gradient to store it in the Swatches panel. Refer to Figure 8-55.

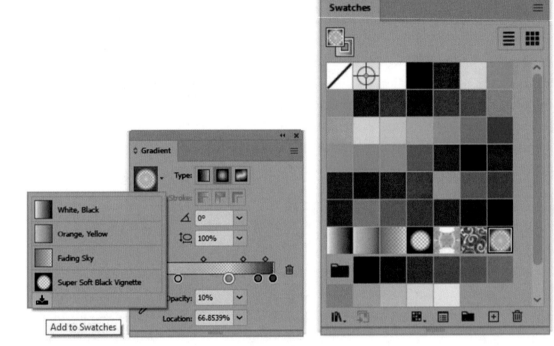

Figure 8-55. *Use the Gradient panel menu to add a swatch to the Swatches panel*

Your selected paths current gradients will continue to display for the fill/stroke in the Gradients panel.

Liner and radial gradients can be further edited using the Gradient tool (G). Drag out a new gradient angle with the tool on your selected path and use the annotator on the path to adjust instead of from the Gradient panel. Refer to Figure 8-56.

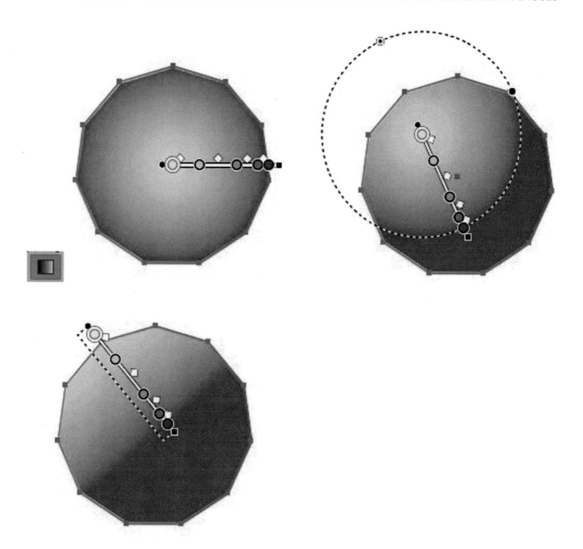

Figure 8-56. *Use the Gradient tool and its annotator to modify the placement and angle of a radial and linear gradient*

The third type of gradient, which we will not be discussing in length in this book, is the newer Freeform gradient. It relies on points and lines to create a type of gradient blend which is very good for creating smooth transitions such as for skin tones or 3D-like shapes, but only for fills and not strokes. These gradients are not stored in the Swatches panel, but you can save them to be used for a graphic style or as part of symbol. Refer to Figure 8-57.

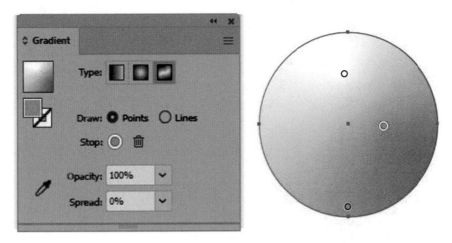

Figure 8-57. *Gradient panel with Freeform Gradient options selected in the panel*

You can learn more about gradients from this page.

`https://helpx.adobe.com/illustrator/using/gradients.html`

To create a new pattern, you can use your Swatches panel as well as your Pattern Options panel to create basic and complex repeating patterns that can be later accessed from the Swatches panel and applied to shapes and paths when the path is selected. Pattern editing mode and the Pattern Options panel can be accessed by double-clicking a pattern in the Swatches panel. Refer to Figure 8-58.

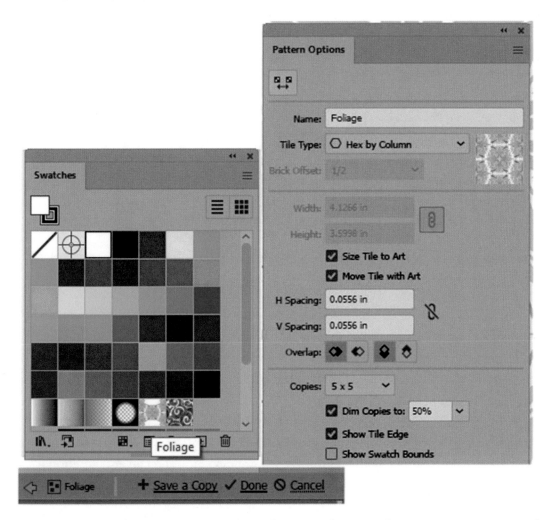

Figure 8-58. *Updating a pattern using the Swatches panel, Pattern Options panel, and exiting pattern editing mode*

However, keep in mind, as mentioned in Chapter 2, patterns underlying text can be a distraction and cause issues with readability, so be aware of this. If you add a pattern to a background, fade the opacity of that selected path using the Control panel. Refer to Figure 8-59.

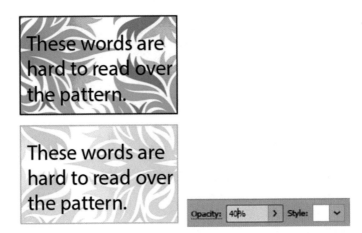

Figure 8-59. *Select the patterned object behind text and use the Control panel to reduce opacity when text is hard to read*

We will look at them in a bit more detail and how they relate to graphs in Volume 2 should you want to apply a simple pattern to your graph. If you are in pattern editing mode, click the Cancel icon in the upper left if you need to exit this area and mode for now. Additional patterns can be found in the Window ➤ Swatch Libraries ➤ Patterns. Refer back to Figure 8-58.

For additional adjustments of transparency and opacity (0%–100%), remember to use the Transparency panel which you can also access while a shape is selected from your Control or Properties panel. In the Transparency panel, you can add additional blending modes from the drop-down list which are similar to the ones found in the Photoshop Layers panel that will blend the upper color shape with the lower color shape. Apply the blend to the upper shape to see the result. This blend will vary from color to color and give a similar Pathfinder panel effect. Normal is the default, and the other options are darken, multiply, color burn, lighten, screen, color dodge, overlay, soft light, hard light, difference, exclusion, hue, saturation, color, and luminosity. Refer to Figure 8-60.

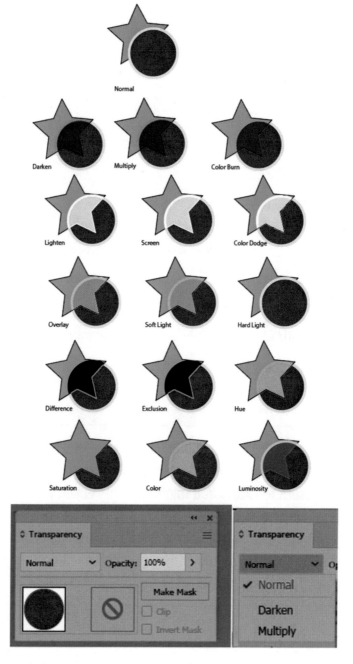

Figure 8-60. *Use the Transparency panel blending mode when on selected objects when you need to have parts of the lower design appear through the upper*

Refer to my file blending_modes.ai to review examples of these options.

Transparency can also have a separate mask applied known as a Transparency mask, for excluding parts it is similar to a clipping mask for a shape. A shape in this case is drawn on the mask. Refer to Figure 8-61.

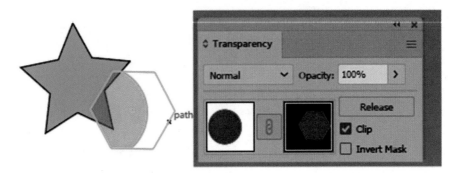

Figure 8-61. *Use the Transparency panel to turn a path or shape into a Transparency mask*

You can read the details of transparency and blending modes at the following link.

https://helpx.adobe.com/illustrator/using/transparency-blending-modes.html

---

Tip   Use the Transparency Overlay setting, such as a blending mode of multiply, on your mock-up placed/linked image, and place that layer above the layer you want to draw on. Be sure to lock it. You might find this easier to work with when tracing, especially if some of your drawn paths or shapes already contain fills or you want to draw on the layer below with a filled path and make adjustments to paths using the Direct Selection tool if they are already filled. Refer to my file blending_mode_layers.ai for an example. Refer to Figure 8-62.

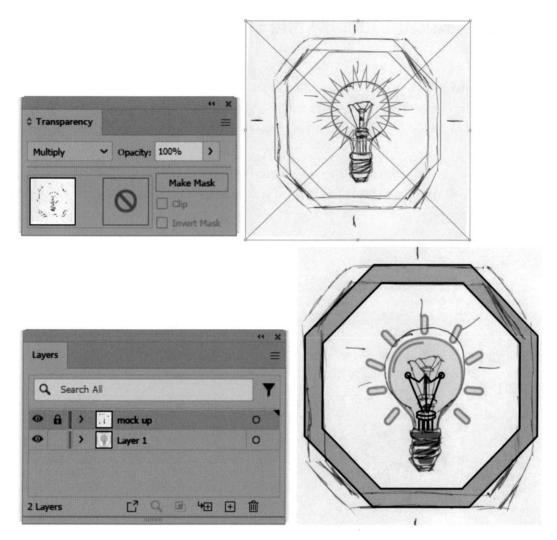

Figure 8-62. *Use the Transparency panel and blending modes on an image so that you can trace under it and still see your colors on another layer using the Layers panel*

Live Paint Bucket Tool (K) and Live Selection Tool (Shift+L)

Another helpful infographic tool for adding color between gaps and squares is the Live Paint Bucket tool. This can be very useful if you want to complete the waffle chart we made earlier using the Rectangular Grid tool or to fill in colors in the Polar Grid in Chapter 6.

Locate your rectangular grid that you created earlier in Chapter 6. If not, refer to these settings. Make sure to press the D key if you need to reset your stroke and fill. Refer to Figure 8-63.

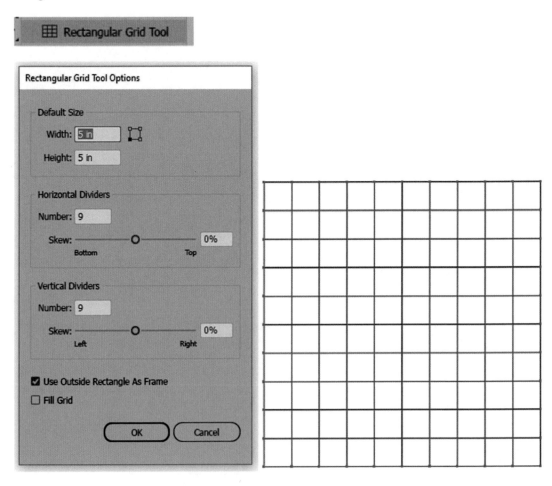

Figure 8-63. *Rectangular Grid Tool Options dialog box and rectangular grid on artboard*

You can then select the grid with your Selection tool and then your Live Paint Bucket tool. Refer to Figure 8-64.

Figure 8-64. *Selection tool and Live Paint Bucket tool*

And click an empty square on the grid to make it a live paint group. Refer to Figure 8-65.

Figure 8-65. *Use the Live Paint Bucket to make the grid a live paint group*

Now use your left and right arrow keys on your keyboard to find the color swatches you want to add to each square and click as you go along. The center color is the color that will be added when you click a grid square. Refer to Figure 8-66.

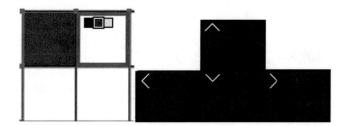

Figure 8-66. *Paint with your Live Paint Bucket and click into swatches into various squares on the grid to paint them. Switch swatches using the arrow keys*

Here we can see how we might represent something that was 48% completed, or perhaps 48 out of the 100 people voted a certain way. Of course, this might need some textual reference in the form of a legend added as well to explain what red and yellow actually represent, but you can see how a simple chart can begin. Refer to Figure 8-67.

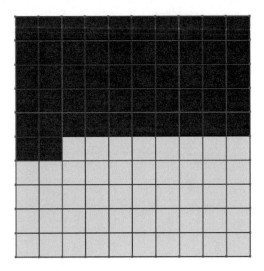

Figure 8-67. *Creating a waffle chart with the Live Paint Bucket tool*

As you work on colors, if you need to switch back to a color in the chart, hold down the Alt/Option key and use the Eyedropper tool to click and switch to a previous color. The Ctrl/CMD key will allow you to switch back to the Selection tool if you need to move your waffle chart.

Later you can use your Live Paint Selection tool if you need to select a square and color it using the Control panel separately. Refer to Figure 8-68.

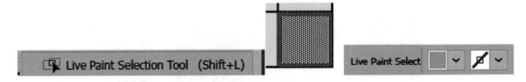

Figure 8-68. *Live Paint Selection tool used to select a square and set a new fill using the Control panel*

For additional settings for Live Paint, you can access them via Object➤Live Paint after you have selected it with the Selection tool. This will allow you to make, merge, or if already created, release back the path to its original state. As well you can set Gap Options if the colors are not filling in on complex shapes correctly, as well as expand the live paint to keep the chart, but now it is no longer a live paint group. Refer to Figure 8-69.

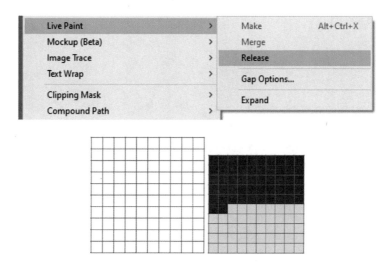

Figure 8-69. *Use Object ➤ Live Paint ➤ Release to return to a blank grid or expand to keep the colors*

You will find Live Paint settings in the Control panel for Gap Options. Refer to Figure 8-70.

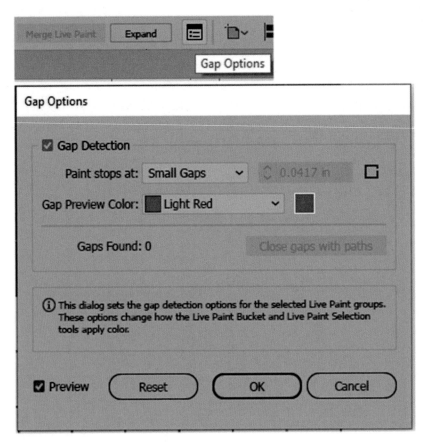

Figure 8-70. *Control panel icon for Live Paint Gap Options and the dialog box*

For individual tool options, you can access these when you double-click each tool in the Toolbars panel. Currently for the Live Paint Bucket Options dialog box, the option for painting strokes is disabled but select strokes is enabled as part of the Live Paint Bucket Selection Options. For the tools the options, Paint Fills or Select Fills is enabled. For the Paint Bucket, you can see the Cursor Swatch Preview. The Highlight color that is part of the selection is light red, and the width is 4 pt. Refer to Figure 8-71.

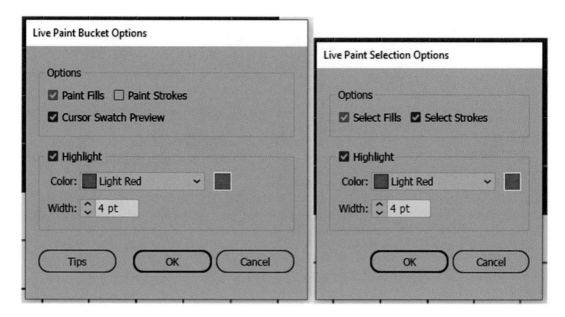

Figure 8-71. *Dialog boxes for Live Paint Bucket Options and Live Paint Selection Options*

Note   The Tips button in the Live Paint Bucket Options dialog box will give you several tips on how to use the tool more efficiently and if you want to merge or add existing paths to a live paint group for your own project. Refer to Figure 8-72.

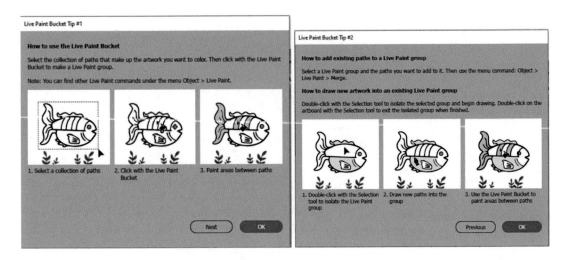

Figure 8-72. *Access various Live Paint Bucket Tips via the Tips button in the dialog box*

You can see how this could work with a Polar Grid that was already turning into a Live Paint object. Object ➤ Live Paint ➤ Make. You could then add an additional line with the Line Segment tool over the top of it and Shift+Click. Select both with the Selection tool and choose Object➤Live Paint ➤ Merge and then continue to color in the gaps. Refer to Figure 8-73.

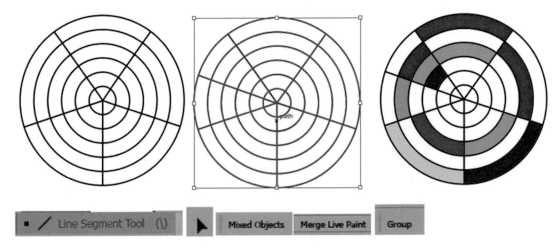

Figure 8-73. *Use the Line Segment tool and the Selection tool to merge the line with the current mixed objects and make them part of the group*

Refer file to Livepaint.ai for reference.

Color Guide Panel

One other main color option that you can use for coloring and recoloring is the Color Guide panel. You will find these settings similar to what we reviewed in Adobe Color, but the options are specifically for Illustrator with swatches. When a grouped shape is selected with multiple colors, this area can be selected in two ways. You could even use the Object ➤ Live Paint ➤ Expand to create a grouped shape or use the live paint group as is. While I will not be going into any major detail on this topic, let me give a general overview. If you have a shape or group shape selected, you can follow along.

The first way is to use the Color Guide panel itself; from the left of the harmony rules drop-down menu, you can observe the base color which can be set by clicking it. It will be different for your own project depending on what colors it contains and the last color that was selected. Refer to Figure 8-74.

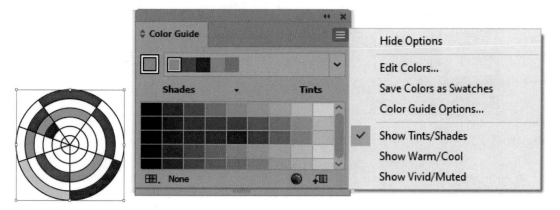

Figure 8-74. *Create a grouped shape with multiple colors to use with your Color Guide panel and menu options*

In the menu, the base color is highlighted in a white outline. Upon expanding the menu, you will discover multiple Harmony rules options, many of which we discussed in Chapter 2 when we worked in Adobe Color. Refer to Figure 8-75.

Figure 8-75. *Color Guide Harmony Rules options which are many*

If individual objects or paths are selected, you can also use this area to edit that color by clicking alternate swatches either in the Harmony Rules area or in the Tints and Shades. Note that the Tints/Shades area can be reset to other swatch combinations from the panel's main menu, such as warm/cool and vivid/muted. I leave this area on Tints/ Shades by default. Color variation options in this area can be further adjusted using the Color Guide Options, but I leave the default setting of 4 steps or transitions and the variation at 100%. Click Cancel to exit. Refer to Figure 8-76.

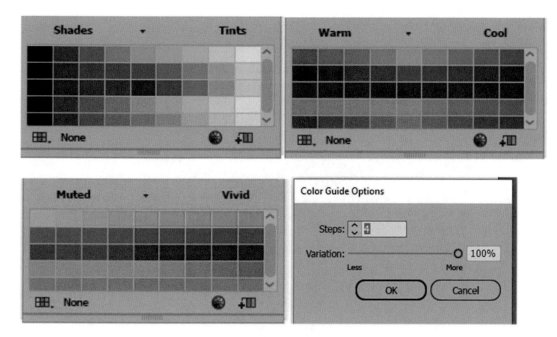

Figure 8-76. *Use the Color Guide menu to set various color settings and options*

The lower buttons on the Color Guide panel allow you to access various libraries to refine your color settings. Currently, it is set to the default of none.

You can then use the next set of buttons on the right. Note that if you do not want to enter the advanced settings yet and just save your current color swatches, then just click the Save color group to Swatch panel button, and it will then appear in the Swatches panel in the color group folder. This does not apply those colors to the shape but merely saves them for use later. Refer to Figure 8-77.

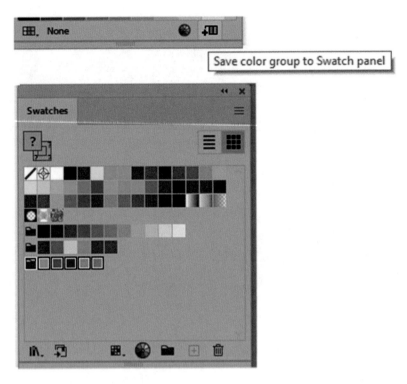

Figure 8-77. *Use the Color Guide panel to save your various colors collections as a color group in the Swatches panel*

Now, if you want to begin entering and altering colors on the selected grouped paths, click the Color Guide Edit or Apply Colors which will also appear in the Swatches panel when the color group is selected. Refer to Figure 8-78.

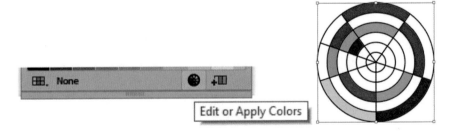

Figure 8-78. *Use the Color Guide panel to edit or apply colors when a grouped shape or path is selected*

You will now have access to the advanced settings of the Recolor Artwork dialog box while the object is selected.

Note   If an item is not selected, you will not have access to all the options and only able to edit colors, and the dialog box will be called Edit Colors instead of Recolor Artwork.

First, we will look at an overview of the Edit tab. Click it if it is not selected. Refer to Figure 8-79.

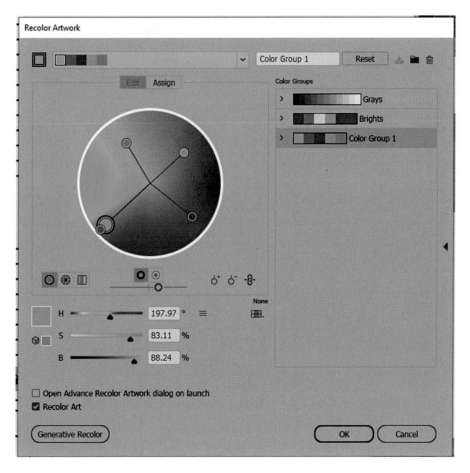

Figure 8-79. *Color Guide's Recolor Artwork dialog box*

The Edit tab allows you to edit your current base color and active colors based on that selection by moving the color swatches around on the color wheel. You can make quick color adjustments using the above harmony rules or move the swatches on the wheel. While the grouped object is selected, this affects the colors in the graphic as you make changes as long as the Recolor Art check box is enabled by default. The option Open Advance Recolor Artwork on launch is disabled by default. Refer to Figure 8-80.

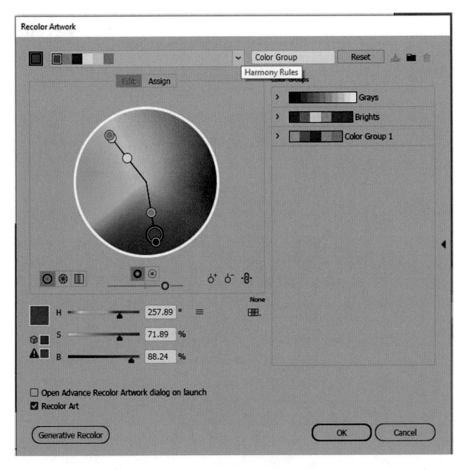

Figure 8-80. *Adjusting color using the Recolor Artwork dialog box*

The area in the Edit tab below the wheel allows you to view color in different settings such as display smooth color wheel, display segmented color wheel, and display color bars. Each has slightly different settings. Refer to Figure 8-81.

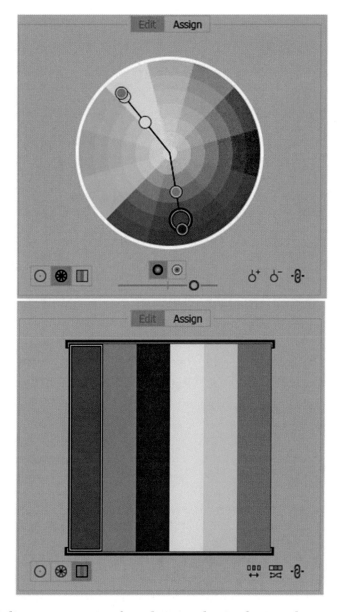

Figure 8-81. *Adjust your setting for editing color in the Recolor Artwork dialog box using segmented color or color bars*

The smooth color wheel allows you to show brightness and hue on the wheel, then adjust the slider for brightness or show saturation and hue on the wheel, and then adjust the saturation. Refer to Figure 8-82.

379

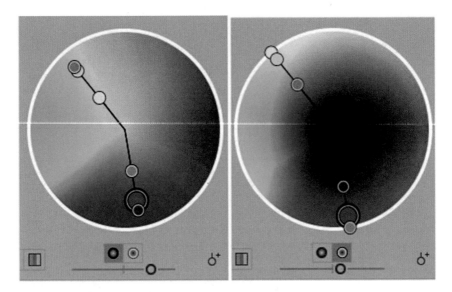

Figure 8-82. *Adjust your setting for editing color in the Recolor Artwork dialog box using icons and sliders below the smooth color wheel*

You can then add a color tool swatch by using the icon and clicking the wheel. Remove a color tool swatch by using that icon and clicking one of the swatches, or unlink the harmony colors when you want to create a custom harmony as you did with Adobe Color. Refer to Figure 8-83.

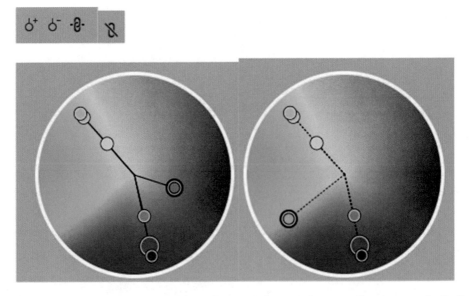

Figure 8-83. *Adjust your setting for editing color in the Recolor Artwork dialog box by adding or removing color tool swatches and link or unlink the swatches*

Color swatches can be dragged or double-clicked on to enter the color picker to edit a color further. Click Cancel to exit the Color Picker dialog box for now. Refer to Figure 8-84.

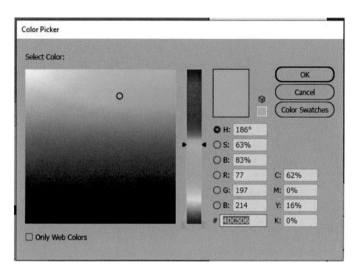

Figure 8-84. *Edit a swatches color using the color picker*

Similar settings are available for the segmented color wheel. Refer to Figure 8-81.

The color bars option on the right allows for settings to randomly change color order, randomly change saturation and brightness, or link/unlink harmony colors. Refer to Figure 8-85.

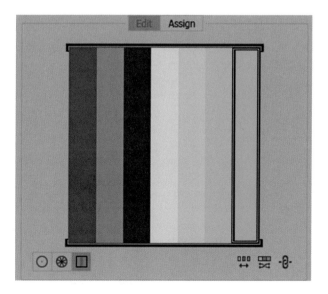

Figure 8-85. *Adjust the color bar order in the Recolor Artwork dialog box*

The bars can be dragged to a new order, or you can adjust the color of one bar by clicking the lower edge to reveal a color picker option within that hue range. Refer to Figure 8-86.

Figure 8-86. *Access the color picker for the color bars in the Recolor Artwork dialog box*

Regardless of what viewing mode you choose, the lower area allows you to use the color modes, in this case, the HSB (hue, saturation, brightness) slider to further adjust the color. Make sure that it does not go out of the gamut (triangle icon with exclamation point) or you have an exact web color (cube icon). You can correct this by clicking the two warnings. Refer to Figure 8-87 and Figure 8-88.

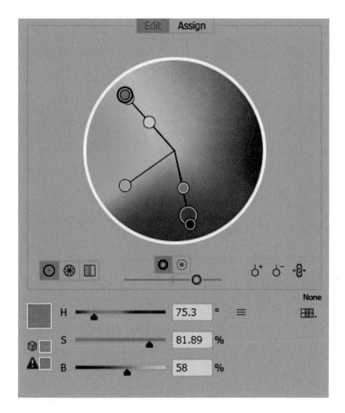

Figure 8-87. *Some color tool swatches may become not web safe or go out of gamut using the HSB sliders*

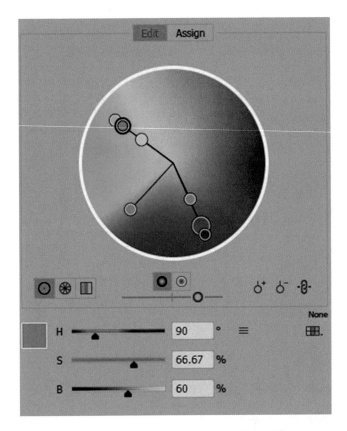

Figure 8-88. *Green color swatch corrected after clicking the warning icons in the Recolor Artwork dialog box*

As you adjust these sliders, if the harmony colors are linked, it may affect the other swatches as well causing them to rotate to a new location with the other colors.

The three dashes open up the menu options if you prefer to work with other color modes and slider options such as RGB, CMYK, Web RGB, Tint (depending on the selection type), and Lab. Global Adjust can be used to correct overall saturation, brightness, temperature, and luminosity (-100, 0, 100%). Refer to Figure 8-89.

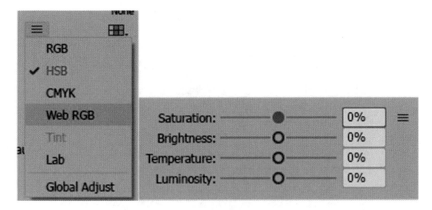

Figure 8-89. *Other color options settings found in the Recolor Artwork dialog box*

When looking at the Color Guide panel, you can limit colors to those available to specific swatch sets in a swatches library. The default is set to none. Refer to Figure 8-90.

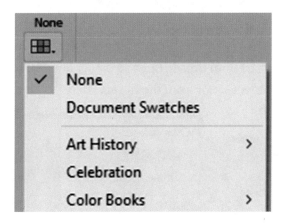

Figure 8-90. *Find other color libraries to limit swatch options in the Recolor Artwork dialog box*

The Assign Tab allows you to assign colors to the current colors of the original artwork. Refer to Figure 8-91.

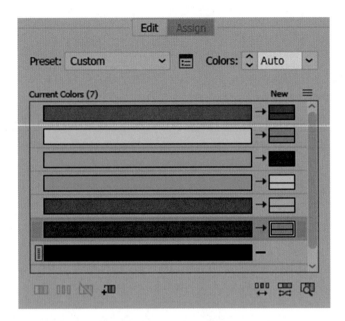

Figure 8-91. *Recolor Artwork dialog box Assign Tab Options*

Currently, it is set to a custom preset, but you can choose other presets from the list. That will allow you to access a color from the library. Refer to Figure 8-92.

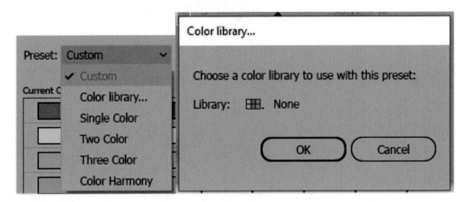

Figure 8-92. *Recolor Artwork dialog box Assign Tab Options choosing a preset or a color library*

Additional color reduction options can be found when clicking the color reductions icon. Refer to Figure 8-93.

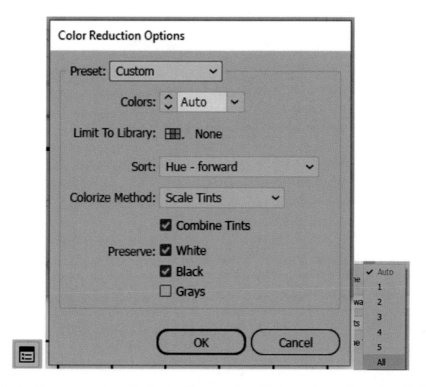

Figure 8-93. *Recolor Artwork dialog box Assign Tab Options choosing Color Reductions Options from the icon and dialog box*

Besides the preset currently set to custom, the colors are currently set to auto which can range from 1 to 5 or all. Next is limit to library, which you looked at earlier that can limit the swatches as well; by default, it is set to none. Refer to Figure 8-93.

You can also sort your current active colors by none, hue-forward, hue-backward, lightness-dark to light, and lightness-light to dark. By default, it is set to hue-forward. Refer to Figure 8-94.

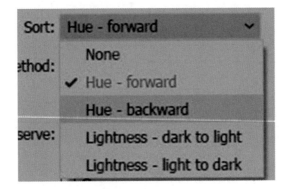

Figure 8-94. *Color Reductions dialog box Sort options*

Colorize method allows you to set exact, preserve tints, scale tints, tints and shades, and hue shift. Refer to Figure 8-95.

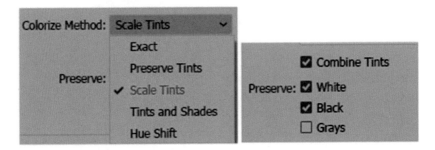

Figure 8-95. *Color Reductions dialog box Colorize Method and Preserve options*

You have the option to combine tints and preserve (white, black, and grays) in your color substitutions. Click OK or Cancel to exit this dialog box. Refer to Figures 8-93 and 4-95.

Outside the dialog box, you can review the current colors on the left and the new ones on the right. Colors with an arrow will convert to the new colors, and those with a dash, such as black, will not convert. Clicking an arrow will prevent conversion and make it a dash or click again to reveal the arrow. Refer to Figure 8-96.

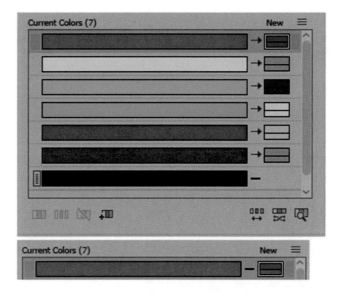

Figure 8-96. *Recolor Artwork Assign Tab setting whether the current color in the row will be colored (arrow) or not (line)*

A few additional tips for this area to remember are as follows:

Current colors can be dragged up and down in the list to be combined with another new color so that both current colors are applied to the new color. Refer to Figure 8-97.

Figure 8-97. *Recolor Artwork Assign Tab, moving current colors to a new row and color*

If you drag on the left end of the colors bar, you can move all colors in the row to another row. Refer to Figure 8-98.

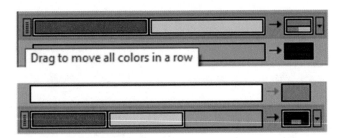

Figure 8-98. *Recolor Artwork Assign Tab, moving all colors to another row*

Or drag a single selected color out of the row and put it back or assign to a new color. Refer to Figure 8-99.

Figure 8-99. *Recolor Artwork Assign Tab, dragging a color back to an original row*

Likewise, you can drag the new swatch up and down as well or double-click to enter the color picker. Refer to Figure 8-100.

Figure 8-100. *Recolor Artwork Assign Tab, reordering the new colors to another row*

The arrow list on the far right side of each new color lets you specify the colorize settings for that color: exact, preserve tints, scale tints, tints and shades, and hue shift. The last two options are only available when Preserve Spot Colors is disabled. In this case, I left the setting of Apply To All colors in the rows enabled. Refer to Figure 8-101.

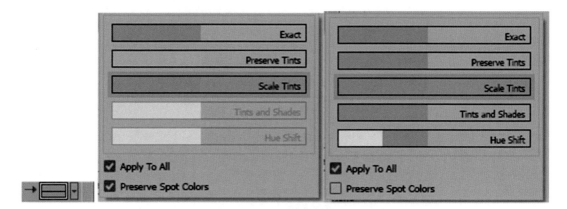

Figure 8-101. *Recolor Artwork Assign Tab, specify colorization method*

Beside the "new" word is a menu for the sort options you saw earlier for sorting the new colors from your active colors in the harmonies. Refer to Figure 8-102.

Figure 8-102. *Recolor Artwork Assign Tab, sort the new colors*

The other settings at the bottom of the Assign Tab allow you, on the lower left, to merge colors into a row, separate colors into different rows, exclude selected colors so they will not be recolored, or create a new row. All the options in this example are available when two colors are selected. Refer to Figure 8-103.

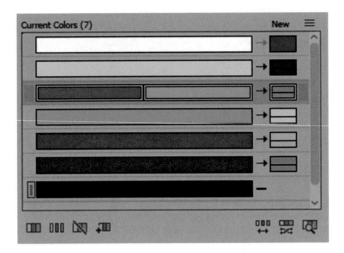

Figure 8-103. *Recolor Artwork Assign Tab, add a new color row*

If, while creating colors, you come up with an extra row you do not require, you can click the colors tab and auto reset. Refer to Figure 8-91. Or to add a new color, click the blank area to the right and click Yes to the message. Then use the color picker to edit the new color. Refer to Figure 8-104.

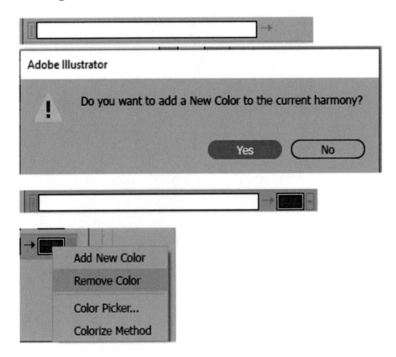

Figure 8-104. *Recolor Artwork Assign Tab, add a new color to the current harmony and alert message and result of clicking Yes*

You can also right-click a new color to add or remove it. Refer to Figure 8-104.

Other color sort settings allow you to randomly change color order, randomly change saturation and brightness, and click colors in the bars to find them in the artwork. Refer to Figure 8-105.

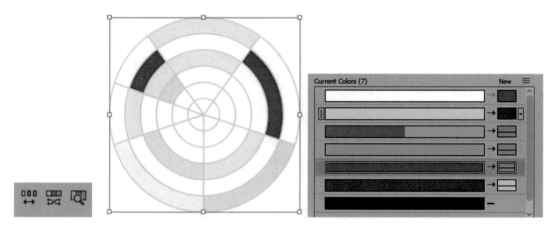

Figure 8-105. *Recolor Artwork Assign Tab, sorting and searching options*

You will notice that the colors in your artwork change as you make adjustments in this dialog box. Refer to Figure 8-106.

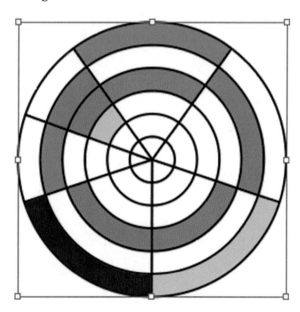

Figure 8-106. *The color in the artwork will change as you apply and edit colors in the Recolor Artwork dialog box*

If you like the color changes you make, as you go along, make sure to save your color swatches that you like frequently. It would be best to work on a copy of your graphic so you don't have to recolor the original again.

You will notice that color groups found in the Swatches panel are stored on the right of the dialog box. Look for the arrow on the right to expand or collapse this area. Refer to Figure 8-107.

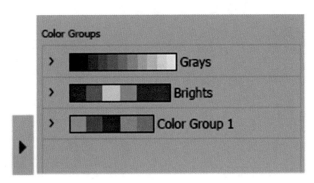

Figure 8-107. *Recolor Artwork dialog box for current color groups*

As you create a group in the upper area, name the group you created, and click the folder to save the group. Refer to Figure 8-108.

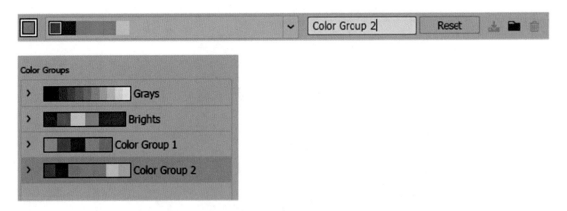

Figure 8-108. *Recolor Artwork dialog box for current color groups adding a new color group*

These color groups can be expanded to see all of the CMYK swatches and settings. Refer to Figure 8-109.

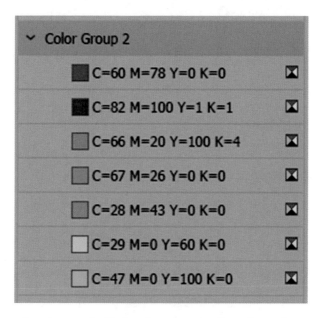

Figure 8-109. *Recolor Artwork dialog box, reviewing the colors within the group*

Other settings are the reset which allows you to restore back to the default colors in the artwork. Refer to Figure 8-110.

Figure 8-110. *Recolor Artwork dialog box, resetting colors in the current group*

If you make changes to a selected color in a group with the HSB sliders, the name will turn italic; you can choose to save your changes to a color group and update the group. Refer to Figure 8-111.

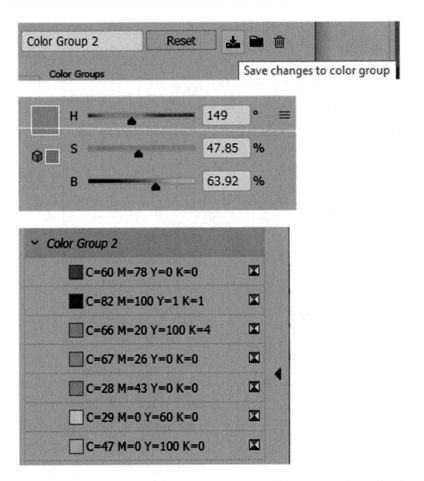

Figure 8-111. *Recolor Artwork dialog box, saving changes to the edited color group*

You can delete a selected color group by clicking the trash can icon or right-clicking the color group or swatch and choose Remove Color Group or remove color. Note that you cannot undo this step, so you may want to save a backup of the swatches group while in the recolor artwork box and give that group another name. Refer to Figure 8-112.

Figure 8-112. *Recolor Artwork dialog box, removing a color group and not a select color*

While active, click the folder icon and then double-click the name of the new swatch to rename the group. Refer to Figure 8-113.

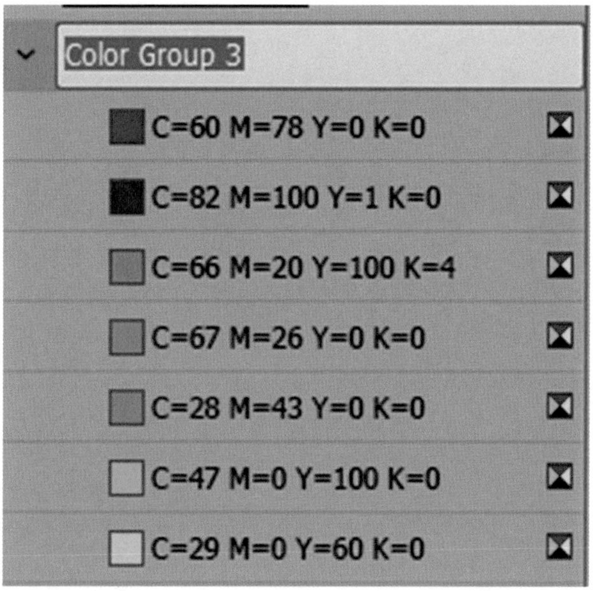

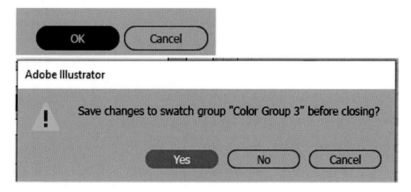

Figure 8-113. *Recolor Artwork dialog box, editing a color group*

Once you have completed working with your swatches, click the OK button to exit so the color groups are officially saved. And click Yes to the message if you have not saved your recent changes to a new group. Refer to Figure 8-114.

Figure 8-114. *Recolor Artwork dialog box. Click OK and then Yes so that the color group is saved*

They now appear in the Swatches panel with the rest of the swatches. Refer to Figure 8-115.

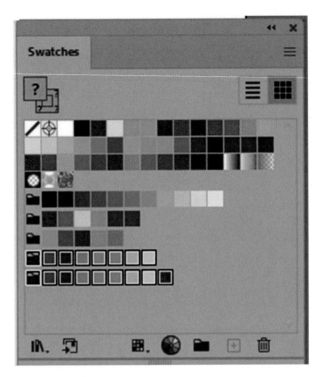

Figure 8-115. *Save colors groups that are created in the Recolor Artwork dialog box are now added to the Swatches panel*

Note   I did not click one button in the Recolor Artwork dialog box, which was the Generative Recolor which we will look at shortly. If I had done that, I may have lost my saved settings in the Recolor Artwork dialog box before I clicked OK to confirm. Refer to Figure 8-116.

Figure 8-116. *Recolor Artwork now has a new button access to Generative Recolor Beta*

Refer to the color_guide.ai file for reference.

Recolor

The second method of recoloring is more simplified, and you may prefer it for quick color changes. This is known as Recolor. I can access the pop-up panel while my artwork is selected using the Control panel and clicking the color wheel icon. Refer to Figure 8-117.

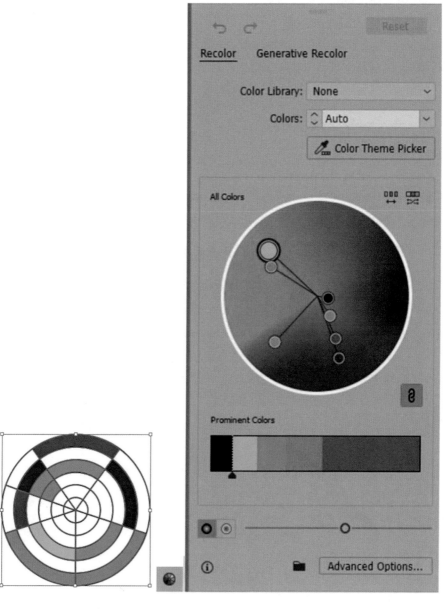

Figure 8-117. *Control panel, Recolor panel to edit colors quickly on the artboard*

Recolor does not worry about color harmonies though you do have access to the color libraries and can set a range of selected colors. Or limit your colors.

Use the color theme picker button when you want to select other colors out of another artwork.

Currently, all colors are active, and like you saw in the Recolor Artwork dialog box and Adobe Color, you can move the swatch sliders around or link or unlink harmony colors using the link icon. This will allow you to move the sliders more freely. There are also options to change the color order randomly or change saturation and brightness randomly. Refer to Figure 8-118.

Figure 8-118. *Recolor panel, change color order or saturation randomly*

You can also adjust your prominent colors by holding and sliding the edge of a color patch to increase/decrease weight of a color in your art though on some artwork, this change may not be noticeable. Refer to Figure 8-119.

Figure 8-119. *Recolor panel, adjust your prominent colors*

The lower buttons allow you to show brightness and hue, or saturation and hue, on the color wheel, and you can use the slider to adjust based on the setting of either brightness or saturation. Refer to Figure 8-120.

Figure 8-120. *Recolor panel, use the icons and the slider to adjust the color on the color wheel*

After making changes, unlike the Recolor Artwork dialog box, here you can use the upper undo, redo, and reset buttons along with the command Edit➤Undo (Ctrl/ CMD+Z). Refer to Figure 8-121.

Figure 8-121. *Recolor panel, use the undo and redo buttons or reset the panel*

Use the folder to save all colors or all prominent colors to the Swatches Panel when you check the option you want from the list. Refer to Figure 8-122.

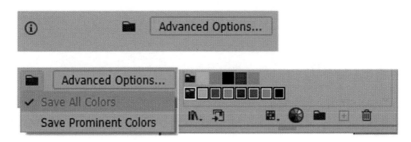

Figure 8-122. *Recolor panel, Save All or Save Prominent Colors to the Swatches panel, click Advanced Options if you want to continue to the Recolor Artwork dialog box*

Note   The Advanced Options button will return you to the Recolor Artwork dialog box and Assign Tab which we already looked at. Refer to that section for review. Refer to this page if you need more details:

`https://helpx.adobe.com/illustrator/using/recolor-artwork.html`

If you need a collection of harmony swatches, refer to the Scientific Library via the Swatches panel. Refer to Figure 8-123.

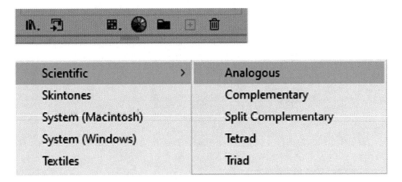

Figure 8-123. *Use the Swatches panel library icon to access more color harmony-related swatches*

Generative Recolor

This is a new feature that has been added to the Recolor area and is recently out of beta development, but you may want to explore it if you are colorizing variations of your artwork. It works based on selection of sample prompts and variations, and currently, it is only available in English, and you need to agree to the user guidelines to use it. Refer to Figure 8-124.

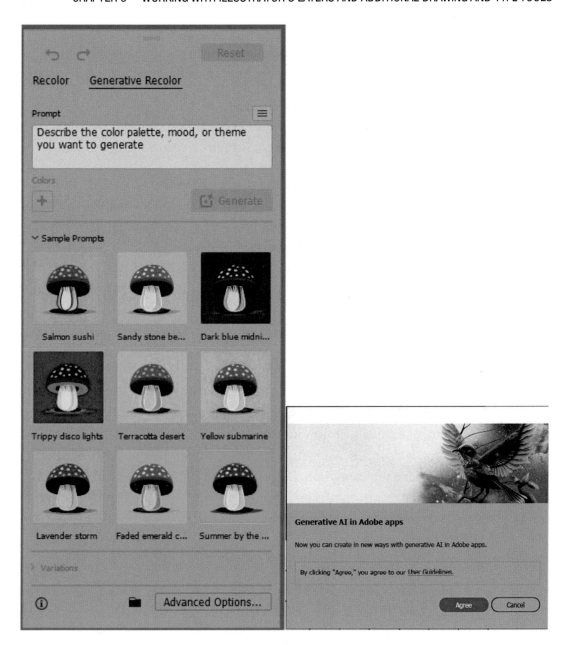

Figure 8-124. *Control panel access to Generative Recolor*

Keep in mind that you must agree to the terms of user guidelines; however, I present it here should you want to test it and create variations of artwork. The is a new way to look at art through using generative AI in future Adobe applications. More details can be found on the following links:

www.adobe.com/legal/licenses-terms/adobe-gen-ai-user-guidelines.html
www.adobe.com/products/illustrator/generative-recolor.html

Note   Swatches can also be added to the Libraries panel and then later checked again in Adobe Color for color blindness or contrast issues as was mentioned in Chapter 2. We will look at the Libraries panel more in Volume 3.

Adding Text with the Type Tool

While the topic of this book is not specifically on type, often your infographic or logo will include some type elements. Text or instruction is always required here and there surrounding any infographic. In other situations, a column or areas of text from a related article or advertisement may be surrounding the infographic. Type can either be set vertically or horizontally using the following Type tools, along with the Control panel and related panels (Character, Paragraph, OpenType, Glyphs) in which similar options can be accessed from the Control panel and Properties panel. Refer to Figure 8-125 and Figure 8-126.

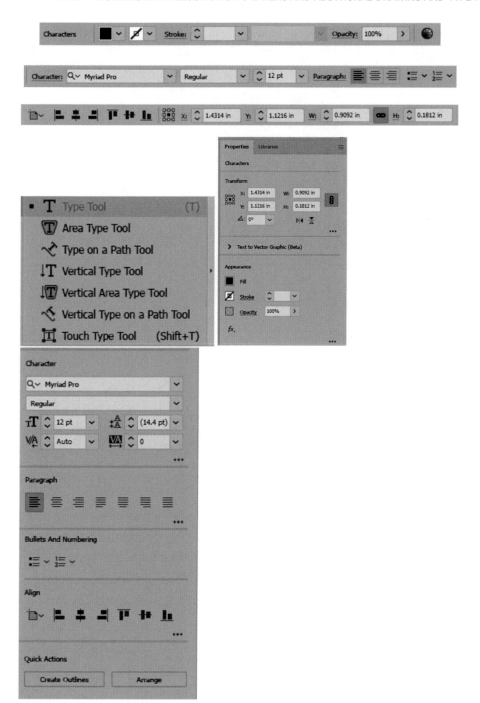

Figure 8-125. *Use the Control Panel and the Type tools with the Properties panel when you want to edit text quickly*

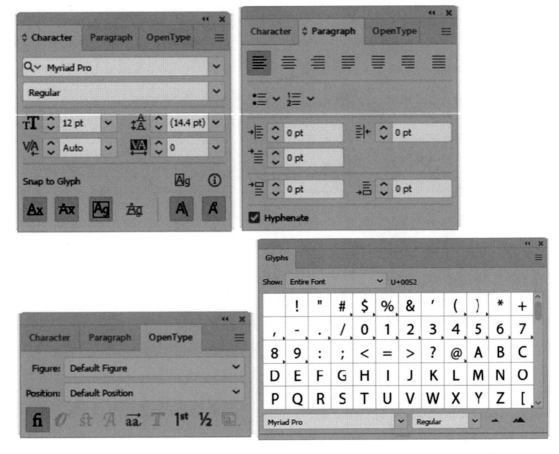

Figure 8-126. *Other related panels for working with Type tools include Character, Paragraph, OpenType, and Glyphs*

I will not be going into any detail on this topic in this chapter other than to give an overview of what these tools and panels are for in relation to the Control and Properties panel. You can find more details on the following pages about Illustrator typography as well as included information on the panels of tabs, character styles, and paragraph styles:

https://helpx.adobe.com/illustrator/using/add-text-work-with-type-objects.html

https://helpx.adobe.com/illustrator/using/tabs.html

https://helpx.adobe.com/illustrator/using/character-paragraph-styles.html

Type Tool and Vertical Type Tool

The Type tool is used to create a type at a select point that you click on the artboard. To add type, select the tool and click anywhere on the artboard, and a highlighted line of type will appear in a supplemental placeholder text. While the text is highlighted, you can then begin to type. Later you can select the text with the Selection tool and scale, rotate, or move the text into a new location. The text will stretch when scaled. Refer to Figure 8-127.

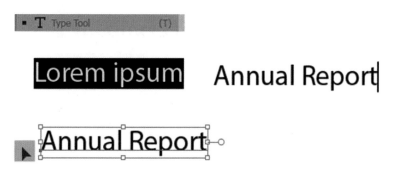

Figure 8-127. *Use the Type tool to type new text when the placeholder text is highlighted and use your Selection tool to move the text to a new location*

If you want the text to fill a very specific rectangular area and don't want the text to stretch when scaled, then with the same tool, drag out a rectangle, and this will create an area of placeholder text. And then begin to type the new text. With the Selection tool, you can then use the bounding box handles to adjust the sides of the text box as well as rotate or move the box to a new location. Refer to Figure 8-128.

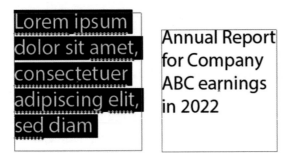

Figure 8-128. *Use the Type tool to create a text area and then use the selection tool to adjust the size of the text area*

Note that the small circle on the right of the text box indicates that this is a text box and not type on a path or a point type. You can double-click this bounding box handle when you need to convert from one kind to another or use Type ➤ Convert to Point Type or Type ➤ Convert to Area Type. The square on the bottom can be double-clicked when you need to collapse the oversized type area. The hollow square on the right indicates the box can still hold text. However, if there is a red plus in it, you will need to either

- Enlarge the area to fill the text with your Selection tool

- Lower the font size using the Type tool and Control panel

- Make another text area when you click the red plus and then click a new location for the text to flow into another text area. This would be known as a text thread which is invisible when printed. Refer to Figure 8-129.

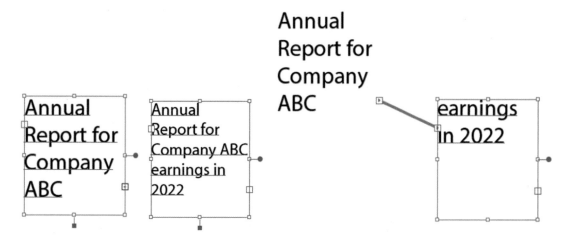

Figure 8-129. *Text area is too small and needs to be expanded; the font made smaller or link to another text area so that the text can flow*

For more details on text threads, see the following page:

https://helpx.adobe.com/illustrator/using/manage-text-area.html

The Vertical Type tool acts in a similar way as the Type tool; however, you can use it to have type move in a vertical path, either from a point when you click the artboard or if you drag out a type area. Note that in the type area, the text moves down and then right to left, so this vertical area type would not be used often for the English characters. Refer to Figure 8-130.

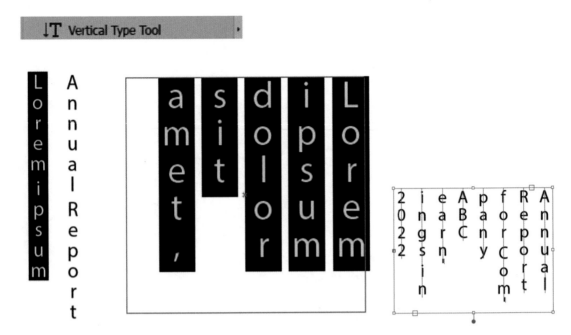

Figure 8-130. *Use the Vertical Type tool to create type on a point or a type area*

For a Quick vertical to horizontal change, you can use Type ➤ Type Orientation and choose horizontal or vertical from the list.

Area Type tool and Vertical Area Type Tool

The Area Type tool is used to type inside rectangular and non-rectangular areas of shapes. You can do this for any basic shape. Refer to Figure 8-131.

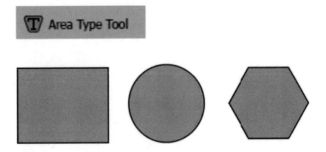

Figure 8-131. *Use the Area Type tool when you want to fill text in rectangular and no rectangular shapes*

With the tool, simply click the stroke or path of a shape that is noncompound and with no mask applied. The shape will then lose its stroke and fill and then fill with placeholder text flowing left to right horizontally. While the text is highlighted, you can begin to type new text. Refer to Figure 8-132.

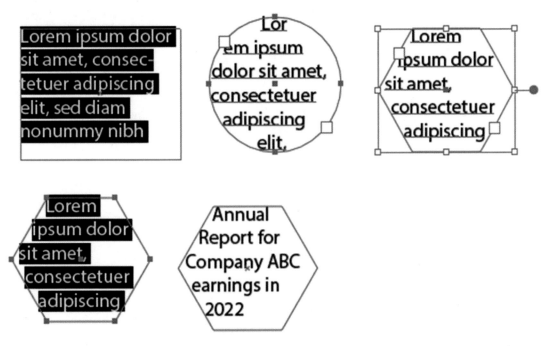

Figure 8-132. *Example of highlighted text in various shapes and while the text is highlighted typing in new text*

Text from these boxes can be threaded to another text box as well.

Use the Selection tool when you want to move, rotate, or scale the area type boxes.

You can, however, use the Direct Selection tool to select the path's stroke and then alter the stroke and fill again using the Swatches panel to select color. Refer to Figure 8-133.

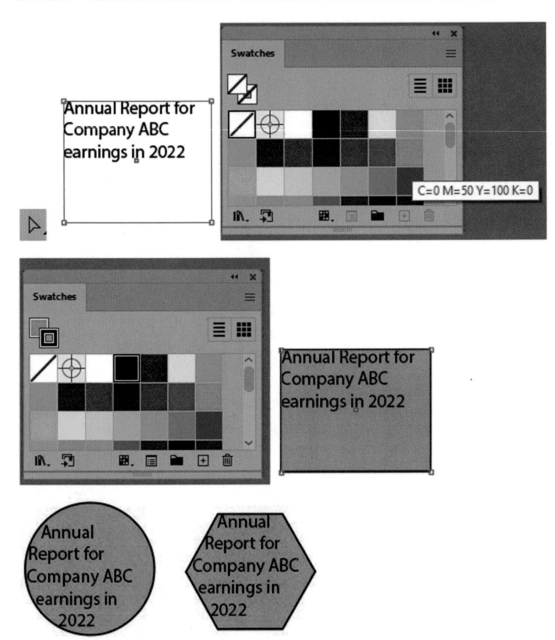

Figure 8-133. *Use the Direct Selection tool to select an area type that you want to alter the fill or stroke using the Swatches panel*

If you need to set additional settings for margins, offset, and alignment for rows and columns, use Type ➤ Area Type Options dialog box to change such things as setting of width, height, number, rows and columns (number, span, and gutter), offset (inset spacing (positive and negative numbers), first baseline, and min), alignment for horizontal and vertical, options for text flow, and auto size for rectangle areas. This dialog box is also available for the Vertical Type Area tool. Refer to Figure 8-134.

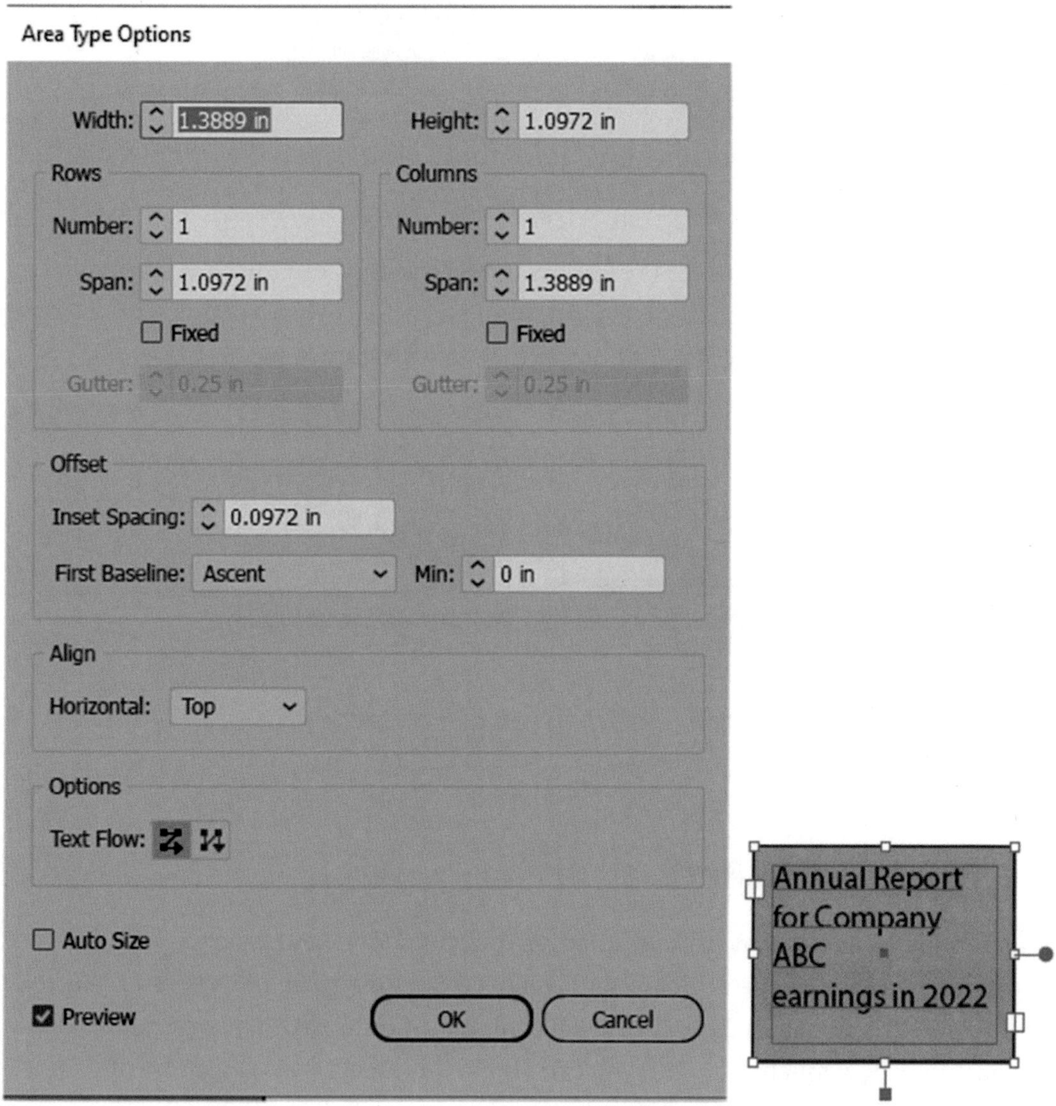

Figure 8-134. *Area Type Options dialog box can be used to adjust the type spacing within an area if its spacing is too close to the stroke*

Some areas, however, may need additional text alignments done using the Control panel and text alignment options as we will see shortly. Refer to Figure 8-135.

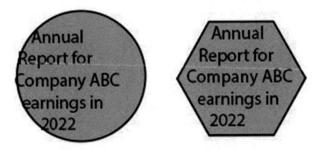

Figure 8-135. *Some shapes may need additional paragraph alignment using the Control panel rather than just the Area Type Options*

The same settings are true for the Vertical Area Type tool, but this time, the type flows in a vertical way though the text, as mentioned earlier, when working with the type tool, may not be best for English-speaking text. Refer to Figure 8-136.

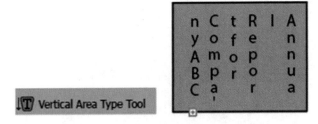

Figure 8-136. *Use the Vertical Area Type tool when you need the type to be aligned vertically in your area, and then you can color the fill and stroke of the area afterward*

Adding Placeholder Text

In some situations, you may want to add more placeholder text to a rectangle or custom shape that is already on the artboard that you have expanded, such as a column. You can use the Area Type tool and then Type ➤ Fill with placeholder text. This will guide you so that you know how much more text you can add to this area. Later with your Type tool, you can highlight this text and type your new information. Refer to Figure 8-137.

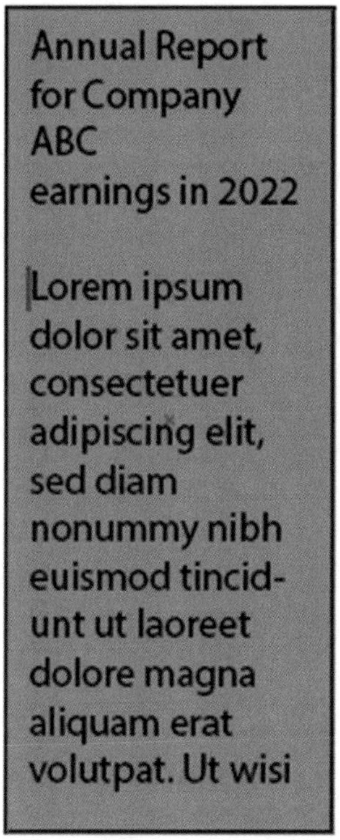

Annual Report for Company ABC earnings in 2022

Lorem ipsum dolor sit amet, consectetuer adipiscing elit, sed diam nonummy nibh euismod tincidunt ut laoreet dolore magna aliquam erat volutpat. Ut wisi

Figure 8-137. *Add placeholder text to review how much space you have available in your type area for your own text*

Type on a Path Tool and Vertical Type on a Path Tool

These options allow you to type on a closed or open path. Refer to Figure 8-138.

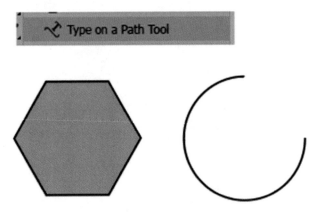

Figure 8-138. *Use the Type on a Path Tool to add type to open and closed paths*

You can use the option by clicking the path of a shape, and it will make the path invisible and add some default placeholder highlighted text. You can type new text to replace it. Refer to Figure 8-139.

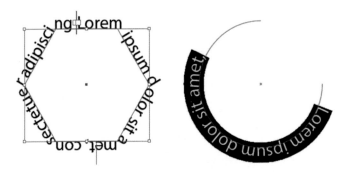

Figure 8-139. *Click the path, and the placeholder text is added to the path*

Using the Selection tool to move the whole path or Direct Selection and the center bracket, you can move the text inside or outside of the shape. Refer to Figure 8-140.

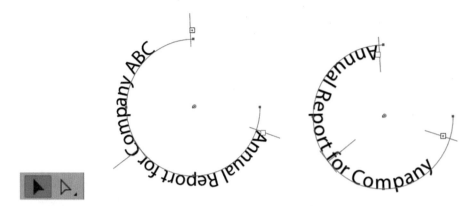

Figure 8-140. *Use the Selection Tool or Direct Selection tool when you need to edit the path or move the text on the path and pull on various brackets (starting, center, ending) to adjust placement*

The starting and ending brackets can also assist if you notice that the text is not fitting, and you need to slide it on the path. When you see the red plus symbol, you can try to expand the path, or if it is still not fitting, you may need to use the Control panel to make the highlighted text smaller. Use the Type on a Path Tool to highlight text. If you find that all the text that is hidden is not highlighted, then while partially highlighted, use Ctrl/CMD+A to select all the text before adjusting the font size using the Control panel. We will look at the control shortly in regard to font size. Refer to Figure 8-141.

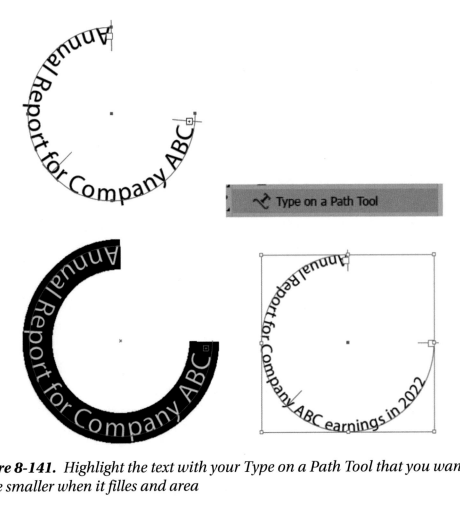

Figure 8-141. *Highlight the text with your Type on a Path Tool that you want to make smaller when it filles and area*

You may need to use your Selection tool to do further adjustments with the center bracket and rotate the path if the text is still not in the right location. However, you can alter the text on the path further under and Type ➤ Type on a Path ➤ Type on a Path Options dialog box for various type effects that stretch, warp the text, adjust path alignment from the default baseline, as well as spacing, and flip the path. The current effect setting that I am using is rainbow. But you may prefer skew, 3D ribbon, stair step, or gravity. Enable Preview to see updated changes. Refer to Figure 8-142.

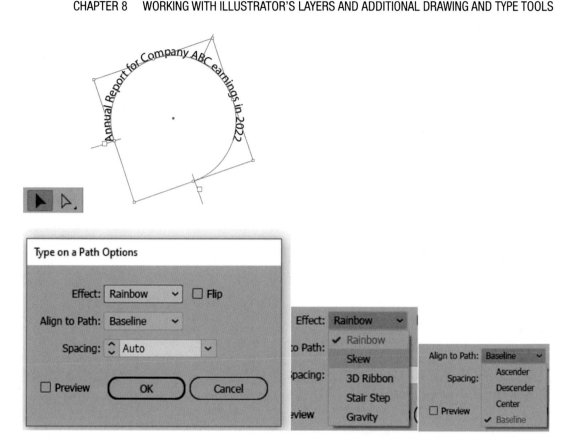

Figure 8-142. *Rotate type and path using Selection tool or use the Type on a Path dialog box*

More details can be found on this page:

https://helpx.adobe.com/illustrator/using/creating-type-path.html

The same settings can be used for the Vertical Type on a Path Tool. But the text will now flow around the edge, half in and out of the path. Due to the new orientation, the text may not fit the path, and you will need to adjust your brackets or font size to accommodate. Refer to the previous link for more details on this. Refer to Figure 8-143.

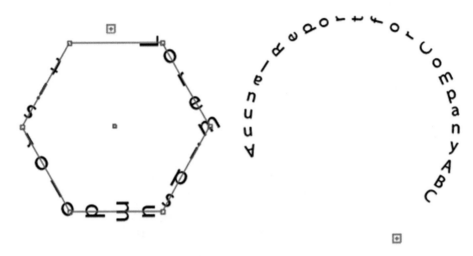

Figure 8-143. *Use the Vertical Type on a Path Tool when you want your text to flow vertically on the path*

Touch Type Tool (Shift +T)

After typing with the Type tool, the Touch Type Tool can be used on individual fonts in a word to cause different alignments and baselines for each letter. Select a letter in a word, and using the bounding box around the selected character, you can move, rotate, enlarge, or scale a separate the letter. Though keep in mind that for not all text or topics would this be a good ideas as your chart heading may start to resemble a ransom note, which does not look very professional. For a less serious topic in a different font surrounded by a related graphic, it might be quite acceptable. Refer to Figure 8-144.

Figure 8-144. *Use the Type tool then the Touch Type tool to edit individual characters on the point or path*

Use Edit ➤ Undo or your History panel if you need to undo some steps. If you would like more details on this tool, refer to the following link:

`https://helpx.adobe.com/illustrator/using/tool-techniques/touch-type-tool.html`

Control Panel, Properties Panel, and Related Panels for Type

The Control panel can now be used to edit selected text in the following ways, and similar options can be selected in the Properties panel if you prefer to use it instead.

Note that the Control panel will change slightly based on whether you have selected text using the Selection tool (Type Options) or used your Type tool (Character Options) to highlight individual characters in the text. To find additional panel options in the Properties panel, click the ellipsis (…). Refer to Figure 8-145.

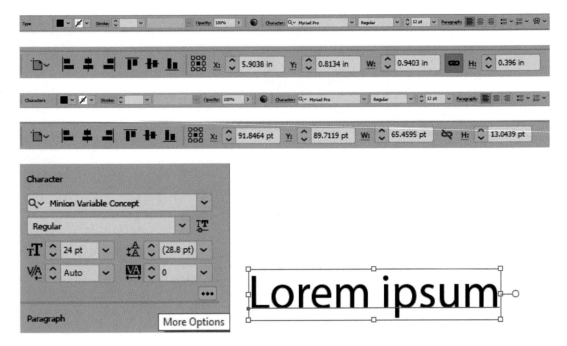

Figure 8-145. *Use the Control panel or Properties panel while text is selected to edit your type and access other panels*

You should be already familiar with most of the settings in the Control panel for alignment; however, this time they are specifically for the type area and aligning a type area with other paths. We will mainly focus on the new settings.

With type, like any shape, you can set its fill and stroke color. Note that by default, a font will be typed without a stroke and only a color fill, which can be altered from the drop-down panel. Refer to Figure 8-146.

Figure 8-146. *Selected text and the Control panel*

If you add a stroke color to a letter or the whole selection, you can then access the Stroke panel to adjust the stroke weight and stroke panel and variable width profile (uniform) for those letters that contain the stroke. Refer to Figure 8-147.

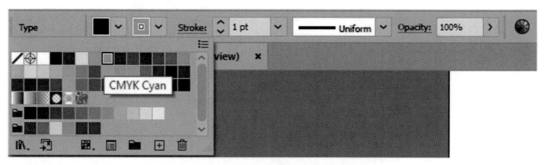

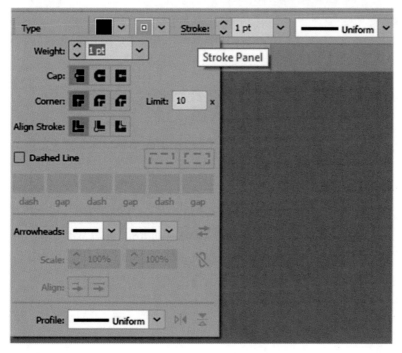

Figure 8-147. *Use the Control panel; change the fill, stroke, and stroke weight of a text; and access the Stroke panel*

From here, you could even make the line around the letter dashed, if required, and lower the weight of the stroke to 0.5pt so that the fill is more visible. Here it is shown with and without the dashed line. Refer to Figure 8-148.

Figure 8-148. *Use the Stroke panel to make text dashed or solid; some stroke colors are more visible when dashed*

Tip   Using a stroke, the same color as the font can make it appear bolder.

From the Control panel, you can also set the overall transparency or opacity (0%–100%) and use the Recolor options we discussed earlier in the chapter. See earlier section "Recolor." Refer to Figure 8-149.

Figure 8-149. *Use the Control panel to add opacity or recolor your text*

Note   When a word is selected, if you notice a question mark (?) in either the fill or stroke, this means that your selection of text has mixed colors. If you want to change this to one color, then from the drop-down panel, choose a new color—it makes all the same. Refer to Figure 8-150.

Figure 8-150. *When fonts have mixed strokes and fills, highlight the font and use the Control panel to set a new fill or stroke*

The next section applies specifically to type. Refer to Figure 8-151.

Figure 8-151. *Use the Control panel to adjust your Character and Paragraph settings*

Selecting the word "Character" will give you more options for sizing, scaling, and rotation which are found as well in the Character panel and its menu. Refer to Figure 8-152.

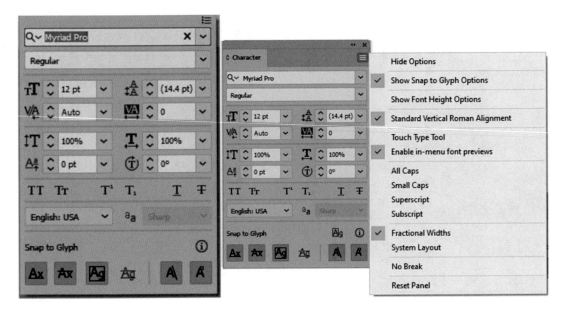

Figure 8-152. *From the Control panel, you can access Character settings as you would from the Character panel and its menu options*

The main settings found in the Control panel that you will use are those to set your font family which allows you to, besides choosing from a large selection, search from; you can then filter for your favorite fonts on your computer or from Adobe fonts (find more). You can also view styles of fonts in various sizes while the selected text is highlighted. Refer to Figure 8-153.

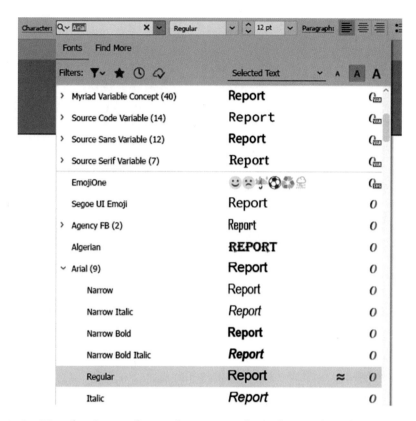

Figure 8-153. *Use the Control panel to set a selected texts font family and style and search for other fonts*

Once you know what font you want, you can then in the next list set your font style (regular, bold, italic, bold italic, or other styles if available). And then choose the font point size which you can either type in a number or select one from the list. Refer to Figure 8-154.

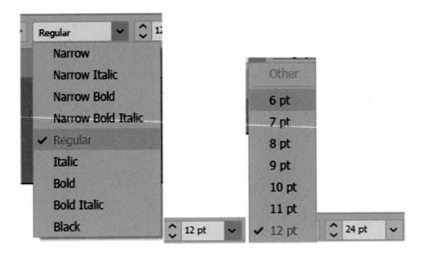

Figure 8-154. *Use the Control panel to set the font style and font size*

Note that if you use a variable font, this will add another setting to your Control panel or Character Panel and will allow for other variable font styling settings such as weight, width, and slant by moving the sliders to adjust. This can vary depending on the variable font chosen as some have optical size or less slider options. Refer to Figure 8-155.

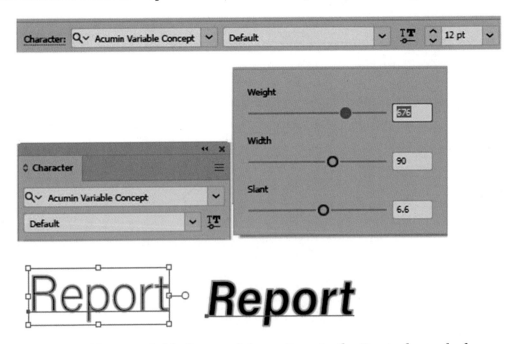

Figure 8-155. *Use a variable font and the options in the Control panel when you want more sizing options*

Tip   Use your Transform panel's shear option when no italic style is available.

For further Character Options, you can also refer to the Window ➤ Type ➤ Open Type panel, which allows for ligature settings and fractions. Refer to Figure 8-156.

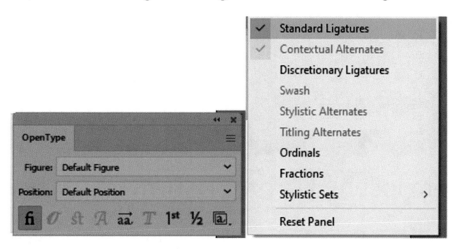

Figure 8-156.   *Use the OpenType panel and menu to access more specialized type options*

For reference, the Character panel and OpenType panel are combined in Photoshop and are not two separate panels as they are in Illustrator.

Note   When you are looking for a specific or special font, use the Glyphs panel and double-click the letter or icon that you want to insert at the insertion point in your text to add the new character. Or highlight the letter with your Type tool you want to change and double-click the Glyphs panel to insert a new letter in that location. Refer to Figure 8-157.

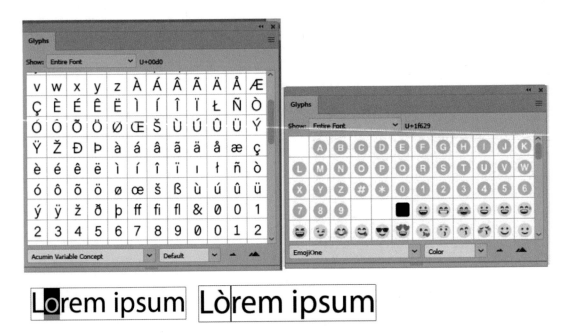

Figure 8-157. *Use the Glyphs panel and your Type tool to select special fonts you want to add*

For more details on individual Character settings, refer to these pages:

https://helpx.adobe.com/illustrator/using/fonts.html

https://helpx.adobe.com/illustrator/using/formatting-type.html

https://helpx.adobe.com/illustrator/using/line-character-spacing.html

https://helpx.adobe.com/illustrator/using/add-advanced-formatting-to-text.html

https://helpx.adobe.com/illustrator/using/special-characters.html

Within that section of the Control or Properties panel is the paragraph, and more options can be found when you click the word Paragraph or the Paragraph panel as you require them for more specific alignment of text, and how changing from left to center may improve the layout of the text within a custom shape. Refer to Figure 8-158.

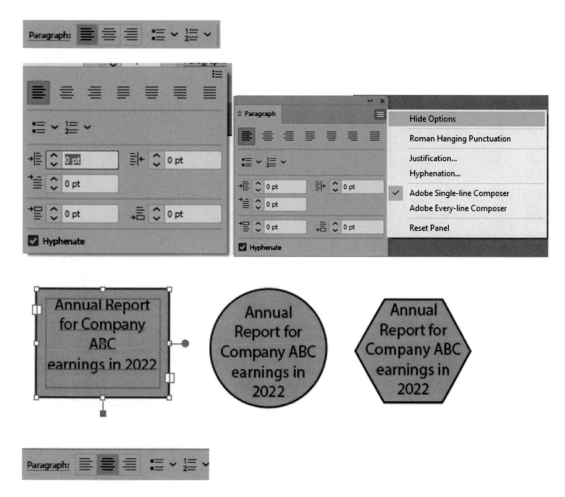

Figure 8-158. *Use the Control panel to set your Paragraph settings or the Paragraph panel to align text from left or right to center*

Keep in mind that this area may appear differently if you are using vertical text. In this case, we are focused on the horizontal text. In the Control panel, you can use the main types of alignment, such as left, center, and right. You can also choose options for bullet shapes and number list bullets. By default, they are set to none, but you can set another option using the drop-down list and access further options under the ellipsis icon (…). Refer to Figure 8-159.

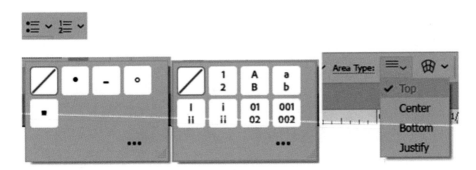

Figure 8-159. *Use the Control panel to add bullets or numbered lists to your text and Area Type Options*

You may also have access to the Area Type Options and related alignment options (top, center, bottom, justify).

For more details on the Paragraph panel and Bullet options, you can refer to the following links:

https://helpx.adobe.com/illustrator/using/bullets-numbering.html

https://helpx.adobe.com/illustrator/using/formatting-paragraphs.html

---

Tip   After working with your Character, Paragraph, OpenType, and Glyphs panels, while no type is selected, make sure to use the panel's menu to reset so that it goes back to its default settings for your next project. Refer to Figure 8-160.

Figure 8-160. *The reset menu on Character, Paragraph, OpenType, and Glyph panels to reset the font back to its base settings*

The next section of the panel allows you to warp a selected type with Warp Options or create your own custom mesh (Make with Mesh). We will not be going into any detail on this topic, but if you're interested, you can refer to the following dialog box; as well I have written a book on this topic for Illustrator, which is mentioned in the introduction for those that are interested in these warping options. Refer to Figure 8-161.

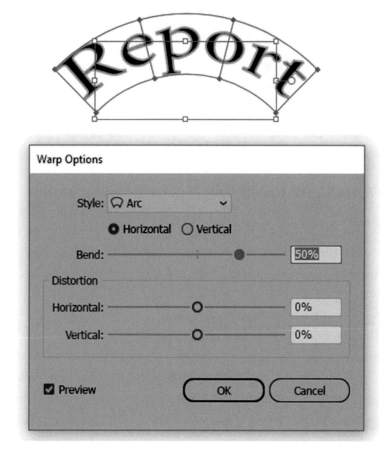

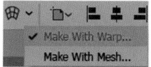

Figure 8-161. *From the Control panel, use Warp Options dialog box when you want to alter the style of some text*

Refer to the following dialog box when your text is selected, and click the warped icon in the Control panel and experiment with various settings and sliders.

The last section of the Control panel, as mentioned earlier, is useful when working with the Selection tool and type if you need to align or distribute your multiple selections of text or individual text to the reference point, x and y coordinate values, or adjust width (W) and height (H) and constrain proportions with the link icon. Refer to Figure 8-162.

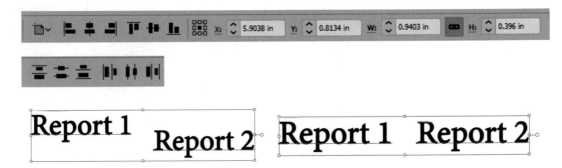

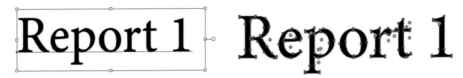

Figure 8-162. *Use the Control panel to align, distribute, and move selected text*

Remember that text, while selected with the Selection tool, can be moved, scaled, and rotated. Shift+Click to select multiple selections of text. Alt/Option+Drag text to create a copy. And while an area of text is selected, you can use the Backspace/Delete key to remove it.

Convert to Type Outlines

Note that for some graphics that you may be sending to a client, if they don't have the font or you do not want to share the font with your client, you can make a copy of the file and choose when the type's bounding box is selected with the Selection tool. Choose Type ➤ Create Outlines (Shift+Ctrl/CMD+O). This turns the font into a vector image, and it can no longer be edited by the Type tool. Refer to Figure 8-163.

Figure 8-163. *Convert text to outlines so it can be no longer edited by the Type tool*

Refer to Type_examples.ai files for reference.

Retype (Beta)

However, a new tool, called Retype (Beta), has been added to Illustrator that may be useful in situations when you need to figure out the type of font that was used for the text. You can select the outlined type and then use the panel by choosing the Enter Retype button to help identify what the original font family was from possible recommended Adobe and non-Adobe fonts. Then activate the font from the cloud if you don't already have it on your computer, and exit the Retype (Beta) panel, and type or apply the identified font to some new text. Refer to Figure 8-164.

Figure 8-164. *Retype (Beta) panel*

Note   Because this panel is in beta, it is subject to change, and recently a new filter option has been added as well as additional features that you can add via the Download icon located at the bottom left near the center of the panel. It has a blue dot before you download the new features. Newer features will allow you to convert static text to live text and other editing capabilities. This would be similar to optical character recognition that is found in Adobe Acrobat Pro and would save some retyping. The Retype panel can also be accessed via your Properties panel in the Quick Actions section. Retype does not recognize all fonts, and it appears to work better with larger text outlines that have not been distorted due to scaling. However, if you want Retype to improve, then share your feedback on this topic at the bottom of the panel. You can learn more about this feature from the following link:

`https://helpx.adobe.com/illustrator/using/retype.html`

Brush Tools That Can Assist in Creating Infographics

Brushes and the Brushes panel are all helpful tools that can be used to add detail or edit a shape or path further. There are three tools that you can use to add painterly-like details along with its related panel. They are the Paintbrush tool (B), Blob Brush tool (Shift+B), and Eraser tool (Shift+E). Note that though not part of the discussion in this book, that the Scissors tool (C) and Knife tool can also be used to cut parts of shapes as well. Refer to Figure 8-165.

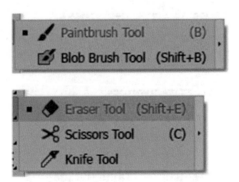

Figure 8-165. *Paintbrush, Blob Brush, and Eraser tools can be used to add or edit a path*

Paintbrush Tool (B) and Brushes Panel

This tool is used for adding painterly effects to strokes, along with your Brushes panel in the five main brush types, and can also be used with the Stroke panel and your Control panel for making a thicker or thinner path. Refer to Figure 8-166.

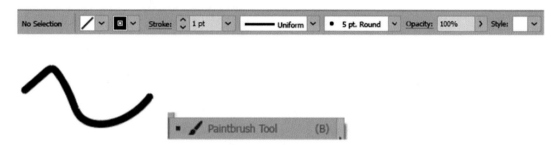

Figure 8-166. *Use the Control panel and the Paintbrush Tool to paint thicker strokes*

To access paintbrush options, double-click the Paintbrush tool in the Toolbars panel, and you can set settings such as fidelity (accurate to smooth); by default, it is set in the center. Options include Fill new brush strokes, Keep Selected, and Edit Selected Paths when you are within a set number of pixels (2–20); by default, it is set to 12. Refer to Figure 8-167.

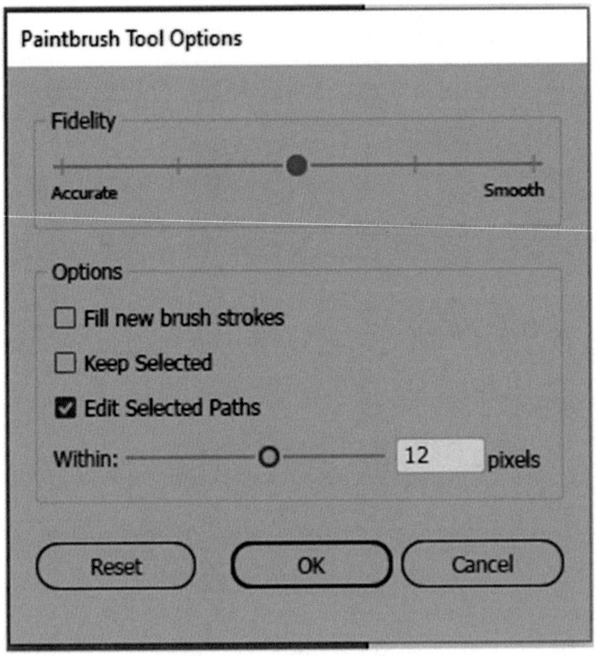

Figure 8-167. *Paintbrush Tool Options dialog box*

To increase and decrease brush size outside the dialog box, use your left bracket ([) to decrease and right bracket (]) to increase. This will also adjust the path that you are painting if still selected. Note that this does not increase the actual stroke weight setting, only the brush definition size, but it is not saved. However, afterward, selecting the stroke and lowering the stroke weight can decrease the appearance of the brush definition. You can also change your variable width profile from the Control panel; the default is uniform. Refer to Figure 8-168.

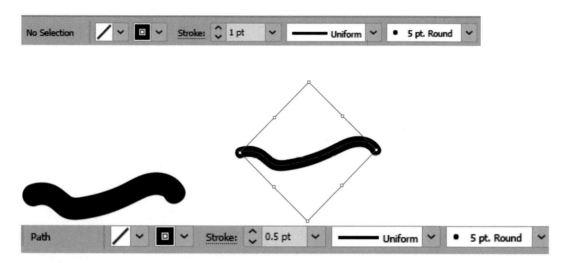

Figure 8-168. *Use the Control panel to alter the stroke weight of the selected path*

The Brushes panel, as mentioned earlier, can be used to set other types of brushes to paint with.

While we will not be going into a lot of detail, the five main brush types that you can use are

- Calligraphic: Which are typically used for thin and thick lines. The basic brush is the default.

- Scatter: For scattering shapes added to the brush.

- Art: Which appears like a charcoal pencil used to make parts of a graphic appear as if they were hand drawn.

- Bristle: Which appears like someone used a paintbrush, and these can often have opacity effects.

- Pattern: Which adds a pattern to the stroke that was created by Adobe or the user. Refer to Figure 8-169.

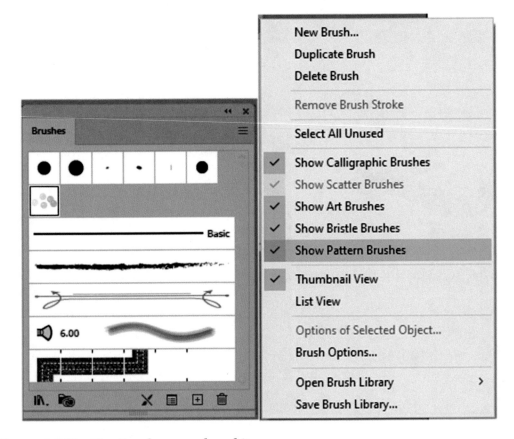

Figure 8-169. *The Brushes panel and its menu*

You can change a path's color and brush definition and opacity (0%–100%) while the path is selected using the Control panel. Refer to Figure 8-170.

Figure 8-170. *Use the Control panel to change the strokes color and brush definition*

You can access more brushes from the panel's library or create your own. For more information on brushes, visit the following page as each type of brush has its own unique creation dialog box and settings:

```
https://helpx.adobe.com/illustrator/using/brushes.html
```

Blob Brush (Shift+B)

This tool does not actually paint a path but more of a shape like a blob though the stroke color is set while the tool is in use. Refer to Figure 8-171.

Figure 8-171. *Use the Blob Brush tool with the Control panel as you would a brush*

This tool is very useful when you have to paint large areas and create a shapeless area or paint in a color to fill an area. Blob Brush tool options can be found when you double-click the tool in the Toolbars panel. Refer to Figure 8-172.

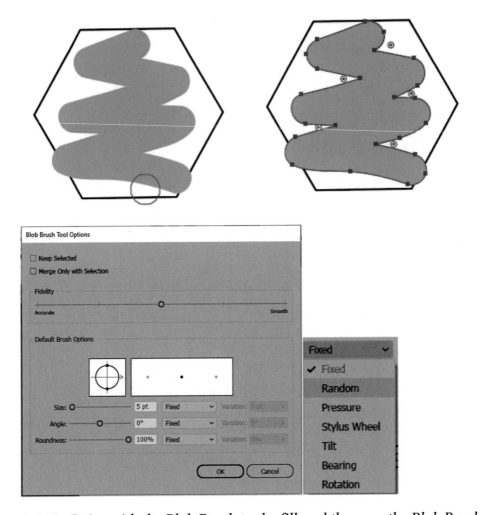

Figure 8-172. *Paint with the Blob Brush tool a fill and then use the Blob Brush Tool Options dialog box and stylus settings*

Settings such as Keep Selected and Merge Only with Selection can be set with check boxes. However, if you already have painted an area with the Blob Brush tool, as long as it is selected and you continue to paint with the same color swatch, the blob will increase; otherwise, it will be a separate blob. If you need to add to a blob area, make sure to select that part of the blob again before you begin to paint, or you might create a new blob. A new blob will be created if you start with a new color.

The Blob Brush Tool Options dialog box also lets you set the fidelity from accurate to smooth and adjust the default brush options, such as size (1–1296) points, angle (-180, 0, 180) degrees, and roundness (0%–100%). The preview image will show what this looks like though you can use the brush shape editor image on the left to adjust the angle and roundness. If you are using a stylus, you can adjust this setting from the default of fixed to another setting such as random, pressure, stylus wheel, tilt, bearing, or rotation. I left it at fixed as I used the mouse. But other settings like random will allow for variation settings (0–180) degrees for angle. You can also set a variation for size and roundness.

Outside the dialog box, when you want to set the brush size, use your left bracket ([) to decrease and right bracket (]) to increase.

The Blob Brush tool can also paint with opacity settings, but you need to set this in your Control panel first before you begin to paint. Refer to Figure 8-173.

Figure 8-173. *Use the Blob Brush tool to paint with opacity*

Eraser Tool (Shift+E)

This tool is great when you need to erase selected areas that you created with the blob brush. If you do not select a path, you may erase parts of your artwork that you did not intend to. Refer to Figure 8-174.

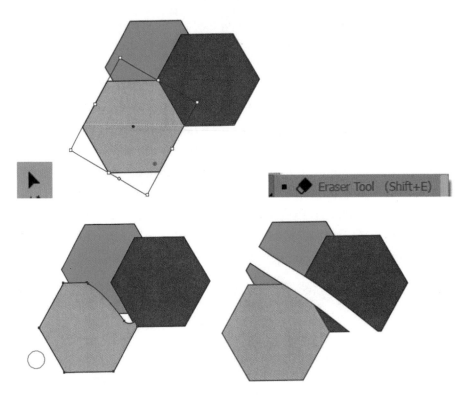

Figure 8-174. *Use the Eraser tool to erase a selected path or through multiple unselected paths*

When you double-click the tool in the Toolbars panel, you can access its various options in the dialog box: the brush shape editor and preview, angle (-180, 0, 180) degrees, roundness (0%–100%), size (0–1296) points, and the reset button. Like the Blob Brush tool, these options can also be set from the default of fixed to another setting with a variation (0–180) degrees for angle if you are using a stylus. You can also set a variation for size and roundness. Refer to Figure 8-175.

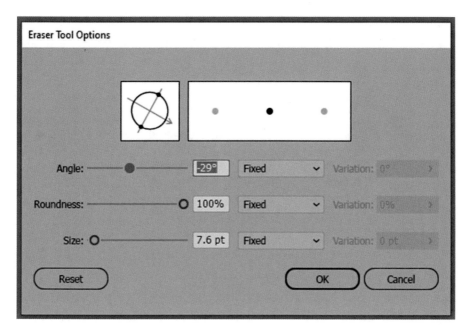

Figure 8-175. *Eraser Tool Options dialog box*

Outside the dialog box, when you want to set the brush size, use your left bracket ([) to decrease and right bracket (]) to increase.

Blend Tool (W)

The Blend tool is a way to take one shape or path and blend a transition into another. This can result in a transition shape that can be later extracted and used for building part of a logo or infographic. Refer to Figure 8-176.

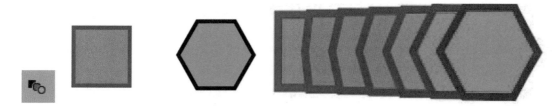

Figure 8-176. *Blend tool and a blend created between two shapes*

The Blend tool works best with basic geometric shapes with solid colors when you want a transition shape, but it can also be used with more complex group shapes in situations where a color or size change is required. Refer to Figure 8-177.

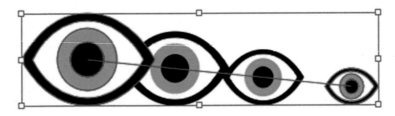

Figure 8-177. *A blend between size and color*

Click one object and then the other to create a blend with a spine. Note that on the second click, if you click a point like the tip of the star rather than the inside of the shape, this will alter the path. The square cursor changes from white to black when on a point. You can use Edit➤Undo (Ctrl/CMD+Z) or your History panel to undo this step. Refer to Figure 8-178.

Figure 8-178. *A blend may appear slightly different if the center of each shape is clicked on or on the second click on the point of a path*

Options for this tool can be found when you double-click the tool in the Toolbars panel or choose Object ➤ Blend➤Blend Options.

Options include smooth color, specified steps in between, or specified distance. Refer to Figure 8-179.

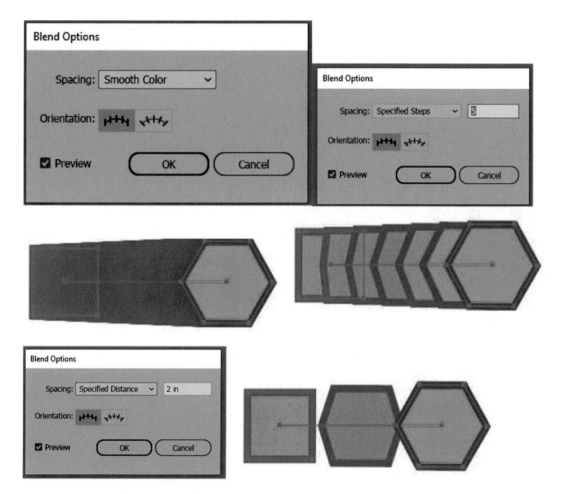

Figure 8-179. *Blend Options in the dialog box and the blend that is produced*

You can then set the orientation to Align to Page or Path. This is more apparent if a point on the path spine has been curved with the Anchor Point tool afterward. Refer to Figure 8-180.

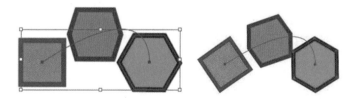

Figure 8-180. *The blend on a curved spine will be different when the Blend Options orientation in the dialog box is changed*

To release shapes from the path, use Object ➤ Blend ➤ Expand. This creates a grouped shape that you can Object ➤ Ungroup and remove the desired paths for further editing using the Selection tool. Refer to Figure 8-181.

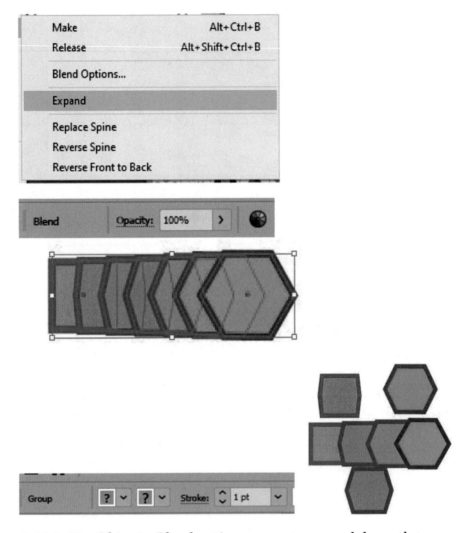

Figure 8-181. *Use Object ➤ Blend settings menu to expand the path to a grouped object and Selection tool to move shapes within the path once it is ungrouped*

This area in the Object ➤ Blend menu also allows you other options to

- Reverse spine or flip.

- Release puts spine back to a path with the original two shapes.

- Replace the spine with another path when you have another path selected with the Selection tool.

- Reverse the blend front to back. Refer to Figure 8-182.

Figure 8-182. *Blend with a reversed path*

You can continue to experiment until you have your ideal shapes or blends. Refer to the blend_examples.ai file for reference.

Object ➤ Intertwine with Lasso Tool

One other new feature for creating logos and parts of infographics, which may be of interest, is the intertwine feature. This setting allows users to overlap parts of a design. It used the Lasso tool which, in the past, was used just to select multiple objects. However, it can select parts of objects to overlap when in intertwine mode. To start, select multiple overlapping shapes using the Selection tool (Shift+Click), and from the menu, choose Object ➤ Intertwine ➤ Make. Refer to Figure 8-183.

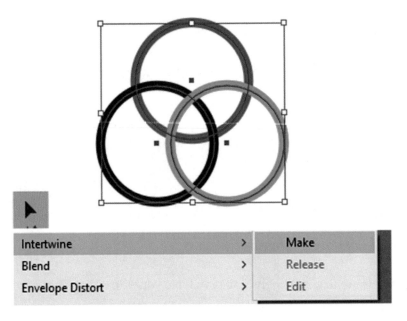

Figure 8-183. *Use the intertwine options to edit paths so that they appear to overlap*

Hover over a crossing area and then click the area that you want to intertwine. You can click this area again if you want to send the overlap back to how it was before. Refer to Figure 8-184.

Figure 8-184. *Intertwine part of a path so that it appears to cross over and then set it back again*

Or you can drag over an area, and the Lasso tool will appear, so you don't have to select it from the Toolbars panel. Then, when you release the mouse after the looping, the area will be overlapped. If you hold down the Shift key, you can make a rectangular selection. Refer to Figure 8-185.

Figure 8-185. *Use the Lasso when you drag in a circle to intertwine; if you draw a straight line, the intertwine is incomplete*

Dragging out a line and not making a loop with the Lasso tool will cause only a partial overlap. Use Edit➤Undo (Ctrl/CMD+Z) or the History panel if this was not your intent.

Right-clicking an area will allow you to choose the order of the intertwine and bring areas to front, bring forward, send backward, or send to back. Refer to Figure 8-186.

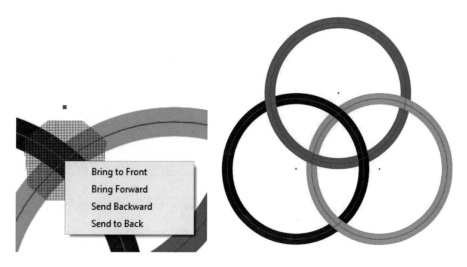

Figure 8-186. *Intertwine selections can be arranged back to front*

You can use Object ➤ Intertwine ➤ Edit if you exit the intertwine mode by mistake by clicking another tool in the Toolbars panel.

This can happen if you click off the shape. Or use Object ➤ Intertwine ➤ Release if you need to make the shape back to paths. You can also enter edit mode or release the intertwine when the item is selected using the Control panel or Properties panel under Quick Actions. Refer to Figure 8-187.

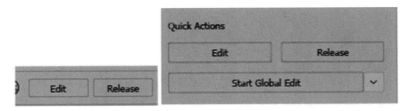

Figure 8-187. *Use the Control panel or Properties panel to edit or release the intertwine*

You will know that your object is intertwined as this name will show up in the Control and Properties panel. As well they are considered an intertwine group in the Layers panel. Refer to Figure 8-188.

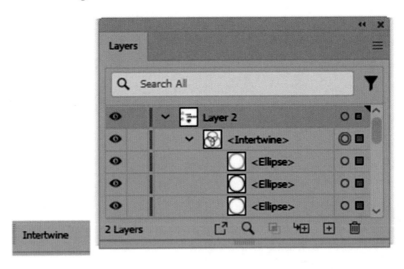

Figure 8-188. *In the Control panel and in the Layers panel, the selected shapes are set as an intertwine*

Adobe states that you cannot use intertwine for the following:

- Intertwine does not work with Object ➤ Live Paint, Object ➤ Repeat, and Object ➤ Graphs.

- Illustrator does not support creating nested intertwines or intertwines from already intertwined objects.

- Intertwine works best with strokes and shapes that have no fills. Otherwise, you may be left with strange overlaps if you apply a fill afterward. Refer to Figure 8-189.

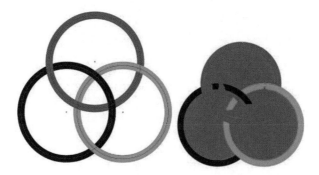

Figure 8-189.   *Intertwine objects are best having only stroke and no fills*

You can learn more about this option on the following page:

https://helpx.adobe.com/illustrator/using/intertwine-objects.html

To make the intertwine permanent, use Object ➤ Expand and click OK to the following setting in the dialog box or click Cancel and undo that step. Refer to Figure 8-190.

Figure 8-190. *Expand dialog box for expanding an intertwine object to a grouped shape*

Refer to file Intertwine.ai for reference.

Applying Appearance

If a path or shape has swatches applied to its stroke or fill, you can continue to add more stroke and fill colors as well as gradients and patterns using the Appearance panel to edit and overlap them. Here are the following things you can add to the Appearance panel. Refer to Figure 8-191.

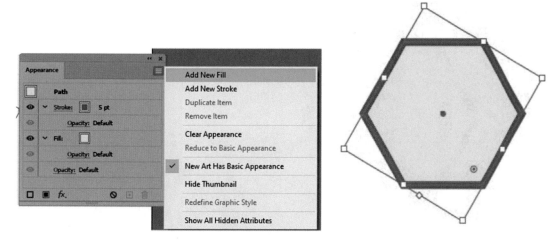

Figure 8-191. *Use the Appearance panel to alter the path's fill and stroke*

Color to Stroke and Fill: This can include solid colors as well as gradients created using the Gradients panel and patterns using the Patterns panel. You can refer to these panels in the section "Additional Ways of Adding Color to an Object's Fill and Stroke," and we will look at patterns in more detail in Volume 2. While the path is selected, click the stroke or fill swatch to alter the color. Click the word Stroke to access the Stroke panel or add a new fill or stroke using the icons on the lower left of the panel. Refer to Figure 8-192.

Figure 8-192. *Use the Appearance panel to set a new stroke and fill or add effects (fx)*

Opacity: This, as well as blending modes, can be adjusted when you click the name and then alter the settings. This can affect the stroke, fill, or over all (0%–100%). Refer to Figure 8-193.

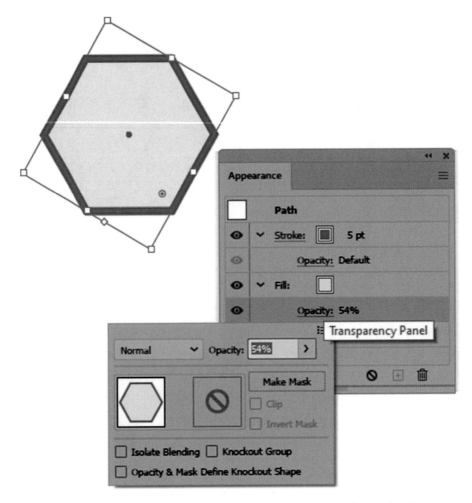

Figure 8-193. *Use the Appearance panel to access setting from the Transparency panel and alter the opacity*

Effects: You can also set various effects (fx) to the appearance such as a drop shadow; we'll look at some effects later in Volume 2, but again they can be applied to a fill, stroke, or overall. You can enter the related dialog box when you click the effect name.

Strokes and fills can be reordered in the Appearance panel by dragging them up or above in the list or down and below.

Once you have completed a style, you can clear the style appearance or duplicate a selected item such as a stroke or fill or delete a selected item using the trash can icon. Refer to Figure 8-194.

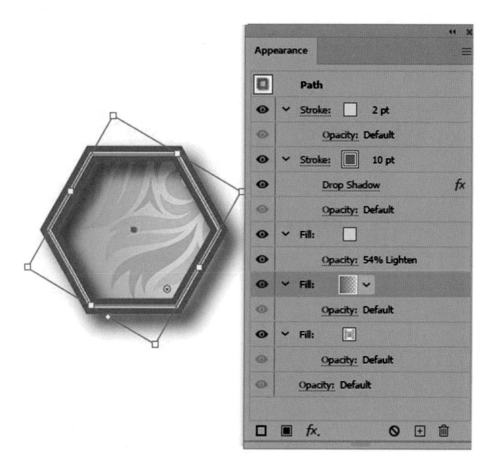

Figure 8-194. *Use the Appearance panel to set multiple fills and strokes*

Once you create your ideal appearance, you can then create a graphic style.

Creating Graphic Styles

The graphic style can be stored in the Graphic Styles panel library and later applied to other shape paths or even type. To add the style to the panel while the path is selected, click the new graphic style icon. Refer to Figure 8-195.

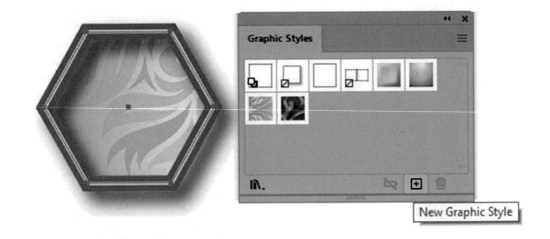

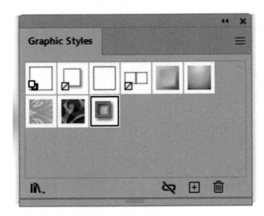

Figure 8-195. *Add an appearance to the Graphic Styles panel*

The graphic style is added, and now you can select another created path or text with your Selection tool and apply that style to it when you click the style again. For some text, the font will have to be very bold in order to apply a style. Refer to Figure 8-196.

Figure 8-196. *Apply a graphic style to paths and text*

With type, keep in mind readability. This may be OK for a larger logo, but not the text within the infographic if there are a lot of smaller fonts. While you can apply a pattern to type as you would a solid swatch, you cannot apply a gradient to type without using a graphic style. Refer to Figure 8-196.

When you need to set the graphic styles back to default for the next selected item or object you plan to draw next, click first style in the upper left corner of the panel. Refer to Figure 8-197.

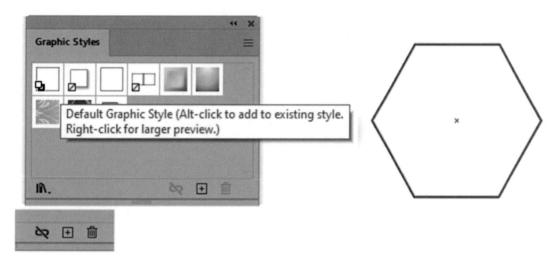

Figure 8-197. *Use the default setting in the Graphic Styles panel to clear, add, and reset the default graphic style*

As in other panels, you can use the library icon to access more graphic styles and use the trash can icon to delete a style. The link icon is used to break the path's appearance link with the library if you plan to create a new style later on. Refer to Figure 8-197

Refer to Graphic_Styles.ai file for reference.

Creating Symbols

Once the graphic is created and you know that you may need it numerous times on your artboard, you can store it in the Symbols folder. Refer to the Symbols_practice.ai file.

For example, if I wanted to use this grouped shape with some text two or more times in my infographic, I would select the shape with my Selection tool and then in the Symbols panel click the New Symbol button. This brings up the New Symbol dialog box. Refer to Figure 8-198.

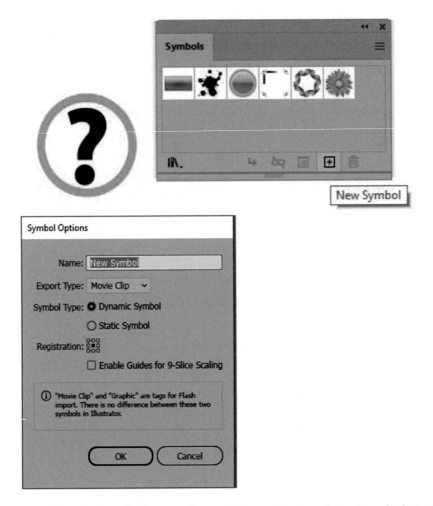

Figure 8-198. *Use the Symbols panel to add a symbol and the Symbol Options dialog box to set the symbol type settings*

While I will not go into all the settings, I will note that here, you can name the symbol. Leave the Export type as Movie Clip or Graphic. It makes no difference, and we are working in Illustrator and not Animate (formerly Flash). You can choose between the options of dynamic or static symbol. Generally, I choose Static, but I will show you what each can do. Keep the registration centered and keep enable guide for 9-slice scaling disabled as that is only for Animate and click OK. And the symbol will appear in the Symbols panel.

Note that a static symbol cannot have its colors altered if dragged onto the artboard from the panel, while a dynamic symbol can have its colors altered only with the Direct Selection tool if you select a stroke or fill, and you will discover that the original symbol in the panel is unaffected. The color change is made by selecting a color in the Swatches panel. The dynamic symbol will appear with a plus icon in the Symbols panel. Refer to Figure 8-199.

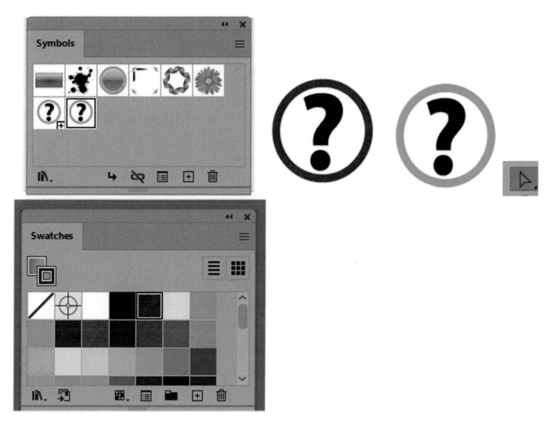

Figure 8-199. *Symbols can be static or dynamic, and you can use the Direct Selection tool and the Swatches panel to alter color*

Warning   Do not use the Recolor option in the Control panel on Symbols as this will affect both the symbol on the artboard and the original in the panel.

On the lower area of the Symbols panel, if you need to place another symbol, use the place symbol instance arrow icon. To break a symbol from the panel, use the broken link icon. Refer to Figure 8-200.

Figure 8-200. *Lower half of the Symbols panel for placing a new symbol on the artboard*

Symbol options can be reviewed for a selected symbol with the list icon. As mentioned, you can use the New Symbol icon to add a new symbol to the panel, or while a symbol is selected in the panel, the plus icon can be used to duplicate it if you drag a symbol onto it. Or delete a selected symbol using the trash can icon. Refer to Figure 8-200.

Note   There are a number of created symbols that can assist you in creating your infographic as well as a starting point, if you need to create an organizational chart or flow chart diagrams, found in the Illuminate Flow Charts and Illuminate Org Chart panels. You can access these and more symbols from the lower left library icon on the Symbols panel, and once the new panel is open, click a new symbol to add them to the Symbols panel. Then drag onto your artboard and break the link to edit. Refer to Figure 8-201.

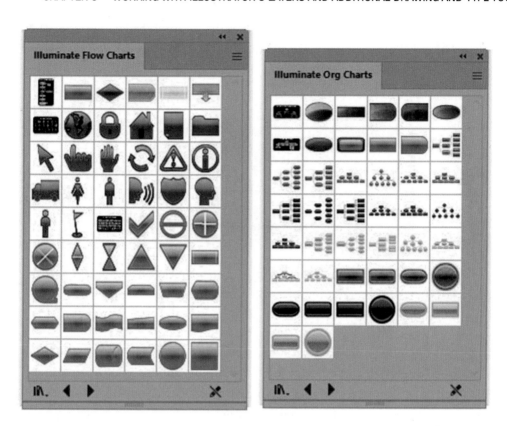

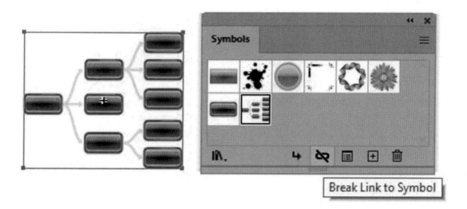

Figure 8-201. *The Symbols panel libraries allow you to add flow diagram and org chart samples to your Symbols panel and then break link to symbol to edit*

Lastly, I will just mention that if you need to edit a symbol, you can double-click it in the Symbols panel to enter the Symbol editing mode. This is indicated in the Layers panel. After you have made any adjustments to your symbol, use the left-pointing arrow icon below the rulers to exit Symbol editing mode. Refer to Figure 8-202.

Figure 8-202. *Use the Symbols panel diagram library to enter Symbol editing mode as seen in the Layers panel, and exit Symbol editing mode using the left-pointing arrow and return to the regular layer mode*

Whether the symbol is static or dynamic, you'll find similar settings in the Control panel. In this case, I left the instance name blank, but from here, you can edit the symbol, break the link, and reset if the symbol on the artboard has been scaled. Replace the symbol on the artboard with another from the symbols or set an overall opacity (0%–100%). Static symbols can only be replaced with other static symbols and dynamic with other dynamic symbols. Refer to Figure 8-203.

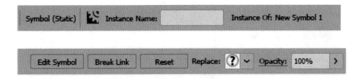

Figure 8-203. *Use the Control panel to edit your symbol further*

Other Control panel options mentioned are for recoloring and alignment when two or more symbols are selected. You can also move your symbol on the (x and y) coordinate values or scaling width (W) and height (H) which can have its width and height proportions constrained with the link icon enabled. These settings are based on the symbol registration point which was set to center earlier and indicated by the cross icon. Refer to Figure 8-204.

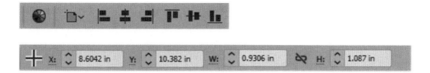

Figure 8-204. *Use the Control panel to align and scale the symbol*

You can learn more about symbols based on the following link:

`https://helpx.adobe.com/illustrator/using/symbols.html`

I will just mention that symbols can be used with the Blend tool for scaling, and you can apply basic appearance effects and graphic styles like drop shadow without altering the original symbol.

Summary

In this chapter, we reviewed the following topics regarding working with layers, adding colors to objects as well as adding type, and creating appearances, graphic styles, and symbols. We also looked at some new color and type options that have recently been added to Illustrator.

In the next chapter, you will be focusing on using the skills you have acquired to create your first infographic projects.

Creating Your First Infographic Projects

Over the last several chapters, you have worked with various tools and panels in Illustrator. You have also looked at how to create objects and paths and add type. In this chapter, you will create and review a few project ideas that can be created with basic shapes, custom shapes, and text. Some of the key steps in those projects I will demonstrate or describe.

Note This chapter contains projects that can be found in the Volume 1 Chapter 9 folder.

In this chapter, we are now going to use the knowledge we gained from the previous chapters in this book to work on your first infographic project as well as look at a second infographic project idea that also focuses on most of the concepts in this book but also add a few more that you may want to explore further in Volume 2.

Project: Creating Your First Infographic

Here I will show you an example of how you can create an infographic resume. In this case, the text has been supplied on the page; on your own, you could add your own symbols or use mine and adapt them as required.

© Jennifer Harder 2023
J. Harder, *Creating Infographics with Adobe Illustrator: Volume 1*,
https://doi.org/10.1007/979-8-8688-0005-4_9

Project Idea 1: Infographic Resume (One Page)

Creating a one-page infographic resume has in recent years become a popular project for graphic designers as a way to show their artistic layout skills. You can do this even if you have never created an infographic before or don't know what topic to research. If you don't have any example of an infographic in your portfolio, why not create an infographic about yourself and what you have accomplished over the years?

To begin, if you already have a text-rich resume, this should give you a starting point for your design.

If not, take a moment to collect some data about yourself. You may not use all of it in the resume, but at least you have some research to begin with.

Topics you may want to cover are

- Your name.

- A short paragraph about yourself which could include some of your highlights and qualifications. It could also be a quote that expresses something about you.

- Your software expertise which could also include Adobe and non-Adobe software.

- Professional employment experience.

- Education and training.

- Hobbies and interests.

- Contact or reference information.

- Languages Spoken: This is optional and could also relate to various software languages (CSS, HTML, JavaScript, or PHP) that you know if required.

Next you need to start your layout. You can refer to my Infographic_resume.ai as I will describe what I did here. However, there are many examples of infographic resumes on the Internet that have varying layouts and later you may find that some of their suggestions may suit your resume better than mine. For now, focus on my layout presented here. Refer to Figure 9-1.

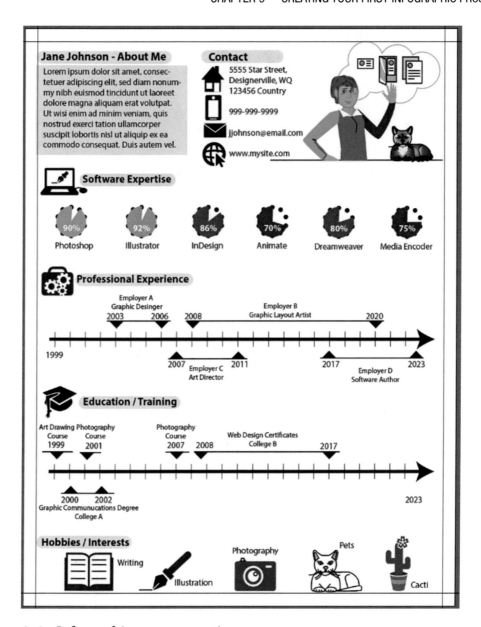

Figure 9-1. *Infographic resume creation*

In my case, I am creating an infographic resume for the fictious client Jane Johnson.

In this case, I create a new Letter-sized Illustrator file which is 8.5 × 11 inches and in a color mode of CMYK as I did in Chapter 4. And I have created a separate guide layer so that I know where my margins are. Refer to Figure 9-2.

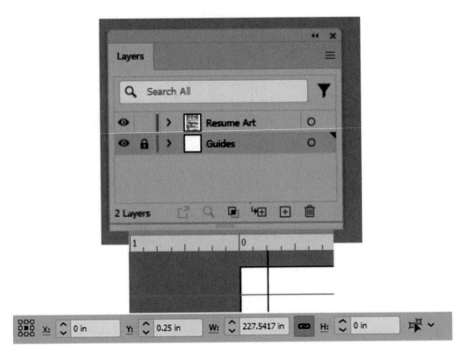

Figure 9-2. *Use the Layers panel and guides to put your guides on a separate locked layer*

In this case, I have the guides placed 0.25 inches surround margin on each side. I dragged these guides out from my ruler and adjusted them using the Control panel and then locked the layer. The guide lines will not print. I used my Control panel to adjust the x and y coordinates of the guides and then locked the layer. Horizontal guides sit at Top X:0 in/Y:0.25 in and the lower at X:0 in/Y:10.75 in. Vertical guides at left X:0.25 in/Y:0 in and the right X:8.25 in/Y:0 in.

Generally, it is assumed for some infographic resumes that they will be made into a PDF file and then just viewed online in the browser or on the desktop of your computer using Acrobat Reader. However, if you are sending the resume to a client that likes to print out copies for their records, I would consider not having a solid color or black background as that will waste a lot of toner. In my case, I just left the background white as white space and the balance of separated items let the eyes rest. The only area I blocked off in a gray area was the About Me section. The 0.25-in margins also ensure that important parts of the design are not cut off like text during printing. Refer to Figure 9-3.

Figure 9-3. *Text area created on the resume and text added edited in the Control panel*

The About Me section and all the artwork are on the top layer "Resume Art." For the text, I just dragged out a rectangular text area with the Type tool over the rectangle background, and it filled with placeholder text. You could then type in a new text with your Type tool when you highlight the text. For consistency, throughout I used one font family in various sizes and the two styles of regular and bold.

Note   Around important headings, I have put a rounded rectangle that is colored and then used the opacity slider to make the text more visible but still add some color behind the type. Refer to Figure 9-4.

Figure 9-4. *Use the Rounded Rectangle tool to add a rectangle behind the text and lower the opacity*

I then used my Pen tool and basic shapes to draw some shapes for my contact area. I then Object ➤ grouped each of them so I could move them as one object on the artboard. With these shapes that I have created, I could then drag them into my Symbols panel and save them for other areas if required on my resume. Refer to Figure 9-5.

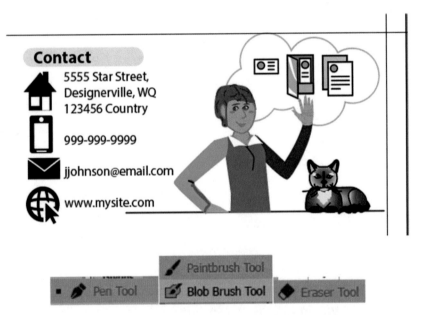

Figure 9-5. *Create icons that you can add to your contact area as well as a logo or illustration of yourself that you create with various brush tools*

As a beginner, if you are having difficulty drawing some more complex shapes for your infographic, you can use the symbols in the various libraries such as web icons or web buttons and bars. Refer to Figure 9-6.

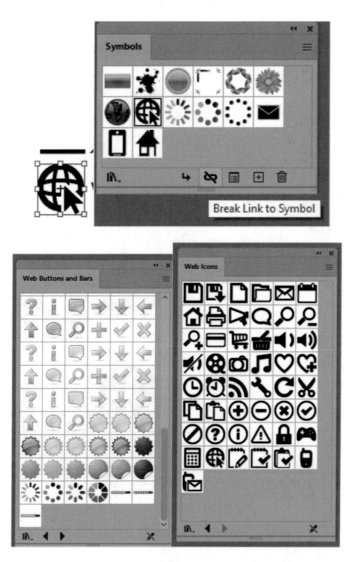

Figure 9-6. *Add the graphics to your Symbols panel from libraries, or break the link and use symbols present in Illustrator's other libraries if you need symbols to practice with*

Once you drag out the symbol onto the artboard, you can then break the link to edit. Refer to Figure 9-6.

Also, other fonts that you can use and then modify for your infographic are Segoe UI Symbol, EmojiOne Color, and Segoe UI Emoji. Use the Type tool and click your artboard, and while the type is highlighted, use your Glyphs panel to add the text and then select it with your Selection tool, then choose Type ➤ Create Outlines. Then you can modify the grouped outline to suit your needs with the use of a combination of the Direct Selection tool and Pathfinder panel and colorize if required using the Control panel. Refer to Figure 9-7.

Figure 9-7. *Use the Glyphs panel to edit fonts that are turned into outlines and then use the Pathfinder tool further to edit and combine your icon shapes and the Direct Selection tool to color some areas using the Control panel*

Note   With color fonts, you may need to first delete all the highlighted placeholder text before you can click to add the emoji to the text path and later create an outline from it. Refer to Figure 9-8.

Lorem ipsum

Figure 9-8. *Delete your placeholder text using the Type tool before you add a color emoji from the Glyphs panel that you plan to outline and edit*

We can see a few examples of created and modified icons throughout this resume; some are placed by the heading to give them more meaning.

In my case, rather than using a photo, I created an illustrated image of Jane Johnson and her cat and then, above her head, placed some of the items she can create for you. I used the Pen tool, Eraser tool, Paintbrush, and Blob Brush tool to create her and the cat.

Likewise, you could put your logo here if you are still working on your drawing skills, or like you traced over the light bulb mock-up, you could trace over a photo which could be placed as a linked file in Illustrator on a separate layer below the art and then be removed afterward or the layer hidden. Refer to Figure 9-5.

While doing research, I noticed that many infographic resumes, when describing software expertise, used a type of pie graph or bar chart to describe the level of skill in that particular software. While we have not discussed pie charts yet, but we will in Volume 2, you can for now use the Ellipse tool to create circles and then use the ellipses start and end pie widgets to divide into wedges or segments to create a pie chart-like affect. In my case, I created a grouped path that consisted of Alt/Option dragged copies of ellipses and, then using the star tool with ten points, moved an ellipse at each point around and grouped the shapes. Refer to Figure 9-9.

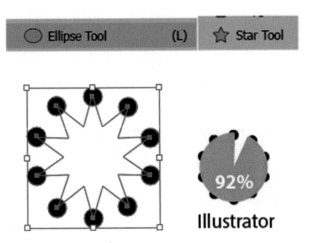

Figure 9-9. *Create a faux pie chart using the Ellipse and Star tool*

This made it easier to drag the handles of my overlying ellipse wedge to the percent I wanted, assuming that 10 points each represents 10%. You could save this guide as a symbol if you plan to use it frequently as I did use it six times. In my case, besides adding the text of each software name in the following, I colored each ellipse to resemble the color of the software icons, and I added a percent as well in case the graph/chart was confusing to the viewer. Refer to Figure 9-10.

| Photoshop | Illustrator | InDesign | Animate | Dreamweaver | Media Encoder |

Figure 9-10. *Create multiple faux pie charts with text to display your skill level in software*

These percentages may be based on a proficiency test you recently took or perhaps your own years of experience, which makes you sure that this is your skill level. In your case, you may want to add other non-software skills such as sketching and drawing. However, you do not want to overwhelm the design with too many pie charts, so pick your top four to six skills.

In this case, I left the charts with the text ungrouped in case you wanted to review my layout. However, remember to use your Selection tool (Shift+Click) for your multiple text or graphics and use the Align panel or the Align options in your Control panel if you want the text to line up and look balanced. Refer to Figure 9-11.

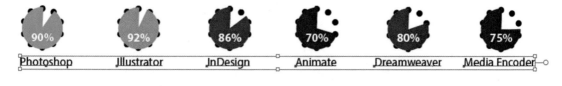

Figure 9-11. *Make sure to align selected text using the Control panel*

Timelines are a simple way as we saw in Chapter 1 of creating a progression of time. Now in this example, you can use a timeline for your professional employment experience as well as education/training. Refer to Figure 9-12.

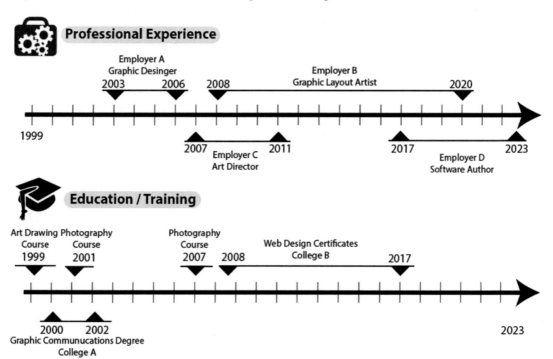

Figure 9-12. *Create a timeline of your professional experience and education*

This can show the reader that you may have worked several jobs at once or that you were taking multiple training courses at the same time, which when just described as text to the reader of the resume could be confusing. A visual timeline will make the events clearer. In this case, I used the Line Segment tool. Refer to Figure 9-12 and Figure 9-13.

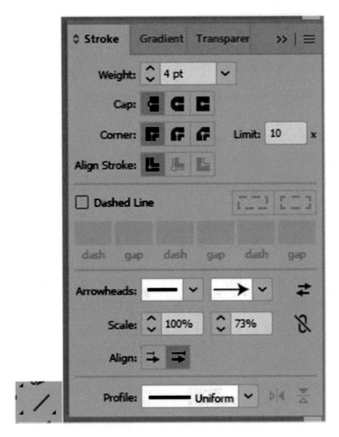

Figure 9-13. *Use the Line Segment tool and the Stroke panel to create a timeline*

Remember, you can add arrowheads to the main line using the Stroke panel and then adjust the arrowhead scale to make it larger or smaller. Likewise, you can group lines and shape polygon triangles together to show a span of time for a particular employment or course. Then add text either at a point or an area type box that expresses such things as dates, the employer, your title, the school's name, or the name of the course you attended.

On the timeline, the dividing lines were evenly spaced using the Blend tool. In this case, we are dealing with the years 1999–2023. So there were 22 specified steps or line spaces in between the start and end line segments, giving us 24 segments. Refer to Figure 9-12 and Figure 9-14.

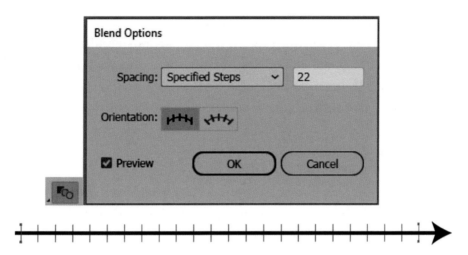

Figure 9-14. *Use the Blend tool to blend lines from one end to the other*

However, in this case she is entering the twenty-fifth year so 2023, which is the start of the arrow as the year in this example is not complete. If wanted another tick, I would have to move the specified steps up to 23. However, I will leave the arrowhead as the last divider.

Creating your dividers for your timeline this way is much easier as you can easily add or subtract lines from the blend if you need to adjust your amount of years when you need to update the resume, for example, to 2024. Or you may prefer for your layout to have a vertical timeline rather than a horizontal one. This way you can easily rotate and scale your lines. Either way, always check the divisions in your timeline and adjust your markers as accurately as possible.

For hobbies/interests, make sure to add a few drawings as they relate to your resume and also make sure to include a title for each. Refer to Figure 9-15.

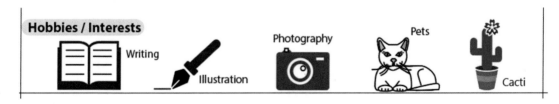

Figure 9-15. *Add designs of your hobbies and interests to the bottom of your infographic resume*

Even if you think you have created the perfect icon that everyone should know what it means, some readers will not, especially if they are not familiar with that kind of technology or maybe a sport. In this case, I put by the cat the word "pets," just in case this was unclear that I like many animals, and "cacti" by the potted plant. However, do not overwhelm the reader with all your interests as your skills and experience are the key items in the resume. That is why I put mine at the bottom of the page and made sure they were the most relevant to my resume.

I then reviewed and added additional text to my resume.

I then File ➤ Save this document as a (.ai) file. Ultimately, I could print this file out or File ➤ Save As a PDF if I wanted to email it to an employer. We'll talk about additional file formats more in Volume 3. Refer to Figure 9-16.

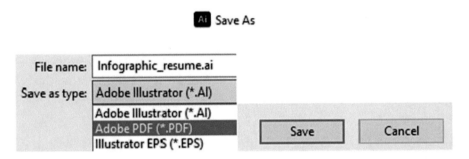

Figure 9-16.   *Use the Save As dialog box if you want to save the file as a PDF*

Taking what you have learned here in these sections about tools and panels, now on your own, take a moment to build your own infographic resume based on your current skills. Consider what you have learned in this chapter and previous chapters so far.

Project Idea 2: Historical Infographic (Mine Map/ Mine Shaft)

Alternatively, for more advanced users, here is another idea you can create if you want to practice with the pen tool to create an infographic on a historical topic you are interested in. Refer to the file Mining_History.ai. I created a more detailed infographic that could be used as a whole or in several parts. It is an illustration of a mine shaft and how miners would extract gold from the mine in the early days in the North, from the permafrost, and then pan the gold afterward. Refer to Figure 9-17.

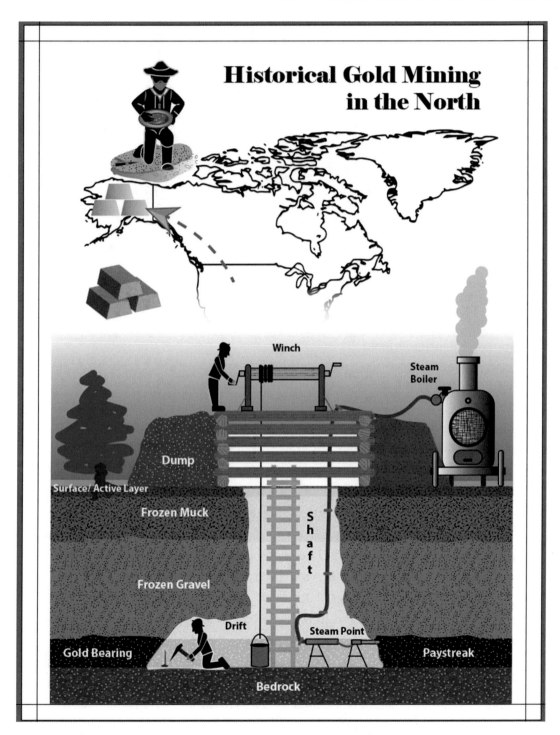

Figure 9-17. *Example of a historical mining map illustration*

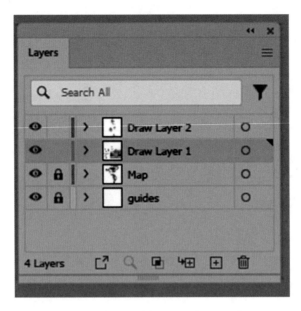

Figure 9-18. *Use the Layers panel to add more layers for organizing your infographic for easier editing*

This mine shaft example was created from looking at and researching the topic of historical mining and viewing various photos of the process used, machinery, maps of that era, and soil layers and then creating a simplified drawing with my own art based on the description of permafrost layers and soil. This design also included part of a world map in the background. You can access a copy of this map, see World_Map.tif, and then use the Image Trace panel to extract a design from a raster image and make it vector art. I will mention how to use the Image Trace panel in Volume 2. For now, if you want to use the current vector map (see Map layer), you can copy it out of the current infographic and paste it into your own file for practice. As you can see in the Layers panel, in this project, more layers were required to organize all the shapes and paths, and some had to be locked so that I could move other paths on the artboard. Refer to Figure 9-17.

As in the previous infographic resume, I used the Pen tool again as well as the Blob Brush and Eraser tool. Some paths had their opacity altered so that the mine shaft appeared as a 3D-like effect. For ladder, I used a lighter color to give a lower contrast so that it was not focused. However, the winch for the bucket and the steam boiler hose were more in focus and used darker colors. Text was made white and bold when it was over darker colors. Refer to Figure 9-19.

Figure 9-19. *Use the Appearance panel to add more overlapping strokes or fills to a path or shape*

I also used the Appearance panel to add to some paths with two different fills so that a pattern with some transparent areas could overlay a solid color and give the appearance of texture. You can find these adapted patterns in the Swatches panel. Many of the originals came from the Swatch Libraries ➤ Patterns ➤ Basic Graphics ➤ Basic Graphics (_Dots, _Lines, _Textures). Refer to Figure 9-20.

Figure 9-20. *The Swatches panel contains many gradients and patterns used in the infographic*

Some default gradients also found in the Swatches panel were also added to the steam boiler as well as the sky, candle, and boiler furnace window. Refer to Figure 9-20.

The Stroke panel was used to add a custom arrow, and it was colored with a blue stroke. Refer to Figure 9-17.

Also in the upper left are a few 3D gold bars which we have not created yet, but we will look at this in more detail in Volume 2 when we look at the 3D and Materials panel. Refer to Figure 9-17. Take a moment to look at these 3D bars in your open file.

I will discuss other uses for this graphic more in Volume 3 in regard to adjustments with Photoshop as well as consideration on how you could add similar graphics to InDesign documents.

On your own, begin working on your own historical infographic using some of the suggestions as well as tools and panels I have mentioned.

This concludes our projects for Volume 1, and you can close any files you have open as well as File ➤ Exit Illustrator.

Summary

In this chapter, we reviewed the topics from previous chapters regarding basic shape drawing tools, moving, selecting, and arranging shapes on the artboard, drawing and editing custom shapes, working with layers, adding colors to objects as well as adding type, and creating symbols. You saw how the concepts from previous chapters could be applied to your first infographics. New ideas were also presented that you may want to explore on your own or proceed to Volumes 2 and 3 and learn more about them as you continue your journey of creating infographics.

In Volume 2, some of the topics that will be covered are

- Focusing on a set of nine tools that are specifically designed to help you create graphs

- Pattern Options panel

- Image Trace panel

- Various 2D and 3D effects that you can apply to your infographics

- Perspective basics

In Volume 3

- Creating interactive infographics with SVG files

- Looking at various layout ideas and concluding our discussion on finalizing and reviewing your infographic with your client

- Next steps that you may want to consider with infographics using other Adobe Creative cloud applications

Index

A

Adobe color application

  Accessibility tools

    color blind tools, 86–88

    contrast checker tool, 79, 80, 83

    contrast text, 78, 79

    determine pass/fail, 81

    deuteranopia, 92

    graphic components, 82, 84

    high/low contrast, 77, 78

    illustration, 89

    import colors button, 82

    protanopia, 90

    recommendations/save
      options, 84, 85

    rod monochromacy
      (achromatopsia), 93, 94

    rods/cones, 90

    tritanopia, 92, 93

  apps tab, 45

  base color, 48, 49

  base color/eyedropper, 64, 65

  color harmony

    analogous and split analogous
      options, 50, 51

    complementary options, 54, 56, 58

    complement options, 58, 59

    compound option, 61, 62

    custom pentagram option, 63, 64

    double split complementary, 56, 57

    monochromatic options, 52

    polychromatic layout, 63, 64

    shades option, 62

    split complementary options, 55

    square/double split complement
      options, 60–62

    triad options, 53–55

  cool zone, 50

  create section, 47

  fonts/color, 95–98

  HEX number/RGB color mode, 66

  HSB/LAB color modes, 67

  layout setup/harmony rule, 48

  libraries panel, 76

  online app, 46

  online app layout, 46

  resource links, 47

  science 2D/3D visualization

    brightness/lightness, 70, 71

    chroma/saturation, 69, 70

    compression chart, 68

    hue, 68, 69

    Munsell color diagram, 71–73

    3D diagram representation, 75

    two-dimensional slice, 73, 74

  temperature, 49

  theme/gradient, 77

  warm colors, 49

  web icon tab, 45

  wheel and base color section, 66, 67

  Wheel tab selection, 47

J. Harder, *Creating Infographics with Adobe Illustrator: Volume 1*,
https://doi.org/10.1007/979-8-8688-0005-4

L, M, N, O

Printed in the United States
by Baker & Taylor Publisher Services